The Practical Guide to Understanding, Leaving and Recovering from Narcissistic Abuse

When Love Goes Wrong,
How to Recover

A M BUCK

Copyright © 2022 A M Buck

All rights reserved. No part of this publication may be reproduced or transmitted in any form or by any means, electronic or mechanical including photocopying, recording or any information storage or retrieval system, without prior permission in writing from the copyright owner, and the publishers.

The right of A M Buck to be identified as the author of this work has been asserted by her in accordance with the Copyright, Designs and Patents Act 1988

The moral right of the author has been asserted.

First published in the United Kingdom in 2022 by
The Choir Press

ISBN 978-1-78963-299-6

This book is not intended to act as a substitute for professional treatment. Opinions contained within this book are from my own experiences, research and observations.

Advice and recommendations given may not be suitable for every situation. Those needing medical advice are advised to consult a qualified medical professional. The recommendations given in this book are solely intended as education and information, and should not be taken as professional advice. Neither the author or the publisher accept any liability or responsibility for errors, omissions, inaccuracies or consequences resulting from advice and information contained within this book.

The series of exercises, visualisations and recommendations in this book are not a form of, or substitute for psychotherapy. You may need professional psychological help. If you choose to perform the exercises and visualisations on your own, and if you experience physical or emotional reactions that feel too intense to manage, you should seek professional help.

The Practical Guide to Understanding, Leaving and Recovery from Narcissistic Abuse

This practical self-help workbook has been developed over twelve years from those who have been through narcissistic abuse, and is written for anyone who is looking to understand their experience, safely leave an abusive relationship or find the fastest and most effective ways to recover.

From experience, this book uniquely defines the sixteen stages of narcissistic abuse, the two pre-leaving stages and the eight recovery stages. It will help you learn how to:

- Identify a narcissist before you get into a relationship with one (even before the love-bombing stage begins).
- Understand why you might be chosen by a narcissist (your personality, unconscious beliefs and schemas).
- Define the narcissistic abuse tactics – from control, food abuse, gaslighting, set-ups, psychological and physical abuse, all the way through to coercive control in a relationship.
- Protect yourself through the UK laws – understanding the coercive control laws in the UK, and how to go to court for a non-molestation or possession order.
- Recognise when you are trapped in an abusive relationship – the TRAP moment.
- Recognise the SNAP moment – when you realise you have to get out of the relationship, but don't know how.
- Safely leave a narcissist (practical recommendations).
- Get the help you need, through charities and narcissistic abuse recovery support networks.
- Help a friend or family member in an abusive relationship (what to say or do).
- Prepare yourself for narcissistic attack after leaving a narcissist – from understanding your strengths, your support network, through to defending yourself from smear campaigns, threats and harassment.
- Validate your experience with people who understand what you have been through.

- Identify how far you have progressed in the eight stages of recovery.
- Find methods of recovery that work for you.

A M Buck has produced podasts about narcissistic abuse, offers free and paid online training and personalised mentoring programmes to help narcissistic abuse recovery. This includes the Intensive Recovery Programme at www.I-recovered.co.uk.

Dedication

Dedicated to all those brave souls who have survived narcissistic abuse before me, those who have been brave enough to share their stories, those who have carried on and suffered in silence and those professionals who have helped the many survivors of narcissistic abuse in their recovery.

It is also dedicated to all the people who have given me courage, help and strength to be able to write this book .

A special mention has to also go an old cat called Chop Lady, whose cantankerous nature has helped me laugh through darker times.

Contents

	Page
Preface	x

Section 1 – Recognising The 16 Stages of Narcissistic Abuse — 1

Phase 1 – Getting Drawn in and Ignoring The Warning Signs — 3

Chapter 1	What a narcissist is likely to be looking for in their partner	4
Chapter 2	How Trusting People are Exploited by Manipulation	7
Chapter 3	How a Narcissist Uncovers Your Needs/Vulnerabilities	10
Chapter 4	Example of how a Narcissist finds Hidden Needs	12
Chapter 5	Love Blindness – First Date Red Flags	18
Chapter 6	More Red Flags – Breaking Boundaries, Pedestalling and Future Dreams	25
Chapter 7	Be Whole, Be Self-Aware Before Being Loved – Wounded Inner Child and Schemas	35

Phase 2 – First Level Control Tactics — 42

Chapter 8	Love-Bombing and Social Engineering	42
Chapter 9	Online Ghosting & Catfishing	52
Chapter 10	Unexpected Withdrawal, Stonewalling and Abandonment	54

Phase 3 – Commitment & Isolating You in The Relationship — 58

Chapter 11	Commitment, Control and Compliance through Assault and Narcissistic Rages	58
Chapter 12	Starting Isolation – Closing Off from Those You Love and Supportive Friendship	66

Phase 4 – Trying To Leave – The TRAP Moment — 76

Chapter 13	The TRAP Moment	76

Phase 5 – Coercive Control Techniques — 82

Chapter 14	Relationship Abuse and Coercive Control	82
Chapter 15	Domestic Abuse and Coercive Control Laws in the UK	88

Phase 6 – Food And Mealtime Abuse — 99

Chapter 16	Food Abuse Tactics	99

viii Contents

Phase 7 – Deepening Coercive Control Methods		**104**
Chapter 17	Gaslighting and Mind Control	105
Chapter 18	Denial of Unfaithfulness	109
Chapter 19	Brainwashing, Interrogation, and Inhumane and Torturous Treaments	112
Chapter 20	Creating False Witnesses and Intimidation	114
Chapter 21	Pathological Lies and Set-Up Lying	118

Phase 8 – Normalising Coercive Control and Narcissistic Abuse   **124**

Chapter 22 No Place Like a Home from Hell   124

Phase 9 – Assaults, Cruelty and Violence   **127**

Chapter 23 Assault and Breaking Point Moments   127
Chapter 24 Cruelty Begins   130

Phase 10 –The On/Off Cycle of Abuse   **133**

Chapter 25 Withdrawal Symptoms/Trauma Bonded   134

Phase 11 – Effects of Abuse on Mind and Wellbeing   **138**

Chapter 26 Effects of Trauma and Abuse – Mental Wellbeing, Addictions and Specialist Help   138

Phase 12 – Preparing To Leave – Evidence   **144**

Chapter 27 Planning Required   144

Phase 13 – Snap Leaving Moment   **149**

Chapter 28 The SNAP Leaving Moment   149
Chapter 29 Non-Molestation Orders, Injunctions and Going to Court   152

Phase 14 – Leaving And The Leaving Dangers   **159**

Chapter 30 Be Prepared for the Worst When You Leave (Danger!)   159

Phase 15 – After The Relationship Breaks Up – Narcisstic Attacks May Increase – Protect Yourself   **172**

Chapter 31 Protect, Protect, Protect Yourself   173

Phase 16 – The End of Narcissistic Abuse   **177**

Contents   ix

Section 2 – The Pre-Leaving Stage – Are You Really Ready To Leave?   **179**

Phase 1 – Am I Really Ready To Do This?   181

Phase 2 – Why I Am Leaving   184

Section 3 – Now You Have Left – The Recovery Begins   **193**

Phase 1 – I'm Out! Now What?   195

Chapter 32 Protecting Yourself   196
Chapter 33 Defending Yourself   208
Chapter 34 Validate Yourself   218

Phase 2 – What Went Wrong?   219

Chapter 35 The Search for Meaning and Courage to Change Yourself   219

Phase 3 – The Help You Need and Getting Your Support Network in Place   222

Chapter 36 Your Support Network   222
Chapter 37 Therapy/Treatment Types   224

Phase 4 – I'm Ready To Speak Up and Defend Myself   247

Chapter 38 Speaking Up – Finding Your Voice   248
Chapter 39 Practicalities of Defending Yourself   249
Chapter 40 Narcissists Weaknesses   258

Phase 5 – My Needs Are The Most Important, They Are ...   261

Chapter 41 What Are Your Needs and Wants?   261
Chapter 42 What Does a 'Normal, Healthy' Relationship Feel Like?   266

Phase 6 – I've Changed And Recovered Enough   271

Chapter 43 Have you Recovered Enough?   271

Phase 7 – I Accept What Happened   274

Chapter 44 Acceptance and Forgiveness   274

Phase 8 – I'm Ready To Move On With My Life   275

References and Other Resources   278

Preface from the Author

Love came fast,
Truth came hard,
Love died slowly,
Sanity went quickly,
Help was hard to find,
Validation was vital,
Hurt took time,
Courage came from within,
Self-protection was learned,
Recovery finally came,
So victim became victor of self,
Empowered again.

After experiencing the trauma of narcissistic abuse, victims will often ask themselves searching questions such as 'Why did they do that to me?', 'What did I do wrong?' or simply 'Why me?'

It is a total shock and victims are often left feeling absolutely devastated, discarded and broken from their ordeal. Your world may have been shattered, your hopes and dreams destroyed and your trust and faith in others may have gone. But this does not need to be your future.

I want you to know that you did nothing wrong to deserve this. It is very difficult to spot a narcissist in the beginning and once embroiled with a narcissist it can be traumatising to leave and get over the experience. **But it can be done**, which is why I want to share with you how that is possible.

This book is for anyone suspecting they might be starting a relationship with a narcissist, in a relationship with one, wanting to leave a narcissistic relationship or trying to overcome the devastation when they have left.

I am writing from a layperson's perspective – I am not trained in psychology – but I share the wisdom imparted by psychologists and legal experts who helped my recovery. Whilst I talk about narcissistic abuse, an expert may describe some of the behaviours described as a psychopath or sociopath. The difference isn't that clear to me, but they have one thing in common – they can be extremely dangerous people to be involved with.

Through this book I am going to be talking about victims of narcissists. The term victim is used in the classic context of:

a. 'a person who is tricked or duped';
b. 'a person harmed, injured or killed as a result of events or actions.'

Preface from the Author   xi

I am also going to be talking about what a narcissist may or may not be thinking. This is subjective and purely from my own viewpoint, observations, questioning and opinion. No-one actually knows what someone else is really thinking. The intention is to be a reflection on how differently someone may think to you, as it is important not to assume that your 'view of the world' is the same as others. The book is written to the extremes of what can happen with a narcissistic relationship and not all narcissists may 'think' or be as extreme as the examples given.

Anyone who has gone through abuse is also a survivor – i.e. someone who has coped well with difficulties in their life and survived the abuse. Please read this book with whatever terminology suits your own experience. I personally felt a victim at the beginning of my journey, but know now that I am a survivor and indeed a victor, and recovered from the experience at the end. Choose your own terminology to replace mine that suits your own needs.

Whilst I have written and given examples about experiences from a male/female gender perspective, a narcissist is a personality disorder not defined by gender, but behaviour. Please read it with my intention of gender neutrality.

I am writing this book after over twelve years from the end of my own personal experiences of narcissistic abuse. It has taken me this amount of time to fully observe the recovery stages for myself and others and share that with you. I hope that by sharing the steps I took, it speeds up recovery for others that have been through narcissistic abuse.

The stories given for Richard and Lisa, Penny and Martin, Ethan and Faye are fictional characters and circumstances and serve only as a demonstration to explain about narcissism in a relationship.

For my own personal recovery journey, one of the hardest parts was having to face myself and my belief systems. It was almost as painful as recalling the abuse itself at times. I could not contemplate some of the things I know now to be true about why I acted or reacted in the way I did – I will share this with you. I certainly did not want to hear that I might have had a personality/behaviour/belief that attracted a narcissist in any way. Categorically I would have told you that it was not my fault. I was totally the victim here and to a large degree I was. I later learned that perhaps I did have something to make me more attractive to an abuser – and if that was the case, I also had the power to change it. Which I did.

My intention is that this book helps you identify someone who may harm you in a relationship, such as a narcissist. More importantly, if you are already in an abusive relationship, to validate your experiences and show you the steps you can take to escape from an abusive relationship (through the UK legal system). The final sections of the book are how I managed to recover from my ordeal, which I hope helps others. Please know that:

One day this will be behind you, and you will be a wiser, stronger and empowered version of yourself again

Section 1: Recognising the 16 Stages of Narcissistic Abuse

Before we talk about the sixteen stages of narcissistic abuse, when put simply narcissistic relationship abuse happens and is possible because of three main elements:

(1) **What a narcissist is looking to GAIN FROM YOU and HOW they go about that;**
(2) **Your PERSONALITY traits;**
(3) **Your CONSCIOUS and UNCONSCIOUS BELIEFS.**

Whilst you cannot change a narcissist, you can and do have the power to change yourself. This is actually very empowering once you realise how you can do this to protect yourself, defend yourself and take steps to help yourself recover from abuse.

When you understand what a narcissist is looking to gain from you and how they go about it, it becomes easier to understand the predictability of their **actions** over their **words**.

This is important because a narcissist is likely to **say anything and do anything** to make themselves attractive to you in the beginning of forming a relationship, and **say anything and do anything** to destroy you at the end of a relationship.

Their needs – what they gain from you – include adoration, praise, elevated social status, domestic servitude, money and property to name but a few when entering into a relationship on a conscious level.

How they go about it includes pathological lying and deceit – from pretending to be the only one to understand and meet your dreams to using their attractiveness, sexuality, humour and charm to manipulate you.

When you understand that their beliefs differ significantly from those they chose to abuse, you can see that they can lie, cheat, manipulate and control because they truly believe that they are superior to other people, are entitled to be treated differently and that everyday rules do not apply to them.

Because narcissists can be incredibly convincing in the beginning of any relationship and seem genuine and authentic, there are very few clues initially about the type of person they really are. It can be easy to become trapped in a relationship or be mercilessly discarded when they consider that you have served your purpose.

Section 1 – Recognising the 16 Stages of Narcissistic Abuse

It is vitally important therefore for victims of narcissistic abuse not to blame themselves for the extreme emotional destruction often experienced after being in a relationship with a narcissist. It is an unparalleled experience, only truly understandable by people who have been through it.

It can be devastating, but please know that you can move on from this, become stronger and more self-aware to prevent it happening again. This can be done by:

(a) Learning how a narcissist operates;
(b) Becoming aware of why you are attractive to a narcissist through your unconscious beliefs;
(c) Being aware of your responses so that it is difficult for you to be manipulated.

Whatever stage of the narcissistic abuse journey you are currently at, there will be information and advice to help and guide you.

The sixteen phases of narcissistic abuse that I have observed include the following stages:

Phase 1 – Getting Drawn in and Early Warning Signs

Phase 2 – First Level Control Tactics

Phase 3 – Commitment, Control and Compliance

Phase 4 – Trying to Leave – The TRAP Moment

Phase 5 – Coercive Control

Phase 6 – Food and Mealtime Abuse

Phase 7 – Deepening Coercive Control Methods

Phase 8 – Normalising Abuse

Phase 9 – Assault, Cruelty and Violence

Phase 10 – The On/Off Cycle of Abuse

Phase 11 – Effects of Abuse on Mind and Wellbeing

Phase 12 – Preparing to Leave – Evidence

Phase 13 – SNAP Leaving Moment

Phase 14 – Leaving and the Leaving Dangers

Phase 15 – Protecting Yourself After Leaving

Phase 16 – The End of Abuse – The Recovery Stages Begin

Phase 1 – Getting Drawn in and Ignoring The Warning Signs

Narcissists form a very small proportion of the population (some estimate around 1%), yet their behaviours cause devastation and heartbreak on a large scale for their romantic partners.

There are many books written about narcissism that describe what narcissism is, and this includes:

- Grandiosity and extreme self-importance
- Excessive need for adoration
- Superficial relationships that feed their ego
- Exploitation of romantic partners and others
- Lack of empathy
- Chronic feelings of emptiness and boredom
- Disregard of other's feelings
- Sense of entitlement – believing they are superior to others and rules don't apply to them
- Manipulative behaviour
- Need for admiration, praise and recognition
- Lack of accountability for their behaviour
- Arrogance
- Often charming and personable

Narcissism is on a spectrum – so some people may have narcissistic traits but not be a narcissist. Narcissism can only be diagnosed by a professional, but typically a narcissist will not seek a diagnosis or even believe anything is wrong with them.

What is important to know is that they have very different belief systems – whether they are aware of them or not.

So when forming a new relationship with someone, some of their behaviours may be actively and consciously chosen (how to manipulate), but others may well be unconscious to them driven by their strong internal beliefs of:

- *Entitlement to be treated differently because they are special;*
- *Their extreme self-importance and superiority to others;*
- *A belief that if they don't control someone, they will be controlled themselves.*

Chapter 1 – What a narcissist is likely to be looking for in their partner

When looking for a new romantic partner, a narcissist seemingly goes about it in a different way to other people. Instead of trying to form a loving, mutually respectful relationship, a narcissist evaluates choosing a romantic partner that will fulfil THEIR needs above everything else. Put simply, they will be evaluating:

(1) **How being in a relationship will help THEM (what they GAIN).**
(2) **How easy YOU are to subtly manipulate.**
(3) **Your PERSONALITY TRAITS, such as being unquestioning and trusting.**
(4) **Your UNCONSCIOUS beliefs and needs.**

When making a selection for a romantic partner, narcissists actually seem to be quite selective about choosing who to form a relationship with, based on the above.

When we also consider that a narcissist's behaviour and choice of partner may be driven by entitlement and superiority-type beliefs, it is easy to see why narcissists have been called sophisticated master manipulators and social predators.

This unfortunately is not readily apparent when you first engage in conversation or start a relationship with a narcissist, because they can go to extraordinary lengths to charm, persuade and pretend to be someone they are not in the beginning of forming a relationship to get their own needs met.

Part of their sophisticated (and often cold-hearted) selection process for a partner therefore may include evaluating:

(1) How you can help them financially, elevate their status or how you can help them get ahead in their life (or make their life easier).
(2) How trusting you are (do you believe their lies).
(3) How easy you can be manipulated through guilt-tripping, through trust, through loyalty or because you are keen to fulfil a life 'need'.

In a nutshell, they are instinctively evaluating what they can gain from you and how easy it is to get that through your personality type, beliefs and vulnerabilities.

It makes sense then, that a narcissist often chooses a person with some of these personality traits as they are easier for to manipulate. Someone who:

(1) Avoids conflict
(2) Is trusting
(3) Is loyal
(4) Takes things at face value and raises few questions
(5) Is kind
(6) Is open and honest
(7) Is selfless or self-sacrificing
(8) Is caring
(9) Is empathic
(10) Is generous and helpful
(11) Is confident and responsible
(12) Is good at what they do
(13) Abides by social norms
(14) Likes to care for other people
(15) Has integrity
(16) Is highly tolerant
(17) Is emotionally mature
(18) Looks for the best in people
(19) But may be malleable in some way – e.g. through guilt-tripping or 'doing the right thing', being the 'rescuer'

Do you see yourself in that list? How do you relate to these personality traits? Are you aware of how you could be manipulated?

When you realise that a narcissist is **only interested in their own needs**, both consciously and unconsciously, these same virtuous personality traits can also be more easily exploited with various methods of manipulation.

A narcissist's true personality is **cold and ruthless** and they truly **do not care about hurting and harming** someone to get their own needs met. They are likely to use charm, lies and a false personality facade to achieve this. For example, by pretending to have the same values, beliefs and things in common with their partner (even if this involves blatant lying), they are able to form quick emotional bonds.

People are naturally drawn to those who think, feel and have the same ideals, values and beliefs as them – and are more likely to open up and form bonds because of this.

The sad fact is that good-natured, kind-hearted and trusting people are an easy target for narcissists. But whilst the aftermath of forming a relationship with someone who is only interested in their own needs is emotionally devastating, it does not mean that it has to be the case in the future.

Chapter 2 – How Trusting People are Exploited by Manipulation

There are several initial techniques that are used by narcissists when evaluating how easy someone is to manipulate. These can include:

(1) Pretending to share the same ideals, beliefs and outlook as their victim (commonality)
(2) False flattery
(3) False empathy
(4) Glib promises – offering people what they need and pretending to be the saviour and rescuer (even if they are not consciously aware of it)

This is because when we believe we have met someone who tells us that they share the same values, beliefs and goals in life, and we are perhaps being praised simply for being who we are, we naturally let our guard down and become more open.

When you look at the list of virtuous personality traits through the eyes of a manipulative narcissist, they would consider them to be **vulnerabilities to be exploited**. Here are some of the ways a narcissist might manipulate someone with the following personality traits:

1. **Kind, caring and helpful – manipulated by guilt-tripping:** A narcissist may try to manipulate through guilt-tripping and exploiting the willingness to help unquestionably. Because kind, caring and helpful people often want to create harmony and peacefulness in relationships, they will also go to extreme lengths to be peacemakers, for example they might want to 'fix' things, even if it is not their fault.
2. **Honesty and looking for the best in people – manipulated by lying and false allegations:** A narcissist may try to manipulate by pathological lying and even false allegations. Because honest people tend to believe other people are inherently honest, even when lies are exposed, an honest person may well try to internally validate the lies as a 'one-off' incident initially. Honest people are not expecting or equipped to deal with false allegations.
3. **Selflessness, generosity and giving more than they receive – manipulated by accusations of selfishness:** A narcissist may happily take as much as is given by someone. Because generous and selfless

people give more than they receive, a narcissist will take this as a green light to take as much as possible and even accuse generous people of being selfish.

4. **Openness - manipulated by blackmail and shame:** A narcissist is likely to take openness as weakness. When someone opens up about their inner thoughts and feelings a narcissist may use any information gleaned as a future blackmail tool. A narcissist will think little of lying about their own situation (they may well create a made-up dramatic situation and ask you to keep it secret), so that a victim opens up more to them about their intimate inner thoughts and feelings. Once intimate information is gleaned from a victim, a narcissist is not above using blackmail and shame to manipulate the situation in their favour.

5. **Empathy and care when someone is hurting - manipulated by sad life stories:** A narcissist is likely to manipulate someone with empathy through obligation and guilt. When first meeting a narcissist, they may well falsely claim to have sad life stories (and indeed believe themselves to be victims) to garner empathy and trust.

6. **High levels of trust - manipulated by being unquestioning:** A narcissist is likely to manipulate trusting people by testing reactions to their lies. Because a trusting person believes the best in people and are inherently honest, they are likely to believe what they are told at face value and are less likely to question a narcissist.

7. **Tolerant, loyal and responsible - manipulated by tolerance and trying to fix things:** A narcissist will be able to manipulate those that are tolerant, loyal and responsible because it generally takes longer for tolerant people to object to bad behaviours. They are likely to remain loyal even when loyalty is not warranted.

8. **Self-sacrificing and humble - manipulated by false flattery and not speaking up:** A narcissist may be able to manipulate someone who is self-sacrificing and humble because they may not be used to speaking up for themselves. Manipulation is therefore possible through false flattery, false empathy and relying on the victim not speaking up.

9. **Confident and good at what they do - manipulated by criticism:** A narcissist is likely to use criticism to manipulate someone who is confident and good at what they do as they will strive to get better.

10. **Abides by social norms - manipulated by underhandedness:** A narcissist can be underhanded, ruthless and a rule-breaker, so would find it easy to manipulate someone who abides by social norms. A victim would simply not expect someone to 'stoop so low' and break the law or rules to get ahead.

What this list actually shows is how a narcissist views virtuous personality traits. The danger is that **expecting** other people to have the same values, beliefs and intentions, can lead to opportunities for a narcissist to exploit people.

Unfortunately, if you stay in a relationship with a narcissist, by the time you come out of the other side you may well find yourself having been seriously abused. Your core can be rocked completely – you may come out doubting yourself, feeling worthless, discarded, emotionally battered and absolutely devastated.

If this is where you are, I am sorry to hear that. It will take some time after abuse for you to trust and rebuild your life again – but it can be done.

Chapter 3 – How a Narcissist Uncovers Your Needs/Vulnerabilities

When looking to manipulate or form a relationship with someone, a narcissist is very adept at quickly identifying people's needs and vulnerabilities – often through questioning and appearing very interested in what you have to say.

If you are not aware of your needs and vulnerabilities, a narcissist certainly will be.

A narcissist is incredibly astute at uncovering people's needs and exploiting them for their advantage. If you are more aware of your needs and vulnerabilities – conscious and unconscious – you are less likely to form an unhealthy relationship with a narcissist.

Your conscious or unconscious needs might be, for example:

(1)   Not wanting to be alone/fear of being alone
(2)   Wanting to share your life with someone who likes the same things
(3)   Wanting someone to rescue you/help to fix something
(4)   Wanting love, marriage, a committed relationship
(5)   Wanting a child/care of children
(6)   Wanting financial security
(7)   Wanting luxury/wealth
(8)   To be taken care of when you are ill
(9)   To enjoy someone else's company
(10)   To travel with someone
(11)   To be rescued/saved from past hurts and emotional wounds
(12)   To be understood and loved for who you are
(13)   To find someone with the same values, beliefs and morals
(14)   Wanting someone faithful and loyal

A narcissist will look to exploit *your needs* as vulnerabilities for their own *gain* and the best way for them to do this is by:

1.   **Pretending to be 'just like you'/mirroring:** Pretending to have a lot in common with you makes it easier for a narcissist to elicit information about your vulnerabilities and needs. They are likely to pretend initially to be just like you, like the same things, have the same values and beliefs to garner important information about you. This is the information gathering stage to be stored and used against you later.

2. **Appearing interested in you:** Initially they might be quite intense – asking probing questions and being intently interested in what you say. You might think that this is because they are interested in you, however, for a narcissist this is merely to find out information to exploit later.
3. **Solution to your needs/saviour:** they may initially provide a seemingly innocent and free solution to your needs or be a saviour. For example, if you disclose that you are having trouble finding something or need some type of help, a narcissist will initially go out of their way to help you. Whilst you might be grateful and thankful, a narcissist will see this as you being **indebted** in the future. It will be stored as a 'favour' that needs to be 'owed back' later.
4. **Glib promises and lies:** They may say whatever you want to hear. For example, if you had disclosed your last partner cheated on you, they would glibly say 'Oh, that's terrible, I would never do that to you!' It would not matter to them that it was a blatant lie (for example they had cheated before) because this gives you the **reassurance** that you have the same values. By lying this way, they gain your trust and means that you more easily let your guard down.
5. **False empathy:** A narcissist may pretend to empathise with you in the beginning. Again this is another tactic that benefits the narcissist because as you share more of your inner thoughts and feelings, they have more information to **manipulate you** with later.
6. **False flattery:** This narcissist technique is used to make a victim initially feel good about themselves. In fact it is likely to be just a ploy to get you to trust them and later in a relationship may be **taken away** to hurt you.
7. **Your vulnerabilities:** A narcissist will want to uncover your vulnerabilities, e.g. isolation, being single, bereavement, not having a support network/friends/family are all considerations a narcissist will make when forming a romantic relationship.

This is why it is so important to understand your own conscious and unconscious needs and vulnerabilities, so that narcissists are less able to exploit them.

Chapter 4 – Example of how a Narcissist finds Hidden Needs

During Phase 1, a narcissist is likely to quickly establish commonality, evoke emotional responses to draw you into conversation and try to establish your needs or vulnerabilities. Narcissists can use charm, wit, humour and friendliness to initially gain trust and they will be very interested in what you have to say.

They may give you a compelling life story to engage with you, arrogantly exaggerate or lie about their life to seem more appealing or mirror back to you the same likes and dislikes. They are likely to tell you anything that you want to hear – even if this means lying to you.

Whatever they say, true or false, seems to be of little concern to the narcissist. They do not seem to care if they are blatantly lying and falsely offering you everything you ever wanted. What the narcissist appears to be looking for is your **response** to the information. This helps establish how easily you could be manipulated. They are calculating someone's vulnerabilities, trust and unquestioning acceptance of what is being said. From this they can establish if that person is likely to meet their own needs.

An example of an initial email exchange on a dating website

The following fictional email exchange demonstrates some of the techniques used to find a potential romantic partner from an online dating website.

In this example, 'Richard' is a narcissist and has left a long-term relationship when he sends a response to 'Lisa'.

Lisa's profile has just a facial photograph. Her profile text, however, contains details that she is currently **vulnerable** having recently moved to a new area. This would be of interest to a narcissist.

Relevant text is highlighted.

Example of how a Narcissist finds Hidden Needs **13**

> ## *Lisa's profile:*
>
> I am an outgoing fun person to be with <u>who has just got a job and moved to London</u> from Essex. Now looking for friends and maybe that 'someone special' to show me the sights.
>
> My friends would describe me as generous, kind and caring.
>
> I love football, fine wine and socialising. Look forward to hearing from you.

Richard's first communication to Lisa:

> **Hi Lisa**
>
> I saw your profile and just thought we had so much in common I had to write. I am a football fan too!
>
> So you are from Essex? Were you born there? ***You look like the archetypal blonde Essex girl, Fit, slim, attractive and intelligent, I would hazard a guess?*** (Well you cannot really say no can you!) And I was absolutely amazed that you have moved to London too. When was that?
>
> I came to London a few years back to work for a large organisation, but it was long hours, which didn't work out. Left the company soon after and started my own ***successful business***.
>
> So what else do you do, ***Susan?*** Lots ***by the look of it, sporty outdoor*** stuff? Maybe some fine dining with a nice glass of Chardonnay, Sov Blanc, Red (delete as appropriate).
>
> Do you go for walks locally? I kind of enjoy that sort of thing, sightseeing etc. It seems to relax me. I used to play football. But just walking around does me good.
>
> I love going to Borough Market with all the food stalls or out for a gourmet meal.
>
> So enough of this drivelling on about me. I would love to talk to you. I know that you may be exhausted on a Friday night so not sure whether to ring you tonight or maybe just over the weekend sometime, maybe Saturday morning even? Seems

that you are working too? _**I am impressed.**_ Do you have a preference?

Perhaps we can text each other to see when you are home or something along those lines. I am at home this evening at the moment. I might be tempted yet to walk over to the local champagne bar and go for a meal later on (my other passion - food). _**I feel a bit lonely on my own though.**_ But the food is usually good. If you want to text me and I will ring you back for example?

In general about me, though, in case you wonder what I am up to on these dating sites, I feel pretty comfortable in myself, but I also know that I am not getting any younger. Equally I am not in a headlong rush into a relationship, but I do seek deeper fulfilment and meaning and to make more friends and perhaps from that _**'someone special' to be with. I don't want to be alone forever.**_

So till later. Hope to chat soon and hope your week has been kind to you.

Richard

What to watch for – How to watch out for early red flags in writing

In the above example it would be difficult to know from just this email if there are any early warning signs that it was sent from a narcissist. Lisa really doesn't know who the person writing it actually is, or if what he (or even she) is saying is true.

If the email is read at face value, it is a chatty conversation style with flattery.

However, if you read the same email with **awareness** that not everyone 'thinks the same way as you' and take a more discerning view, there are a number of red flags that jump out of that initial email communication:

1. **Early instigation of a 'sad' story:** This included: _I feel a bit lonely on my own though_; and _I don't want to be alone forever._
2. **False flattery:** This included: _You look like the archetypal blonde Essex girl;_ Seems that you are working too? _I am impressed._

3. **Speculation/mind-reading assumption:** _Fit, slim, attractive and intelligent I would hazard a guess? By the look of it sporty outdoor_ (he is speculating because he only has a facial picture to go on.)
4. **Sense of urgency:** _Ring you tonight or maybe just over the weekend; Perhaps we can text each other; If you want to text me and I will ring you back. Hope to chat soon._
5. **Verbose and guess work:** A clever use of guess work including all options, so that one will be correct, e.g. _nice glass of Chardonnay, Sov Blanc, Red (delete as appropriate)._
6. **Wrong use of name in the text:** Richard uses the name 'Susan' in the text. This is a clear indicator this has been 'cut and pasted' and is not tailored to Lisa at all.
7. **Commonality:** Richard immediately advises that he has something in common with Lisa. Her profile has stated she has moved to the area and likes football, socialising and fine wine. He **mirrors** back with words that fulfil those **needs** in her profile by stating: I am a football fan too! _absolutely amazed that you have moved to London too; Chardonnay, Sov Blanc, Red (delete as appropriate)._

Practical Advice – How to navigate sad stories, false flattery and being aware of your needs

There are several methods of initial manipulation that a narcissist uses – a couple of these are sad life stories, false flattery and the speed of trying to control.

Of course, it is very hard to distinguish between genuine people who have gone through difficult periods in their life and narcissists using sad stories/false flattery to find out how easy you are to manipulate.

It is extremely difficult to tell the difference between the two initially.

Sad life stories of people you are just getting to know – What you can do:

(1) **Watch for people who instigate sad life stories** very early on when getting to know you. Make a note of how you respond. Do you believe them without questioning further? Do you avoid the conversation as it is uncomfortable? Do you feel compelled to help? How do you react? What are your emotions?

   a. A narcissist is looking for your **reaction**, in particular looking for someone with **empathy and sympathy**.

b. You can show empathy and sympathy for another person without having to be **drawn into their situation and offering to help.** E.g. 'I am sorry that happened to you.'

(2) **Ask plenty of questions** to establish the facts. Narcissists can lie fluently and dislike being questioned or being presented with facts. Careful questioning can help you find out if someone is telling the truth or not.

(3) **Narcissistic sad life stories lack accountability:** When they tell their story, note if they:
   a. Blame other people for their situation without taking any accountability themselves.
   b. If there are any facts to back up what they say: Is there anyone else you can ask to see if this sad story is the truth?
   c. Generalise: Make sweeping generalisations that cannot be verified.

(4) **Do your homework and don't automatically believe what you are told to be the truth.**
   a. For narcissists can tell GRANDIOSE lies to elicit your response. If you are the personality type that is overly trusting, it is in your best interests to validate the facts yourself.

False Flattery – What you can do:

(1) **Be wary of false flattery.** Think about WHY someone is being very flattering to you - what do they seek to GAIN? Is what they are saying over the top? Does it seem 'too good to be true'. Do they seem genuinely believable?

> **Ask direct questions** such as:
> 'Thank you. What makes you say that?'
>
> **If you suspect it is false flattery, challenge it.**
> 'Are you trying to butter me up for some reason?'

Being aware of your own needs/vulnerabilities – What you can do is:

(1) Become **aware** of what your own needs are, both conscious and unconscious.

(2) Be **careful what information you share** that might make you unwittingly vulnerable, e.g. you are lonely, alone, moved home or area or that you have money or assets. Make sure you are not sharing this information early on.

Before taking conversations offline quickly from dating sites – What you can do:

(1) Keep **conversations on the dating site** for as long as possible. It is especially important because you cannot always be sure of who you are actually speaking to online or even their gender or age. Because most dating websites don't offer robust screening services (you do not have to prove who you are to be on there), profiles, people and photos could be fake.

(2) **Ask for help from other people – Get their opinions:** Make sure you get other people's opinions if you are starting a romantic relationship online; often they can see what you cannot.

(3) **Look at fraud tactics:** Go to websites such as Action Fraud and Take Five.

(4) **Reverse photo searches:** This may bring up a different identity, so make sure you are checking. Go to Google Images to do this.

(5) **Checking their details:** Ask for specifics about who they are before you meet and clarify that online independently.

Chapter 5 – Love Blindness – First Date Red Flags

When considering a first date, there are a number of 'red flags' to be aware of. The most important 'red flag' is being aware of how you are feeling.

Did you feel uncomfortable in any way? Why was that? Did the person seem like a nice person, but there was 'something' you couldn't quite put your finger on it? Your gut feelings and intuition are really important.

What can be difficult, however, is when you are getting conflicting messages. Your date may appear intently interested in you, charming or even funny. They may be saying all the right things and telling you how much you may have in common. However, there is that subtle 'something' that doesn't quite feel right.

This is where it is really important to observe the FACTS on a date. What is actually happening rather than letting your heart get too carried away before getting to know someone.

Red flags can come out of observations:

- **How is the person treating those around you?** Are they being nice to everyone? How are they treating waiters/waitresses? Are they angry with anyone? Are they making disparaging remarks?
- **Are they talking badly about their ex-partner?** What are they saying? Is it dramatic? How quickly did they bring their ex-partner into the conversation? Do they take any accountability for the break-down of the relationship? How?
- **How are they treating you?** Are they asking lots of questions? Are they leading the conversation? Are they asking about personal things early on?
- **How do they connect with you physically?** Do they take your hand/elbow/shoulder and lead you in a particular direction? Are they subtly trying to control where you go?
- **Do they take control?** Do they 'tell' rather than 'ask' you what you want? Do they choose for you? Do they presume to know your needs without asking?
- **Do they bring in a sad life story**? What is the purpose of the story? What are your reactions to it? Do they watch how you respond?
- **Are they funny?** Do they make you laugh? Are the jokes at someone else's expense, or funny in a different way?

- **Are they charming?** Do they give you lots of over-the-top compliments? Do they listen intently to what you have to say? Do they bring in commonalities to the conversation quickly?
- **Were there any initial 'lies'?** Was there anything they said or didn't say that was different to previous conversations? What was that? What did you do or say?
- **Did they use phrases like:** 'You think ...' (Mind-reading.)
- **Did they over-talk?**
- **Did they include any type of guilt-tripping in the conversation?** Did they complain about the cost of anything? Did you feel guilty for anything, e.g. for being slightly late?
- **What did they want you to know about them?** When you came away from the date, what were the impression(s) that they gave you? Was it grandiose in any way? Was it almost unbelievable? Were you shocked? Were you very impressed by their job/career/car/way they dressed?

What to watch for – How to watch out for red flags on a date with a narcissist

Red flags on a date

Here are some of the tactics that can be used by narcissists on a first date to watch out for:

- **Intensity:** Narcissists can be persistent and very intense. It is likely to appear that you are the total focus of their attention.
- **Taking control:** Subtle and not so subtle methods of taking control. This might include suggestions, directing where people sit, ordering drinks and food without asking and subtle manipulation phrases like 'I would never ...'; 'If, I was you, I would ...'
- **Self-pity:** One tactic a narcissist may use is a self-pity sad story to evaluate your empathy levels. Empathetic people can be easier to manipulate.
- **Offering you something you need:** A narcissist is likely to evaluate if there is something you 'need' – a simple example might be offering to fix your car if it is having problems for free (but really a narcissist is offering something that can be used as a bargaining chip later and are likely to consider that they are 'owed' something in return – i.e. it is not real generosity, it has a catch).
- **Charm and flattery:** A narcissist is likely to be aware that people will

let their guard down and open up more when they use charm and flattery.

- **Glib promises:** Insincere and glib promises may be used to try to gain quick commonality and put the victim at ease. This, for example, might be promises such as 'I would never treat you like your ex,' if you mention that you have broken up.
- **Lying and believing everyone lies:** Because a narcissist's belief system can be that there is nothing wrong with lying, they may also assume that everyone else lies.
- **Observing reaction to lies and misleading information:** This technique can be used by narcissists to establish how easy someone is to manipulate. Someone who challenges misleading information or lies is unlikely to be considered a viable future 'victim'.
- **Mind-reading:** This technique can be used to try to elicit information. The approach is stating 'You think …' and then the narcissist will state information they believe to be correct. In this way the victim feels like a narcissist may well 'know them well' or conversely correct them – either way this tactic can gain a narcissist important information about what someone is really thinking.
- **Playing the victim role:** This may be used to gain sympathy. They may be fine actors or actresses when they tell a compelling story about how they have been victimised. The story that they tell could be completely fake or dramatized for effect, but their performance of the story (tears, sadness, feeling sorry for themselves) will be quite believable.
- **Meanness and guilt-tripping:** Narcissists can show their true qualities, e.g. by being mean to other people. If you observe the way that they treat staff or other people is disrespectful, demanding or degrading it is a sure sign that this is how they are likely to treat you later on.

Red flag – Conversations being led

There is a big difference between someone being self-absorbed or selfish and someone being a narcissist.

The self-absorbed may frequently respond to a topic of conversation you are having with 'I know, when I …' and then may take over the conversation from their own perspective (even if it is irrelevant to what you have just been saying). Irritating, but not necessarily a narcissist.

A narcissist can enjoy the sound of their own voice with grandiose talking about themselves, but I have also observed that they also have another tactic to lead the conversations in a certain way. They are doing it for a different reason – to see how you respond to lies and glean information about your reaction.

This might include:

1. **Raising a question at the end of a statement/long story to glean information:** For example a narcissist might make a statement/story about themselves and then ask a specific question to see which aspects of their story/statement took your interest. It can differ from normal conversation because the first part is egotistical and self-absorbed and the second aspect – the question – is helping them identify if you 'go along' with their story. It seems to be an initial step to help a narcissist identify if you can be manipulated. For example, if a narcissist was lying about their career, they might state:

   'When I was in travelling with the military, top of my game you know, a captain at the time, I was awarded a long service medal in the end. In the attic now, I think. Not that we speak about it, you know, but as I was saying the buildings were amazing. The architecture so precise, don't you think?'

   Here we have the grandiose statements 'captain', 'long service medal', 'top of my game' ending with a question about the architecture. This gets the 'story' into the conversation (and your mind). The end question cleverly deflects all the lies about their career so that the 'story' itself is not challenged.

   Someone more easily manipulated might just answer the question about architecture at the end to politely follow on conversation (and take the previous information as factual).

2. **Making multi-choice statements to get your opinion:** The purpose of this is like a funnelling effect where the narcissist states multiple options to help them understand your particular interests or 'hooks' in the conversation. The technique helps them hone into areas that interest you. They are aware that commonality helps you open up and therefore ensures a better flow of information. This technique is also used by people in general. The difference being most people are looking for commonality to share, whereas a narcissist is looking for commonality to find opportunities to exploit later.

3. **Burying controversial topics in the middle of the conversation sentence:** This technique is used to steer the conversation their own

way. This is done by bringing in a contentious/controversial issue into the middle of the conversation and then deliberately continuing to talk about something normal. It appears to be a method that narcissists use to *understand if this makes their audience uncomfortable or confused about how to respond.* E.g. 'Nice weather today, well I'm an expert weatherman you know, but I do think the good weather will continue, don't you?'

4. **Using silence to influence and steer group conversations:** This is an interesting technique that narcissists seem to use to get their views and opinions out, without anyone in a group contradicting them in public. The aim is for them to steer the conversation so that lies can be hidden or change the viewpoint of the group into one that they want the group to agree to.

   When they take control of the conversation, they state lies or half lies as if they were truth and facts. When done in front of other people, they are fully aware that most people will not contradict them in public. The lies tend to stick as truth because no one speaks up at the time. E.g. a narcissist speaking about his wife, Eleanor, in front of new friends:

   > *'As I said to Eleanor the other day, when she made the decision that we had to leave the area because it wasn't upmarket enough for her. You know, I said, Eleanor, you are right. So, that's why we moved here and are new to the area. Thanks for inviting us over!'*

   This statement implies that Eleanor is to blame for the decision to move to a more upmarket area. The reason for the move (the facts) were that the narcissist had lost his previous job and they were forced to relocate. With Eleanor sitting in on the same conversation with new friends, it would be difficult for Eleanor to speak out and call the lie out. The reason for moving 'her need for an upmarket area' becomes 'the truth' because Eleanor was uncomfortable (or pressured) by the narcissist to say nothing.

5. **Saying deliberately controversial things:** This is another interesting technique used. When a narcissist wants more attention, opinion or reaction, they may say something controversial to gain that attention. It is also seems to be used by narcissists to explore who responds to controversy and who calls them to account.

If you see any of the above behaviours on the first few dates, be cautious.

Practical advice – Narcissistic lies and conversations being led

Narcissistic lies

People do lie, people do make genuine errors and people do exaggerate on dating profiles to put their best foot forward. With a narcissist the difference seems to be that they have no emotional attachment to what effect their lies might have on other people. They do not seem to care. They also appear to assume other people are lying. What they seem to be looking for is the response to the lies.

So, how can you tell the difference between someone telling a small white lie or a narcissist? It's difficult. What I have observed is that they can become defensive when challenged – including getting angry (so that you back down on your questions), putting out false allegations that you then need to defend or answering a question with a question to evade having to answer it.

A lie is a lie is a lie? Maybe. My question would be, if someone has lied about this [small thing], what else might they not be telling the truth about?

Your best option seems to be to decide what your personal values are about lying. This might include zero tolerance or it being acceptable to have someone in your life who tells small white lies (e.g. through embarrassment or to not hurt you), but not someone who lies because they are wanting to manipulate those around them or those who habitually lie.

When you observe a lie, you can decide not to call them up on the lie immediately, but make a mental and physical note of what was said differently and ask them the same question another time. When asking the question, take care how you ask it:

(1) **Be specific about the lie** – 'I'm a little confused, why did you say xyz, when you said abc before?' A narcissist may minimise/trivialise the lie and say something like 'Oh, it doesn't matter anyway', 'It was only a little lie', or 'I don't recall I said that. Are you sure?'

(2) **Ask directly** – Did you just lie to me?

> WARNING: A narcissist will hate to be called up on their lies and can become defensive and/or angry or try to deflect the question right back. Typical responses might be 'No, I did not lie!', 'Are you calling me a liar?', 'Don't you believe me?' or 'No, why would you think that?' They will want you to back down.
>
> Responding to a question with a question is a defensive stance. It

puts the onus of providing an answer back on the person asking the original question. It can be rather tricky to navigate out of it without getting drawn into a defensive conversation, so I would suggest ignoring any 'why' questions back with clarity on your own question.

Be specific about the lie itself and not the person lying:

a. 'No need to get defensive, I am just trying to clarify why you said previously xyz and now you are saying abc.'

b. 'You previously said xyz and now you are saying abc.'

These are important strategies regarding a narcissist because they are very often not accountable for their words and may be very defensive when found to be lying.

Red flag – Conversations being led

If you notice that conversations are being led – someone is over-talking or talking excessively about themselves, consider taking the relationship much more slowly to evaluate things. A narcissist will want to charge ahead quickly, so taking your time to consider how you feel first is important. Don't be rushed.

Remember a date is to **find out about someone** and to see if this fits with your **values, beliefs, wants and needs**. Love cannot be rushed.

Chapter 6 – More red flags – Breaking Boundaries, Pedestalling and Future Dreams

If a narcissist is interested in you, the next set of red flags to observe are:

(1) Do they break personal, social or legal boundaries?
(2) Do they 'pedestal' you with declarations of love and devotion early on?
(3) Do they talk enthusiastically about future dreams?

Any of these could potentially be a 'red flag' and point to a narcissist. In particular you will notice that these things happen normally **together and at speed**.

An example of boundary breaking and pedestalling

After just one date, Richard, a narcissist, has become **intense** with Lisa.

Lisa has advised Richard where she works, but not to contact her there. However, Richard ignores her request and sends an email which **breaks her boundary, uses flattery, pressurise her to meet and early instigation of pedestalling**: Relevant text is highlighted.

> **To:** Lisa
> **Subject:** Good morning gorgeous
> Hiya.
>
> What a pleasure to meet someone so special last night, <u>I feel you are morphing into my soul mate</u>. You have been absolutely on my mind. I enjoyed the wine, the company. It is an experience and a privilege. <u>You looked so stunning and beautiful. And, so understanding and compassionate.</u>
>
> I have to meet you again. No pressure and I totally understand if you say no. <u>I just had such a strong feeling that we should see each other again soon.</u>
>
> <u>Now why do I risk telling you this at work?</u> Well, A) I can't wait until Saturday, B) I miss you already, C) I really mean it.
>
> Richard

26 Section 1 – Recognising the 16 Stages of Narcissistic Abuse

The way that Lisa responds will help Richard determine:

- **How she asserts her personal boundaries;**
- **What she does when Richard deliberately breaks her boundary;**
- **How she reacts to flattery and over-the-top praise;**
- **How she reacts to pedastalling;**
- **How she responds to pressure to meet.**

In this example, Lisa responds in a weakly assertive way rather than enforcing her own boundaries:

> **To:** Richard
> **Subject:** Good morning gorgeous
> Hello there
>
> It would be lovely to see you again soon. I'll call you tonight. I'm at work at the moment and I've lots of meetings today. Lisa x
>
> PS We're not really supposed to send personal emails at work – so I don't want to get into any trouble!

This weakly assertive response is unlikely to be a deterrent to a narcissist. This response, could lead onto the love-bombing stage (see Chapter 8). This is likely to include:

(1) Increased intensity of contact
(2) Gifts
(3) Declarations of undying love and devotion
(4) Promises for the future/future dreams
(5) Telling someone how perfect they are

What to watch for – Narcissists Breaking Boundaries

Narcissists do not appear to be as constrained by legal, moral, social or personal boundaries as other people (because they get in the way of their needs or they are superior and do not need to abide by the same rules as other people).

Because of this, you are likely to notice some of the following:

- **'So what?' attitude**: You might notice if you ask a narcissist why they break the rules, a narcissist will respond with a 'so what?' attitude. They appear to minimise breaking boundaries. If there are little or few consequences to breaking rules, regulations or even the law, their attitude is one of 'I will do what I please!'
- **Following rules and regulations is inconvenient at best and angering at worst:** Because a narcissist's NEEDS are the most important thing to them, rules, laws and regulations at best are inconvenient to follow (if they chose to) and at worst it is like a red rag to a bull – absolutely unacceptable in their mind that these rules, regulations and law could get in the way of their needs.
- **Narcissists seem to test everyone around them on their boundaries to see how strong they are:** It may seem quite minor, but a narcissist tests everyone around them to see who conforms to rules, laws and regulations and who does not. More importantly, they are also checking you out to see whether you give way to your own principles.
- **Narcissists may pressurise you and test your boundaries further:** Because your boundaries can get in the way of narcissist's needs, if you strongly enforce your personal boundaries expect responses which can **mock, trivialise, shame and challenge you.** Expect to hear things like, 'Oh, go on, what's the harm in it?' or 'Who cares! Really, you shouldn't be so concerned about that!', 'Who's going to know?', 'It doesn't really matter that much does it?', 'Oh come on, who's going to find out?' or 'So what?' They may even pretend it's a joke, 'Oh come on, don't you have a sense of humour?', 'Lighten up, it was just a prank!'
- **Subtle control – Making exceptions:** You might hear something along the lines of 'Oh, could you make an exception and do it just this once for me?' which is part of a narcissist's entitlement.

The techniques of blatantly breaking rules, regulations or laws differ from other people. Narcissists break rules, regulations or laws because it inconveniently gets in the way of their needs and wants, and they are not afraid of the consequences.

'Not all rule and boundary breakers are narcissists, but narcissists will nearly always break boundaries and rules.' A M Buck

Practical advice – Speaking out assertively and setting healthy boundaries

It is important to have your own strong personal boundaries – those things you will accept and those things that you won't accept. People with weak(er) boundaries are more easily manipulated by narcissists.

At times, it is necessary to speak assertively – especially when someone is breaking your healthy boundaries. But it may not be natural for you and actually feel uncomfortable. It is important to learn these skills if they do not come naturally. Training is available to assist with speaking out and setting healthy boundaries (be it counsellors or through online courses).

It is especially important to have extremely strong, impenetrable boundaries with a narcissist as they are likely to try to break them early on and break them down further the longer you are in a relationship.

Remember, narcissists work in a completely different way to many people. To them boundaries exist as an inconvenience, or if they do adhere to them it is because they are forced to do so. Meeting their own needs is more important than your personal boundaries or indeed social, moral or legal boundaries.

When we look at the response that Lisa sent in her email, she could have had a more assertive response:

(1) **Assertive responses:**
   a. Richard, please do not contact me at work. I asked you not to. Will speak later. (Much firmer.)
   b. Blocked his email and not responded until she was out of work.
   c. Realised this was unhealthy boundary breaking and question it.

Practical advice – Other typical boundary breaking techniques

Here are some of the other subtle ways narcissists (and other manipulative people), try to get you to break your own boundaries:

1. **Guilt-tripping against vague 'general' or 'popular' opinions:** A manipulative person is aware that guilt is a great way to manipulate other people. If you try to assert a boundary, they might for example say something along the lines of 'Really?', 'Oh, come on, no one cares about that' or 'Who's really going to find out?' The answer to this needs

to be personalised to your own boundaries:

(a) Statement of fact – 'I care, it matters to me.'

(b) Statement of fact – 'I will know, and I don't agree with that.'

(c) Generalise – 'When did you start thinking everyone breaks the rules?'

This will undoubtedly lead to further attempts at guilt-tripping, but you will need to end the conversation – perhaps saying directly, 'No. My opinion will not change,' and repeat it over and over again if necessary.

2. **Minimising or trivialising rule breaking:** Typically, they might say 'So, what?', 'No-one cares about it' or 'Look, other people do it all the time – what's your problem?' The narcissist is likely to be adamant that breaking rules are to be trivialised. This is because they do not have the same concerns as other people about the consequences. By encouraging you to break your own boundaries it gives the narcissist a useful advantage to use against you later. To prevent this, stating your boundaries is important. For example: 'Come on, just this once. What's the problem?'

Statement of fact: 'I am not breaking the rules for you or anyone else'

Generalise: 'When did you start thinking that I had a problem?'

3. **Wanting to change the rules in his or her favour:** This may take the form of making the 'rule' or 'boundary' stupid, wrong or not worthwhile because it makes it more difficult for a narcissist to get their own way and get what they need more efficiently. It differs from someone who has inadvertently broken rules, as they are more likely to be apologetic if confronted. This might include when someone says, 'The rules are stupid anyway – why are you following them?' You could respond with:

Statement of fact: 'The rules may be stupid, but we still need to abide by them'

4. **Charm:** This one is particularly useful to a narcissist. They are aware that when they use charm, it is far easier to manipulate someone. Stage 1 is always to get people to like them and this is applied through false flattery and finding things in common. This technique is used very calmly by a narcissist, e.g. smiling, they might ask, 'Oh, I know I'm asking you to break the rules, but this is really an exception and I know you hate enforcing those rules really.' To overcome this, again boundaries need to be enforced using statements of fact.

Statement of fact: There are no exceptions, this is what you need to do.

5. **Sexual and flirtatious manipulation:** This technique equally applies to male and female narcissists. For example, slowing down speech in a seductive way, smiles, subtle touches of the lips, hair flicking, dressing provocatively, intense eye contact, fluttering eyelashes, strutting, preening or sitting in a seductive way. The technique is used then to ask for what they want; typically they would like an 'exception' made for them e.g. queue jumping. If a narcissist is attempting queue jumping, a firm no will likely result in contempt, false accusations and anger. A more subtle rejection could be:

No response to flirtation: 'If you could wait in line for your turn please.'

6. **Asking for help with small things/directing people:** This technique is used to get someone to do something. It can be something as small as 'Can you hang my coat up please?', 'Would you just help me with xyz?' Or 'would you make me a cup of coffee?' This can also be used by non-narcissists, the difference being that with a narcissist once you have done the 'little something', the requests get bigger.

About pedestalling and future dreams

What do we mean by pedestalling and future dreams? They are terms used to describe **over the top, intense and great grandiose displays of love and devotion early on.** During the pedestalling and future dreams stage, a narcissist will go to great lengths to make you feel wonderful and totally loved and appreciated for who you are. This may also be accompanied by gifts, treats and compliments. What differentiates a narcissist is the **promise of future dreams.**

When you are being pedestalled you may feel **overwhelmingly loved and euphoric that someone cares that much about you.** This is sadly just a phase and is not real-love at all.

During the pedestalling and future dreams stage a narcissist is likely to be very romantic, charming and share intimate and personal details, proclaim undying love and use phrases such as 'soulmates', 'belong together' or 'you are "the one" I have searched for all my life'. It can be very intense and convincing.

This is an example of a typical future dreams email that might be received. These 'scripts' are often downloaded from the internet. For this example, Martin is the victim to Penny, a narcissist.

> Dear Martin
>
> I want you to know that I love you and I am going to love you in your weakest moments to your strongest ones.
>
> I am going to love you when you are happy and I am going to love you when you are sad, just like I always have.
>
> We are going to have the most wonderful life together, you and me and create all those dreams.
>
> I will show you my love and never give up on something this special. I am here and not going anywhere.
>
> You mean the world to me and I want you with your imperfections – I just want you simply for being you.
>
> Forever yours – I will always be by your side, loving you with everything I have.
>
> Penny xxxxxxx

In this example, Penny is actually a narcissist looking for money from Martin. She proclaims to be out of an abusive relationship, which plays to Martin's unconscious 'rescuer' nature. This, however, is untrue. He wants to help her, to rescue her and be her hero. The relationship, however, is only ever over the internet and by phone, so Martin has yet to meet Penny.

Initially she feeds into all his unconscious needs and she reinforces the message that he is the one who has rescued her and elaborates details of the abuse to gain his sympathy. She declares her love to Martin in the pedestalling and future dreams stage. Later she starts sending Martin gifts to build up trust that she is genuine and generous. Penny uses this as a ploy in the beginning and only starts asking for more money some time later after Martin is 'hooked' (the TRAP moment).

Practical advice – How to navigate pedestalling

Pedestalling

When you are being pedestalled, it is a very personal and private situation that is rarely shared with other people. It is a quick, fast, way for a narcissist to form a bond with you – **that is, away from anyone else**. It can be intense, intoxicating and is designed to give you the feeling of love and euphoria. You might feel **included, special and that this is the love of your life.**

32 Section 1 – Recognising the 16 Stages of Narcissistic Abuse

However, for a narcissist, their 'words' very often have no real substance, meaning or even deep feelings. They are simply tools in a narcissist's arsenal which allows them to gain control.

They may, in fact, say whatever you want to really, deeply hear about yourself.

Let's look at some of the warning signs, that you might consider red flags at the pedestalling stage and how to navigate these:

1. **Extreme compliments and loving sentiments:** These are generally 'over the top' for someone that you have recently met. For example, in the email sent by Richard to Lisa – *'I feel you are morphing into my soul mate'* – is a very strong statement after only meeting for a first date. This should be quite a strong warning sign to Lisa to be cautious. To make sure that you are not being pedestalled, it is important to:

   a. **Pause, take a step back:** Whilst it is flattering to be adored, taking a step back and taking things slowly will save you heartache later on. Rarely is it ever love at first sight and someone who is genuinely interested in you will wait.

   b. **Asking someone else you trust if this is unusual:** Asking a trusted friend or family member can help validate if the compliments and loving sentiments are over the top. It is easier for someone else to see pedestalling. If a trusted friend or family member thinks that it is over the top, they might ask you questions such as 'What does that person want?' or 'What are they after?' Be prepared for this as it is a fair question.

   c. **Listen to your gut feeling and only take advice from trusted others:** If you are someone who is easily swayed, or indecisive, it is imperative you take time to process what you are actually feeling. Writing pros and cons down even.

2. **Flattery is intense and can be exactly what you had inadvertently said you needed:** Before the pedestalling stage, a narcissist may well have been asking a lot of questions and listening intently to some things more than others. For example if you complained that your last partner 'never gave you compliments', then the narcissist is likely to initially fake empathy and at the pedestalling stage is going to make sure that they give you a huge amount of compliments.

   This can be intoxicating, because you may feel you have been heard and listened to and it is everything you ever wanted from a partner. Sadly, with a narcissist, this is likely to be information gathering rather than real. If in doubt, ask yourself, what would a sensible other person say about the flattery you are receiving?

3. **Speed:** This is the biggest warning sign. A narcissist may well want to overwhelm you with loving emotions at the earliest possible opportunity. In fact, by making you believe you are loved, is a very fast way to take down your defences and even negate your own nagging doubts. Whilst pedestalling is likely to invoke your genuine feelings, the narcissist is probably not feeling the same way. They are just words to them.

This is why it is so important to take a new relationship slowly, giving yourself time to process everything.

The way to overcome pedestalling is insisting on taking your time in a new relationship and ensuring you talk about the relationship with trusted friends and family. This would be the last thing a narcissist wants, and they may either try even harder or simply walk away from the relationship swiftly.

A narcissist may put added pressure on you, saying things like 'I have enough love for the two of us', 'How can anyone else know what a special thing we have here?', 'Why wait – I love you?', 'Our love is so amazing, no one else could know.' The answer to this is:

a. **Statement of fact:** 'This has happened so fast. Love grows over time, so there's no rush at all – we have our future together. Let's take things slowly at a pace I am comfortable with.'

A genuine person would respect this. A narcissist would be angered and possibly walk away.

Practical advice – How to balance future dreams

Future dreams

In the future dreams stage, a narcissist will create imaginary **future dreams** which hook into **every dream you ever desired or wanted**.

It is like a fairy tale because you may be **promised the life you want, the dreams you want, the lifestyle you want, the love and devotion you want**.

However, these future dreams are sadly just that: **DREAMS at worst**, or **come with huge consequences at best**.

34 Section 1 – Recognising the 16 Stages of Narcissistic Abuse

From a narcissistic perspective, they are designed to make you:

(1) Let your guard down.
(2) Believe you have found 'the one' person in your life that really understands and gets you.
(3) Get you to think about the future instead of what is going on in the present moment.
(4) Get you to commit more fully to the relationship (so that they can isolate you later).

And because many narcissists are **very often successful** in life because of their personality traits (or lie that they are successful), they do often come with the seemingly attractive package of:

(1) Wealth/security.
(2) Great lifestyles.
(3) Fame.

But, the question is how much you are willing to pay for the dreams being offered (if they are true). Even grandiose statements like 'I don't care where we live as long as I am with you' should send out alarm bells.

The practical way to deal with these future dreams, particularly if you are being pedestalled at the beginning of the relationship is to:

Slow down the relationship. Take your time.

Evaluate how possible the future dream actually is. Who is paying for the future dream? Who is benefiting from it? What is in the dream for you? What if the future dream is untrue?

Chapter 7 - Be Whole, Be Self-Aware Before Being Loved - Wounded Inner Child and Schemas

The wounded inner child is a term I use to describe vulnerable emotional aspects of someone's personality. For example, if a child had been left home alone for long periods of time as a child, the child is likely to grow up with a wounded inner child of 'abandonment'. When the child becomes an adult, they are likely to feel distress when someone withdraws/leaves, unconsciously triggering deep fears that they are repeating the incident from childhood.

I define schemas for this book as pre-existing thoughts, which are a set of 'beliefs' used by your mind to interpret the information around you. These are generally unconscious beliefs which can influence behaviour. They tend to reinforce existing beliefs (from experience).

For example, if one of your unconscious schemas (beliefs) is that 'other people are unreliable', then you are more likely to focus your attention on validating that belief. Even when people are reliable, you can dismiss this as being 'unusual'. The mind filtered information to fit your belief.

What to watch for – Be whole, be self-aware before being loved – identifying your inner child and your schemas

Before forming a relationship, it is important to work out your own inner child (needs) and your unconscious schemas. This work is best done with the help of a qualified psychologist.

I would personally recommend reading the book by Wendy T Behary, LCSW *Disarming the Narcissist, Surviving and Thriving with the Self-Absorbed*, which has a much fuller explanation of schemas.

In this book, schemas are reproduced from work by Jeffrey Young, PhD and grouped into eighteen early maladaptive schemas identified. by Jeffrey Young.

Schemas

This is how I interpret schemas from a layperson's perspective, 'thoughts' used by your mind to interpret information around you:

Schema	What you might be thinking/feeling if you have this type of schema
Self-Sacrifice to the point of suppressing your own needs	'I don't like asking for what I need' 'I feel guilty when I ask for what I need' 'I try to prevent causing pain to others' 'I feel guilty when I am selfish'
Other people's needs come first	I put other people's feelings first' 'I put other people's needs 'above mine'' 'I am compliant' 'My feelings and opinions are not important to others'
Suppressing how you really feel	'I keep my feelings to myself' 'I control my emotions' 'I don't tell people how bad I am really feeling'
Unreliable support around you	'I am afraid of being rejected' 'I am afraid of being alone' 'Other people are unreliable' 'I expect to be abandoned in my relationship'
Imperfect and flawed belief	'I am not good enough' 'I buy into criticism' 'I have many flaws' 'I am inferior to others' 'I am very self-conscious'
Emotional support is lacking around you	'I am not sure that anyone really understands me' 'I don't get the affection and attention I need' 'I don't know if there is anyone out there that can meet my emotional needs' 'I don't believe there is anyone who can protect me'
Expecting mistrust and being hurt	'I expect others to hurt me' 'I am familiar with abuse' 'I give in under emotional pressure' 'I have to people please to avoid anger/punishment'
High Standards to avoid criticism	'I try very hard to be the perfect partner' 'I know what is expected of me as a partner' 'I will compromise some pleasure to please someone else'

Do some of these resonate with you? If so, you may have discovered something very important about yourself and how you **unconsciously** view the world. These belief systems also make you attractive to a narcissist.

Narcissists also have schemas – but theirs seem to be quite opposite to their victim and include things like entitlement, grandiosity, insufficient self-control and punishing others to name but a few.

Typical schemas narcissists have may run along the lines of:

- 'I am entitled to that because ...'
- 'I know better because ...'
- 'I don't have to stick to the rules because ...'
- 'I refuse to be constrained by ...'
- 'You are being nice to me because you want something'
- 'I am special because ...'
- 'I have to control this situation/person because ...'
- 'I know you are lying to me ....'

In addition, because their voice needs to be heard, they are likely to behave in a way that is constantly attention-seeking (good or bad), looking for recognition of their status/wealth/achievements and this may also drive their perfectionism (because they believe they are entitled to the best of things).

When you consider how **DIFFERENT** narcissistic schemas are, then you can see why people who are self-sacrificing, have low self-esteem, weak personal boundaries, are people-pleasing, empathetic and trusting, to name but a few, can be manipulated by a narcissist.

Narcissist's unconscious beliefs?	How a narcissist might test a victim's suitability	Type of person that is likely to be of interest to a narcissist
'I am special, self-important and better than other people.'	– Reactions to their claims of superiority. – Reactions to statements such as 'I would never ...', 'You should ...' and 'You think ...'	Those who are: – Impressed by a narcissist's grandiosity/status/confidence. – Self-sacrificing so that they put the needs of a narcissist before their own. – Adore the narcissist and help them achieve their goals. – Apologetic. Easily led by someone.

38 Section 1 – Recognising the 16 Stages of Narcissistic Abuse

Narcissist's unconscious beliefs?	How a narcissist might test a victim's suitability	Type of person that is likely to be of interest to a narcissist
'I expect to be recognised and treated differently.'	– Reactions to statements such as 'I am better than . . .', 'You can make an exception for me can't you?', 'We have to do it this way.'	– Someone who praises narcissist's achievements and downplays their own. – Someone who wants the best in people and strives to help achieve that. – Someone who doesn't speak up when boundaries are crossed. – People-pleasing.
'I am entitled to special treatment.'	– Reactions to their victimhood sad stories – whether true or false. Statements like 'You wouldn't do that would you?' – Reactions to their grandiose statements such as 'We will change the world ...', 'We are so much better than other people ...', 'We can make a difference ...'	– Someone who has an abundance of empathy. – Someone who can be manipulated by guilt. – Someone who is looking for a greater meaning in life.
'I don't trust other people's motives.'	– Reactions to statements such as 'Everyone lies don't they?' or 'Everyone is out for themselves.'	– Someone who will go out of the way to prove that they are trustworthy by being open and honest. – Someone who is prepared to be tolerant and loyal to demonstrate trust. – Someone who wants to love another and feel better through their love.
'People want something from me.'	– Reactions to statements such as 'We don't need agreements between ourselves.'	– Someone who has something a narcissist wants e.g. wealth, status, servitude. – Someone that takes things at face value. – Someone who doesn't insist on contracts.

Narcissist's unconscious beliefs?	How a narcissist might test a victim's suitability	Type of person that is likely to be of interest to a narcissist
'I will control you before you control me.'	– Reactions to taking the lead to 'Make us a cup of tea would you', – 'Would you hang my coat up please?'	– Someone influenced by subtle initial control.
'I want things done perfectly and I want the best of everything.'	– Reactions to demands of how things 'should and must' be done. – Reactions to wanting the best things in life.	– Someone who is conscientious and prepared to make changes to themselves to meet the narcissist's needs. – Someone who is prepared to pay for lavish items.
'There is no harm in lying to get what I want.'	– Reactions to deliberate lies are studied carefully to establish if they are believed.	– Someone who believes what they are told. – Someone who asks few questions.

This is why it is really important for you to be self-aware and whole before forming new relationships. In particular, you will be attractive to a narcissist if you:

- **Show signs of a lack of self-esteem/confidence/vulnerability:** This might include if you have few friends/family or no support network. This might include personality types, such as 'people pleasers' or someone who has moved to a new area.
- **Put others first:** This one is important to a narcissist because it makes someone more malleable and more easily manipulated. Narcissists do not date narcissists. They are seeking someone who puts others' needs first. The carers and 'nice' people of the world.
- **Have had previous trauma:** It seems to be useful to a narcissist to find someone who has had a childhood trauma, dysfunctional family environment or difficult upbringing. This gives them the knowledge that it is likely that submissive patterns have already been ingrained a long time ago.
- **Do not speak out:** Someone who is not confident speaking up for themselves, maybe because they want to **avoid conflict**, can be manipulated by implanting views or opinions.

- **Are loyal:** This is extremely important to a narcissist. Very early on, they are likely to establish loyalty by giving out personal information such as a 'secret'. This information may or may not be true, but the test is if you are loyal enough to keep the information secret. If someone keeps loyal, they are more likely to keep bad behaviour by the narcissist a secret as well.
- **Have empathy:** Running parallel to the 'sad' stories, a narcissist is looking for someone who has empathy. They want to be able to manipulate the emotions of guilt, shame and 'feeling sorry' for someone else or 'the rescuer' or 'saviour'.
- **Avoids conflict/are polite:** Another attribute a narcissist is looking for is avoidance of conflict and politeness. These two personality traits mean that you are less likely to stand up to them.

Practical advice – How to identify your own wounded inner child and schemas

Wounded inner child and schemas

There are plenty of great resources out there that are likely to help you identify your own wounded inner child and schemas. It is my opinion that once you are made more aware of your schemas, it can help you understand yourself better and what drives you as a person. Here is where you can get some help:

1. **Self-help books:** These can be very insightful in identifying some of your wounded inner child and schemas – but seek professional help changing or adjusting them to something more positive. These make you more aware of yourself. One of the best books I have found for this is called *Disarming the Narcissist: Surviving and Thriving with the Self-Absorbed* by Wendy T Behary, LCSW. The eighteen maladaptive schemas described are reproduced in her book with the permission of Jeffrey Young, PhD.
2. **Meditation/visualisation:** These types of methods can help you to identify your wounded inner child. Advocates of this include great books from Cooper, Diana. 1998. *Transform your life: a step-by-step programme for change*. This popular approach can make you more self-aware.
3. **Counselling/psychotherapy:** The right psychotherapist or councillors are properly trained to help with identification and self-awareness of your schemas in a safe supportive environment. Make sure you do your

research because some counsellors/psychotherapists are better than others – specifically relating to abuse, trauma and narcissists.

A good counsellor and psychotherapist will not only help you become more aware of your schemas and wounded inner child but offer practical assistance in observing your vulnerabilities and recovery from it. Ask what their experience is and qualifications regarding narcissism. What type of counselling/therapy do they do? Some offer excellent regression therapies which use visualisations to go back and change your perception of events (such as rewind techniques, NLP and CBT).

Phase 2 – First Level Control Tactics

Chapter 8 – Love-Bombing and Social Engineering – Manipulation of Those Around the Victim

Love-bombing is a term often used when talking about narcissism and is typically about 'over the top' compliments and gestures. It is used by a narcissist to make sure that they 'secure you' as their object of desire and can 'control you' in the future. It is typically characterised by:

- Over-the-top compliments
- Excessive communication/intensity
- Constant showering of affection and attention
- 'Soul-mate' and other 'meant to be' claims
- Demanding commitment/premises of devotion
- Disrespecting boundaries
- Neediness
- Gifting and grand gestures (but these may not be what you want)
- Making you feel so special just for being you
- Expecting prompt responses
- Feelings of intoxication and euphoria
- Declarations of love and devotion
- Future dreams

What narcissists seem to be doing at this stage is the start of emotional abuse and is extremely dangerous. It creates an unhealthy dependency if you are unable to set boundaries.

Unfortunately with a narcissist this can feel like a 'euphoric' stage, but is the start of the cycle of abuse – all the nice compliments, gifts and attention is later on painfully replaced with criticising, minimising, gaslighting or any other of the many techniques used.

What isn't discussed always is in addition to the love-bombing, **a** narcissist is also **MANIPULATING the social environment** of the victim by influencing friends, family, neighbours and colleagues.

Example of love-bombing – Richard and Lisa

Richard has stepped up his pursuit of Lisa with the following love-bombing techniques:

- Texting and emailing Lisa an unhealthy number of times a day
- Declaring his love for Lisa with words like:
    - ✧ 'I love you so much, you make my life complete.'
    - ✧ 'I need you, Lisa, in my life.'
    - ✧ 'I just miss you so much when you are not around.'
    - ✧ 'I just can't be without you in my life. You are my soul mate.'
    - ✧ 'I need you closer to me.'
- Writing poetry for Lisa declaring his love
- Treating Lisa to expensive restaurant meals, football games and jewellery

In addition, Richard is starting to put unhealthy pressure and guilt-tripping on Lisa to demand commitment. This includes:

- **Unhealthy Pressure/Guilt-Tripping:** Richard is stating 'I love you so much, but it is so hard to keep this relationship going when you live so far away from me. It would be so much easier for us to get closer when you live with me. I am not sure how much longer I can keep commuting that far to see you.' If you are here, we can help each other through the bad times.

Richard is pressuring Lisa to move in with him as quickly as possible: a sure sign of love-bombing.

Example of love-bombing – Martin and Penny

The love-bombing stage for Martin and Penny intensifies with gifts and long phone conversations. They talk online and by telephone for hours every day. Martin believes he is helping her and has fallen in love. Martin is given no time to think in the love-bombing stage.

Penny plays into Martin's unconscious rescuer personality type:

- **'Pity me' stories:** Each time Penny lies about the terrible abuse she suffered at the hands of her ex-partner, Martin wants to 'rescue' her

and be her hero by being the opposite. She tells elaborate lies about the abuse and how he has taken all her money and left her penniless. In fact Penny was the abuser in the last relationship and is adept at financial manipulation, but Martin does not know this yet.
- **'False praise':** Penny deepens her control on Martin by declaring she can 'never cope without him', he is 'the kindest man she has ever met' and she feels 'so protected and loved' having him in her life.

What to watch for – Love-bombing and subtle control

These are examples of classic love-bombing:

- For Richard and Lisa – On the one hand gifts, excessive contact and overwhelming declarations of love and on the other guilt-tripping and pressure to quickly move the relationship on.
- For Martin and Penny – On the one hand there are extreme declarations of love and on the other Martin is being manipulated with untrue 'pity me' stories. He believes he is saving Penny, when in fact he is being set up to send Penny money later.

There is a big difference between romantic love and love-bombing. Here are a few things initially to watch out for:

1. **Grandiose declarations of love:** This can be terms such as 'soul mate' used very early on in the relationship. It is likely to be positioned as unique and exceptional love.
2. **Speed and intensity:** The big difference between romantic love and love-bombing is the intensity and how quickly it happens. Romantic love gives people space and time to grow together, learn to trust one another and build a relationship slowly with foundations and understanding.
3. **Adoration and gifting:** The love-bombing stage will be filled with adoration and over-the-top gifting. In a romantic relationship the difference is the gifting is freely given, in a narcissistic relationship the gifts have a purpose, which will have to be 'paid for' in the future..
4. **Idyllic future dreams:** When being love bombed, a victim is likely to feel hooked into the grand and 'idyllic' future together.
5. **Subtle (and not so subtle) emotional manipulation:** In the example with Richard's communication to Lisa, he was really saying the following:
   a. **Threat to cause alarm, distress and guilt:** Richard was subtly

Love-Bombing and Social Engineering– Manipulation of Those Around the Victim 45

threatening to take his 'love' away because of the distance between them; he didn't want to keep commuting that far.

    b.   **Looking for an easy way for him:** Richard was saying that it was easier for him if Lisa lived with him.

6.   **Pity me stories:** Penny is cruelly making up a horrific story of past abuse by her ex-partner to entrap Martin. These are, however, lies. She is trying to play to his empathy and protective nature to gain trust and later money.

7.   **Gifts with conditions:** It may feel very loving to have gifts given at early stages of a relationship. This may come with grandiose statements of 'That's what I do for someone I love' and 'You have never been properly loved have you?'

    The gifts, however, whilst representing control for the narcissist, are often what they want and not what you want. For example, they might get you a necklace in green, when you love red. But they are likely to insist that necklace suits you better. They might give you a pen with the words 'I am so deeply falling in love with you, this pen is my gift to you. It's a [designer name], but it is for you.' They might get you a surprise ticket or an item you need for your home. But the clue is that they are going to choose the gift that they *think* you want, and it is unlikely to be a gift that you *really do* want.

    The gifts also form part of their ownership of you and might include statements like 'Oh, no only the best for you.' The gifts might also be gifts of your favourite restaurant, but the subtlety here is likely to be, for example, insisting on a certain type of wine, music or even what you eat. *It is likely to be grandiose and possibly over the top for a new relationship.*

    The difference between someone 'genuinely' in love and a narcissist is about expectations and control. The gifts are not given by a narcissist lightly – they are likely to be given as a future token and demonstration of their own power to control others. The gifts are stored as favours and may well have to be paid for in the future. Indeed, the gifts may well be taken back at a later stage if they do not get what they consider they are entitled to.

8.   **Pet names, soulmate reference, twin flame references, destiny, astrology:** Sometimes a narcissist may use reference to 'higher powers' or loving terms to make the relationship seem special or unique early on.

In addition to the love-bombing, a narcissist is highly likely to also be manipulating the people around the victim – to minimise external influences. This might include:

1. **Offers of help to those closest to you:** This may be used as a continuation of their ownership and control of you. This does not seem to be done because they want to necessarily get along with your family or friends, it may instead be a method for eliciting further information about you, finding weaknesses in your relationships with others to exploit later or a way to gain 'support' for themselves against the victim later on. If a narcissist has used charm towards friends and family, the victim can be isolated against their friends and family in the future. If a narcissist has found relationship weaknesses, these can be used to persuade the victim to discard family and friend support and isolate the victim.
2. **Lying about how much they care and love the victim to others:** This aspect of narcissistic abuse can involve convincing friends and family (and sometimes even neighbours) how much they care about the victim. The purpose of this is that it is easier to control a victim if the people around think that the narcissist really is a nice person who genuinely cares about their 'victim'. If the narcissist later takes advantage of the victim, the victim will find that friends and family are less likely to believe them.
3. **Trying to cause friction or divisions with family and friends.** This technique focusses on slights, hurts and divisions between friends and family rather than being a peace-maker. In this way it ensures that a victim is more isolated because they break the ties from friends and family themselves.

What to watch for – Why you can't hear friends or family advice in the love-bombing and subtle control phase

At the same time that you may be getting good advice from friends (to leave), an intense narcissist could also be wanting to know about all your conversations with other people. This is the part that is very clever from a narcissist's point of view, because they may well anticipate objections from those close to you and try to minimise their views in a number of ways. Your trusted friend or advisor might tell you:

a. **Wait/slow the relationship down:** However, a victim will not want to wait because they have already been programmed that their 'love' may be taken away if they don't move things forward or that 'their love' is exceptional and no one else could understand how they feel. It may be hard for a victim to hear that they should wait from friends and family, but it is sound advice. It is highly likely that this advice will be ignored, because the victim is 'hooked' into the 'future dream' and 'exceptional love'.

b. **End the relationship:** Very wise advice if a friend or family member advises this, but unfortunately at this point in a narcissistic relationship, too much emotion may have been invested and it may be difficult for a victim to hear. If the love-bombing was very intense a victim can initially feel absolutely 'adored'.

c. **Try to dismiss your fears:** If your friend/family/trusted advisor does not understand that this person is a narcissist, they may well dismiss your fears and encourage you to go for it. This might be, for example, saying, 'We all have off days.' This can be extremely dangerous, but unfortunately, we are not equipped to detect narcissists in everyday life.

Why is it so difficult to leave at the Love-Bombing stage?

At this stage, you are already under the control of a narcissist. A narcissist furthermore will be **prepared for this stage and have a number of other techniques to keep you under their control**.

They will have already anticipated objections to the relationship from those close to you and will have already subtly (or not so subtly) tried to minimise other people's points of view and any outside influences.

From a narcissistic point of view, they have invested heavily already at this stage and will want to hold on to their 'victim'. Expect some or all of these behaviours/techniques if you try to get away from a narcissist at this point:

a. **False devotion - Charming friends and family:** If they are concerned that friends and family are a threat in any way they may choose to talk to them and influence their views using false devotion. They might tell them 'how wonderfully amazing, beautiful, intelligent' their friend/family member is to disarm them and give them the impression that they are taking care of the victim. This gives friends and family the illusion that the victim is being cared for. It prevents the friends/family members from interfering in their 'narcissistic supply' (the victim) and also means that when the victim complains or has doubts, their friends and

48 Section 1 – Recognising the 16 Stages of Narcissistic Abuse

family act as the narcissist's 'back up' and help to quell any doubts.

b. **Expecting other people to see through them:** A narcissist is likely to be concerned that other people can see through them. They may well cling even more tightly to the relationship at this point, not wanting to give up their chosen 'victim' easily. They are likely to be extra manipulative at this time.

c. **Helping out friends/neighbours/family for free:** This tactic is used to make them seem helpful and useful. This means that anything negative said about the narcissist by the victim is likely to be disbelieved. By precuring free favours and giving people things they need, the narcissist starts to make themselves invaluable to people around the victim. This can make it more difficult for the victim to get away.

d. **Starting to put deliberate doubts in minds – Twisting facts:** This tactic is used to plant 'concepts/ideas/concerns' in the minds of others. Two examples of this might be:

   (1) **Appearing genuinely concerned for the loved one:** Take the example of the narcissist saying to a friend/family member/neighbour: 'Oh, I was really worried about xyz the other day, she really seemed out of sorts – did you notice anything?' This can appear as genuine concern, when really the tactic is to implant the thought that they need to focus their attention on the victim 'being out of sorts'. This ensures the focus is away from the narcissist and limits any suspicion that they might be out of sorts *because* of the narcissist.

   (2) **Focusing on jealousy or other negative attributes:** This might play out such as 'You know, Martin, I've noticed that your friends interfere with what you do. Are they jealous of you or something? Do you think they are trying to stop us being together?' This also is highly manipulative and puts an 'element of doubt' in the victim's mind. This means when someone tries to warn a victim that they might be entering an abusive relationship, the victim perceives the information as jealousy and interference instead of concern. This element cannot be underestimated. Narcissists are expert manipulators of people and have an uncanny knack of knowing how to create confusion and doubt.

e. **Expecting other people to want to stop them:** The narcissist may be looking for ways to ensure other people do not stop their relationship. Already at this stage the narcissist considers their love interest (the victim) their own and their own supply. A narcissist may therefore use a number of techniques to make sure no doubt is put in the mind of the intended victim.

(1) **Extra charm:** When they charm people close to and around the victim as well as the victim, they know that when they do behave differently, it is less likely to be challenged.

(2) **Divisive of other relationships:** For example, if you had previously told a narcissist you 'love your friend', but 'wish they didn't talk over you sometimes', the narcissist would focus all their attention on the 'talking over you' concern. Rather than trying to say, 'that happens in all friendships sometimes', they would use it as a tool to increase friction in the relationship and cause divisions.

(3) **Finding ways to avoid the victim meeting up with other people/starting to close down other influences in the victim's life:** This tactic can include cancelling at the last minute (e.g. feigning illness if jointly meeting up), so that the victim cancels the plans. This can also include more love-bombing and intensity, including suggestions that they are going to miss the victim 'so much it is unbearable' if they try to meet people alone. This guilt-tripping is a technique used to stop contact with other people. Another method may be deliberately booking a special treat or surprise on the same day that the narcissist knows the victim has other plans. This is intended to manipulate the victim by guilt and loyalty.

f. **Getting frustrated with keeping up their false public personality:** It can be such an effort for the narcissist to continually keep up their false persona; it can become frustrating for them. Whilst they may well try to contain it, sudden outbursts that may seem out of character to their victim are actually just the real personality bursting through. In these moments, when the narcissist is afraid of being caught out and they do not want to lose their victim, they are likely to talk their way out of it.

g. **Needing to control the situation – their own schemas play out:** In their unconscious mind, because of their own schemas, such as 'I am entitled to this person' (the victim) and 'I have to have control', they are likely to genuinely believe that they must 'control or be controlled' in their mind. This drives many of the unpleasant actions, manipulations and lies.

h. **Entitlement – Other relationships, possessions:** Although it may appear that the relationship is exclusive of other people, at this stage, the narcissist is potentially likely to have 'other people in reserve' in the background. This is just in case they do not secure the victim as an ongoing supply. Because narcissists have their own schemas – such as entitlement – they may not even feel guilt or shame about doing this because their entitlement is more important than anyone else's feelings. Entitlement may also extend to their partner's possessions and property. It is highly unlikely that their 'victim' is aware a narcissist can consider them a 'possession' at this early stage.

i. **Withdrawal symptoms from not getting constant attention:** The narcissist is likely to be having intense withdrawal symptoms when not getting constant adoration.

Practical advice – How friends and family can help in the love-bombing and subtle control phase

It is important for friends and family to realise that in the love-bombing stage of a relationship with a narcissist, the 'victim' is already invested in the relationship. They are likely to be infatuated and not seeing reality. They may already be keeping quiet about concerns and showing loyalty to the narcissist very quickly. The narcissist may have already taken control and is ensuring conversations with other people are reported back to them (in the guise of being open and honest in the relationship).

This is also a difficult time for friends and family, who can feel rejected when their advice is ignored and may withdraw their support. It is actually a critical time when friends and family support is very important. If you think you have a friend or family member about to enter a relationship with a narcissist consider these approaches:

1. **Remind them that you care about them:** In the background the narcissist is likely to be trying hard to minimise outside influences. The best option is to tell a friend or family member that you care about them but are worried for them.
2. **Expect not to be heard:** Because a victim is 'intoxicated' with false love, expect that you may not be heard or even criticised for your point of view.
3. **Tell them the door is open for them:** Letting someone know that there is a way to exit the relationship will give someone a safety net if needed.
4. **Tell them what may happen next:** This is a shock tactic that might get through. It must be said calmly. Along the lines of:

a. 'My greatest fear is that this person may be a narcissist and I fear you are entering a relationship of coercive control. If this is the case, what is likely to happen next is that they will try to distance you from me or ask for money. They might try to minimise our relationship and state this is because of jealousy or another factor. I want to remind you that I love you and am here for you no matter what and I want you to know that I will help you. Just promise me that you will look out for warning signs of a narcissist and take your time. A person who loves you will always wait for you.'

5. **Tell them how to get out if this happens:** This includes giving them information about support lines and domestic abuse helplines. You will need to give them telephone numbers or send them articles that are relevant. Be prepared that they will not hear you and even by this point their phone or email may be monitored by the narcissist.

6. **Tell them you have noticed 'out of character' changes in them:** This includes that you might feel rejected or distanced from them since they were in the relationship with the narcissist.

7. **Intervention:** If there is solid evidence that someone is entering a relationship with an abusive person, intervention may be an option. This is an extreme method, which may mean helping someone stop all contact with the narcissist and will require professional help. It is likely to be akin to drug withdrawal and may not be a welcome approach in the short term.

Chapter 9 - Online Ghosting and Catfishing

It is worth mentioning that with the advances in technology, a whole new type of abuse is available on the internet.

When people are not meeting up 'face to face' but using the internet, terms such as ghosting and catfishing are commonly used for abusive behaviours.

Whilst ghosting (when someone online or you knew personally suddenly stops communication with you and gives no reason or explanation) can be emotionally painful, it does not mean this was done by a narcissist. Equally, those who 'catfish' look for sources of income from people online pretending to be someone may not be a narcissist.

Example: Martin and Penny – Penny is catfishing for money

After some time, Martin wants to meet Penny and Skype her so that he can see her, but each time he tries to book travel or to set up a Skype meeting, Penny claims to be computer illiterate and always makes excuses of why they cannot meet.

Penny continues to play to Martin's 'rescuer' personality and asks him for money for food and housing as she proclaims she is penniless after leaving her 'abusive' relationship. There is no abusive relationship, but Penny is a very convincing narcissistic liar. Martin sends her money for the bills, believing he is helping her.

In this case, Penny has no intention of meeting up with Martin or for him to see her on Skype because it is easier for Penny to manipulate Martin by phone and internet alone.

Practical advice – Make sure you know who you are communicating with online

If you have not met someone, are getting emotionally drawn into an 'online relationship', you are at risk of being 'catfished' for money or goods (or even to help someone else commit fraud).

For this reason, make sure that you take time to get to know someone online and use first-line defence tactics such as reverse image searches.

I strongly recommend that you END online relationships where you are asked in any way for money or goods without knowing or having met them.

Chapter 10 – Unexpected Withdrawals, Stonewalling and Abandonment

After the love-bombing stage, there is nearly always a withdrawal period which leaves victims of narcissistic abuse 'shocked and confused'.

Alternatively, if the love-bombing stage has not gone the narcissist's way (e.g. they have been questioned or asked to wait), a victim is likely to experience very painful emotional stonewalling and even abandonment.

Withdrawal/Return

Withdrawal happens when the narcissist deliberately and suddenly withdraws from the relationship (often after some intense love-bombing) without any prior warning and refuses to respond to any attempts of communication. The victim is left in a very uncertain state of why this might be. There are different types of withdrawal:

(1) Withdrawal to ascertain the response/for enjoyment.
(2) Withdrawal because they don't care if they hurt someone and are only focused on their own needs.
(3) Withdrawal because the false self is too hard to keep up.
(4) Withdrawal to cover up lies.
(5) Withdrawal to get money or items.

Withdrawal/return to ascertain the response for enjoyment

This type of withdrawal seems to be done for perverse enjoyment by the narcissist to ascertain the response. The objective is to inflict emotional pain on the victim in some way. This could trigger feelings of abandonment, lack of self-worth and powerlessness in the victim.

When they return to communication, without any apology or reason for the withdrawal, it forces the victim to respond. If the response is assertive, the narcissist may switch the blame back onto the victim for being needy. If the response is passive and the victim does not say anything, the narcissist is then aware that the victim can be manipulated by withdrawal. This technique helps a narcissist gain some level of control in the relationship.

Withdrawal because the narcissist is only focused on their own needs

This withdrawal type may be when a narcissist is purely focused on their own needs and entitlement without any regard for their partner. It may well bring up feelings in their partner of being unimportant, unappreciated, abandoned and not loved.

When the narcissist returns after this type of withdrawal, their likely expectation is that the victim does not say anything about how their behaviour made them they feel. They may even expect the victim to validate them in their choice to abandon. For example, they may expect their victim to agree with them that they can abandon the relationship and withdraw as and when they please or even to take the blame for their painful withdrawal.

Withdrawal because the false self is too hard to keep up

This withdrawal type may be when a narcissist is actually enraged and needs to withdraw so that their false self is not discovered. This may typically be when a narcissist is trying to funnel a victim into meeting their real needs – such as marrying for money or moving in so they can exert control. They may be feeling angry that they are being asked to be accountable, so the sudden withdrawal allows them to compose themselves before going back to the relationship.

On return, a narcissist is likely to be extremely apologetic and charming and promise not to do it ever again. They may not even try not to withdraw again up until the point they are in control, e.g. married or moved in together.

Withdrawal to cover up lies

This method of deliberate withdrawal helps a narcissist establish if the victim is malleable to lies, and what their reaction might be. Withdrawal to cover up lies include:

1. **Turning the lie around in their favour:** This technique is where the lie about the sudden withdrawal is turned back on the victim as another 'sad' story. For example this might be when a narcissist has spent the night with another person, but lies that the reason they withdrew was because they were ill. (gaslighting).

56 Section 1 – Recognising the 16 Stages of Narcissistic Abuse

With most of these withdrawal types, the narcissist is likely to get very annoyed if you challenge them or ask them to be accountable for their withdrawal. Because they are likely to feel entitled to pull away from a relationship at any time, you would typically see:

a. **Deflected anger:** They may well accuse you of cheating/not trusting them/making things up and turn the conversation round in their favour until they become the 'false' victim.

b. **Enlisting others to cover for the lies:** This can be when a narcissist deliberately enlists the help of innocent other people with charm to cover their lies. For example, they might convince a receptionist not to mention they got in late.

c. **Refusal to back down – Smoke screens:** The other narcissistic defence mechanisms can be circular conversations and deflection. This is where conversations cannot be concluded. Questions are answered with questions, or the conversation is deflected – often by accusing the victim of something not related. All of these are smoke screens to prevent the lies being seen.

Withdrawal to get money or items

After the initial love-bombing stage has started to wear off, a narcissist may withdraw suddenly and then return with 'urgent' requests. This can be done quite casually, manipulatively or asked for in the guise of an 'urgent' situation. For example a narcissist might make up an urgent situation where money is required – for items, flights, accommodation etc. Whilst these can seem plausible and believable to the victim, it is often a guise to get money or items.

Other unexpected requests might be anything from using the victim's bank account for money laundering/fraud, or getting cards/gift cards set up in your name. The withdrawal can be a painful void for a victim.

Stonewalling and Relationship Abandonment

Stonewalling and abandonment of the relationship can happen if the narcissist realises that they have:

(1) Been seen for who they really are
(2) Cannot manipulate someone as they thought that they could
(3) Have been forced to be accountable in some way
(4) Are feeling controlled
(5) Realised that their lying has been uncovered
(6) Been made to wait for what they want

If a narcissist abandons you, this is a blessing in disguise. It may not feel like it to the victim, but stonewalling and sudden abandonment of the relationship indicates that you have successfully:

(1) Believed yourself and your instincts
(2) Stood up for yourself and been assertive in some way
(3) Researched the background and history of the narcissist and told them you know the truth
(4) Have put your own needs first and communicated them to the narcissist
(5) Enforced your own boundaries
(6) Have put the brakes on a relationship when in doubt

If this is the case, congratulations, you have done well to get away.

It may well, however, cause you, the victim, to be traumatised and possibly trauma bonded from the experience. A victim may well find it devastating to be discarded, yet still be interested in forming a relationship again with the narcissist or frantically searching what the narcissist is doing and if they have been 'callously' replaced. It is a search for why?

Practical advice: How to cope with withdrawals and sudden abandonment

Anyone who has invested time, energy and love into a relationship and finds themselves abandoned and love being withdrawn is going to experience aspects of trauma.

If this is the case, it is important for you to get some form of closure and assistance. It is far more painful because you have:

- Lost your future dreams
- Invested time, money and love
- Will feel intensely hurt and humiliated
- Will need to find resolution and comfort
- May feel ostracised from friends, family and community

You additionally may want a 'closure' conversation and be denied it. If this is the case for you, you will benefit from going through the recovery steps in Section 2 and 3.

The effects of withdrawals and sudden abandonment after love-bombing cannot be underestimated – it is simply not the same as withdrawal from other types of relationships because of the devastating emotional trauma caused.

Phase 3 – Commitment and Isolating You in The Relationship

Chapter 11 – Commitment, Control and Compliance through Assault and Narcissistic Rages

Once you have committed yourself to the relationship, perhaps by moving in with a narcissist, you are effectively 'trapped and controlled' in their environment. This is often when the abuse starts.

One of the first demonstrations of the control in the relationship is witnessing a narcissistic rage. These are extreme and about controlling their victim. The timing is always when the narcissist believes that their victim is 'hooked' or 'vulnerable' or under their 'control' in some way.

The narcissist gains two things:

- Control by FEAR
- Compliance of the victim

Compliance and control by fear

- After (and during) a narcissistic rage, the narcissist gains compliance and control from the victim through fear and confusion.
- The narcissist also gains an understanding of which methods of control work specific to the victim. How the victim responds at this point is key for a narcissist to understand how far they can 'control' their victim.

Example: Lisa experiences Richard's narcissistic rage

After being pressured Lisa has agreed to move in with Richard. She gives up her home and moves in with Richard. Initially the love-bombing continues, but shortly after moving in Lisa is shocked by an unexpected narcissistic rage.

The incandescent rage is about autumnal leaves falling on a driveway. He is so angry that leaves keep falling and he has to clear them up that he hammers his fists on the table, shouts and swears and stomps his feet on the ground for fifteen minutes. Lisa is naturally shocked. Richard is fully aware of the impact the narcissistic rage is likely to have on Lisa (confusion and control). Whilst Lisa tries many different techniques to calm Richard down, Richard will not accept offers of help, Lisa cannot distract him or placate him from his rage in any way. Just as quickly as it started, Richard switches back to being calm and pleasant just as if the rage never happened. Lisa is left shocked, scared and confused.

Richard, however, has learned that Lisa will try to placate a rage with pleading, placating and distracting – all of which would not work because the purpose of the rage is control.

Example: Ethan and Faye assault

Ethan is a hardworking young man who is careful about who he gets into a relationship with and just started his first job. He is a proud man and also very loyal to those he loves.

Faye is a narcissist. Ethan is very flattered that she has taken an interest in him. To gain his trust, Faye has lied about her past to Ethan, proclaiming her last relationship was abusive and she had to leave for the safety of her child. This appealed to his unconscious hidden need to protect the vulnerable and for a family. Faye was initially very charming and insisted that her 'child needed him' and he could 'be a real father' to her child. Faye's real intention was to find ways so that she did not have to work and be provided for and she realised that Ethan could fulfil that role.

After a few months of Faye convincing him, love-bombing him and declaring her love for him, Ethan had moved into her house to become the father figure to her child. Shortly after moving in, however, Faye had her first narcissistic rage. After Faye had goaded and belittled Ethan for over an hour, he tried to walk out of the house and away. Faye, however, was so angry in rage that he tried to leave the house that she attacks Ethan physically, causing bruising.

He walks away shocked with Faye shouting after him that 'No one would believe him' if he mentioned the physical assault.

Later Faye has cooked his favourite meal and is very charming. She has switched back to being doting, interested in his day and flirtatious. She glosses over the earlier incident by refusing to acknowledge it happened.

Faye has learned that Ethan does not report her for the assault, so she has the 'power' and control over him. Furthermore, she has learned that

What to watch for – The first shock tactics of control

When a narcissist feels like they have their intended victim in a suitably vulnerable position (feeling love, commitment), the narcissist is able to start relaxing into their real personality. In this phase the narcissist may start changing from their public personality (charming) gradually back into their real personality. This is what to watch for:

Typical behaviours:

1. **Shock tactics – a demonstration of power and control:** This tactic is used only when a narcissist feels more secure that their victim isn't going anywhere else. This could include demonstrations of power and control such as narcissistic rage, or deliberately letting the victim overhear threats of violence or actual violence to other people (or animals). The point of the shock tactic is that it causes fear. Fear is a major manipulation tool for a narcissist. The timing and waiting until a victim is under their control also chillingly _implies that a narcissist clearly knows what they are doing._

2. **Overreactions/extreme reactions to things outside of their control:** This might include anything from the weather to what someone else has said or done. A narcissist may genuinely feel entitled to overreact because it is about something they have not been able to control. This may appear to be quite illogical or irrational to another person who knows you cannot control everything, but to a narcissist they have to 'control or be controlled'.

3. **Offers of help and solutions are rejected:** Offers of help and solutions can actually annoy a narcissist because in their mind they seem to think that they know better than anyone else, and their way of doing things is the only way.

4. **Deliberately refusing to deflect, deflate or disarm a rage:** The purpose of a rage is for self-gratification and control. It is also attention seeking, so the narcissist has little or no reason to want to find a resolution that can be deflected, deflated or disarmed in any way.

5. **Glibly talking about breaking the law:** A narcissist might glibly talk about breaking the law. Because they simply do not care about legalities that might get in the way of what they want or need, they expect others to think in the same way. They may minimise law

breaking, the likelihood of being caught and not be afraid of the consequences. They appear to be not concerned about breaking the law if it gets them what they want and are likely to encourage their victim to do the same.

6. **Talk about physical or psychological harm to others/animals:** A narcissist can have little or no remorse about harming other people or animals. They may start to talk about killing animals – for sport, pleasure or revenge or even boast about what they have done to other people who have crossed them. This doubles as a warning to the victim (low level threat), but also appears to enable the narcissist to explore the victim's reactions.

7. **Constant antagonisation:** This can include gauging reactions to goading, belittling, cruel remarks. The level of antagonism seems to keep going until there is a strong reaction. When someone is in distress, and the narcissist is seemingly enjoying antagonising them, they have no real motivation to end this behaviour. In fact, prolonging the incident seems to give them more attention.

What the narcissist seems to gain from the shock tactic:

(1) **Watched purposefully, seemingly enjoyed:** The first shock tactics seem to be so extreme that it will cause major internal concern or even terror. It is unlike an argument or disagreement, which are quite normal in relationships; it is the absolute shock factor which differentiates it. It also differs from other relationships in that the abuser is looking for the reaction very closely. The purpose for a narcissist is to elicit fear as a control tactic and can even make them smile (as it seems to be pleasurable for them on some level).

Timing of the shock tactic:

1. **During the love-bombing/early part of the relationship, to cause utter confusion:** This first shock tactic is also likely to be done when the victim has strong emotional bonds to the narcissist. This tactic would not work earlier on in the relationship, because the intended victim would pull away.

2. **Privately/behind closed doors:** The first shock tactics are likely to be done privately behind closed doors, or if there are witnesses, people that do not matter to the narcissist. The reason is that the narcissist cannot be seen to damage their external public reputation.

3. **Done at a time when the influence of others is not as powerful:** The

Behaviour after the shock tactic

1. **Desire to know how the victim felt, but no meaningful commitment to change:** A narcissist may want to know how a victim felt after a rage. This might even be done apologetically in a way that can appear that the narcissist was remorseful and cared about how their rage had impacted the victim. However, seems to teach the narcissist how easy it is to control the victim through rage. Whilst it is likely that a narcissist might make promises to change, this is only superficial and there is no real meaningful commitment to change.
2. **Lack of remorse:** A narcissist will feel little remorse when other people have been harmed or hurt. They know, however, that they need to show remorse in public, so some narcissists learn to mimic remorse. Even in an intimate relationship, a narcissist can be an extremely good actor or actress and can easily mimic remorse even when they don't feel remorse.
3. **Deeply apologetic and pseudo tears:** This step doesn't always happen, but a narcissist can be seemingly apologetic and even have pseudo tears after the first rage/shock tactic.
4. **Enjoyment of inflicting harm:** A narcissist may actually enjoy inflicting hurt, pain, suffering and fear on their intended victim as a method of control. They appear intent on harm. They may quite literally laugh out loud when they watch people in emotional pain, smirk or smile to themselves. This can also come with claims of 'But I would never do that to you.' This is not to be believed - observe actions over words.

Practical advice – How to identify narcissistic rage

Narcissistic rage – identifying

Narcissistic rage is very different to healthy relationship disagreements or arguments because of its intention and ferocity. Narcissistic rage is characterised by:

1. **Intention behind the rage:** The intention of the rage is to win against another person. The winning prize that the narcissist seeks is attention and a demonstration of their power over another. This seems to give

satisfaction and even happiness to the narcissist because it proves that they are indeed 'more powerful', 'better', 'in control' of another person.

2. **Behind closed doors:** Very often narcissistic rages are hidden behind closed doors, so that no one would suspect the 'change in character'.

3. **Can easily be switched 'off' by a narcissist:** If during a rage a narcissist is at risk of being seen by someone outside of their control (e.g. those that they like to influence positively), they can actually turn their temper and rage off instantly. They can even go from snarling and menacing to smiling, calm and chirpy if someone unexpectedly interrupts them.

4. **Said in a way that deliberately does not respect the victim:** The point of the narcissistic rage seems to be completely self-absorbed and lacks any respect to the victim. There are several other more constructive ways to communicate frustration or anger, but the narcissistic rage is the top end of the spectrum of anger and disrespects entirely the recipient. It is ferocious.

5. **Refusal to de-escalate or stop the argument/rage:** To stop the argument or rage would mean that the narcissist stops getting narcissistic supply (a reward of attention). Whilst the rage continues and the victim uses methods of placating, pleading, remaining quiet or distraction – it still feeds into the narcissist's need for attention. In a healthy relationship, these methods would be more effective and give an opportunity for both parties to begin de-escalation.

6. **Counterattacks do not work:** This method equally does not work when a narcissist is in a narcissistic rage because again the focus remains on the narcissist. Indeed, if a narcissist is good at arguing points, they may well take enjoyment of the attention and watching their victim flounder.

7. **Disengaging – Time out may not be allowed to calm down:** This element is very frustrating for a victim because the narcissist is reliant on prolonging the matter. Time out (e.g. putting the phone down and calling back later or leaving the house), can sometimes not be permitted by the narcissist as it takes away the point of the rage (control). Walking away from a rage (or putting the phone down) is likely to enrage a narcissist further because they expect to be heard during their rages. It can even lead to further escalation and repeated attempts by the narcissist to inflame the situation e.g. using additional verbal attacks to provoke goading such as 'shame', 'regret', 'worthlessness' in their victim. This might include phrases like:

    a.   'That's right, walk away – you always [xyz] anyway!' (Used to goad.)

    b.   'You're not leaving – we need to sort this out now!' (Used as power and control.)

Section 1 – Recognising the 16 Stages of Narcissistic Abuse

    c.   'If you don't finish this argument now, I am going to …' (Threat.)

    d.   'What type of man/woman are you! Can't you take an argument?' (Goading.)

8.   **Personal nature of the rage:** The rages are deeply personal and can blindside victims because it is unexpected from someone they think loves them:

    a.   **The subject of the rage may not be the point of the rage:** In the example given, autumnal leaves falling on a driveway caused the rage, but the point of the rage was to elicit control.

    b.   **Perfectly aware of the consequences of the rage on others:** Narcissists know that their rages are highly likely to control other people and have a negative personal effect on another person.

9.   **The rage will be 'your fault':** With a narcissist, after the rage has occurred, their behaviour can be characterised by suddenly changing back to being happy and charming as if nothing had happened. The victim is often bewildered but a narcissist is unlikely to give an explanation or is likely to try to 'skip over' what has happened or even rationalise it as being the victim's fault in some way: 'If you hadn't …'

Narcissistic rage – Disarming

This is a specialist area and for most people would require specialist training. Techniques require victims to have confidence in what they say and do – which very often they don't have in an abusive relationship. Also for the abuser (the narcissist) to be able to hear. The problem is that the narcissist does not necessarily want to hear or disarm the situation. There may also be a greater risk of violence, so care needs to be taken.

The following may be useful (assuming you cannot walk away – which is always the first choice):

1.   **Stay calm, repeat the subject matter:** This would require a repetition of the same phrases and being able to block all the triggers inside you during a narcissistic rage. Extremely difficult, for the example given with Lisa she could use phrases like **'It is irritating when the leaves fall in autumn'** and refuse to try to placate or distract from the rage.

2.   **Verbal linguistics:** This requires re-training yourself in verbal self-defence. One of the books that is particularly helpful about this topic is from Suzette Haden Elgin who provides an eight-step programme of verbal self-defence. This puts the power of your words and intonation back in your own hands and circumvents pleading,

placating or negating what has happened. It is completely different to assertiveness training.
3. **Body language:** This also may require professional training to ensure that your words and body language give off the impression of assertiveness.
4. **Record the rage:** If you can do so safely, record the rage on your phone or recording device.
5. **In danger?** If you think that you might be in physical danger call the police on 999 in the UK. The call will be recorded, and specialists will be able to help.
6. **Get out and away:** After a narcissistic rage, no matter how 'sorry' they are, it is highly likely to happen again. The best option is to get out of the relationship.

Chapter 12 – Starting Isolation – Closing Off from Those you Love and Supportive Friendships

The other devastating aspect of forming a relationship with a narcissist is how they start to isolate you and close down support from outside the relationship to further their control.

Friends and family may well be very concerned and be the first to start to notice subtle differences to the normal self of victims – but this may already be too late.

Part and parcel of the isolation process is causing divisions or charming friends and family so that they do not suspect what is really going on:

1. **Charming friends and family to seed concerns:** By being utterly charming to friends and family, when a victim starts acting out of character because of the abuse, the narcissist can imply that they are worried about the victim. This gives the benefit of looking sincere, when in fact the objective is to alienate the victim from support and provide lies as explanations for the changes in behaviour of the victim.

2. **Deliberately causing further relationship rifts:** A narcissist may deliberately implant ideas about friends and family over time. This subtle approach of repetition of an idea will eventually become your own. This might include things like – your dad 'never really loved you'. Said enough times, combined with alienating friends and family members by the narcissist's controlling behaviour (e.g. causing deliberate cancellation of pre-agreed meetings), friends and family do finally withdraw or get angry with the victim. This is a deliberate set-up.

3. **Installing conditional thinking:** When this method is used on a victim, it would typically include things like 'If, xyz really loved/liked you then [they would have treated you better in some way/done something different].' This method focusses attention on the negative traits of a relationship deliberately, so that it appears worse perhaps than it really is.

4. **More love-bombing to stop someone going out:** This is the initial go-to position and would typically include 'But, I am so going to miss you … Can't you put it off for another time?' Said once or twice in a healthy relationship may be true, but a narcissist is likely to use this manipulation technique the majority of the time.

5. **Threats of abandonment:** This method further instils fear of rejection and abandonment. Typically, a narcissist might say, 'If you chose to listen to their word above me and don't listen to me then [threat to leave].'

6. **Constant attention-seeking and emotional blackmail:** This technique is used as emotional blackmail to stop a victim going out to see other people if other techniques of 'missing you' don't work. This might include a narcissist saying, 'If you go out and leave me alone tonight, then I will [emotional blackmail, e.g. generally about seeing someone else].'

7. **Withdrawal if not getting own way and guilt-tripping:** This is another method used. Typically, this might include agreeing to the victim going out, but then sulking and guilt-tripping later, e.g. 'So, did you have a good time tonight when I was all alone and lonely?'

8. **Monitoring phone conversations for compliance:** A narcissist may covertly monitor phone conversations/texts to understand if the friend or family member is for or against them. Whilst they are likely to try to influence the thoughts of friends or family to be positive about them, if charm is not working, they may instead deliberately try driving a wedge between the victim and friends/family.

9. **Leading conversations in public so that the victim does not have a voice:** A narcissist may lead the conversations in public. In this way their version of events and lies can be communicated easily because the victim has already been trained not to contradict or publicly respond because of the consequences later.

10. **Blame and lies to discredit the victim:** A narcissist may use a technique of blame, deliberate confusion or lies about their victim to other people. By repeating the same lies many times, it starts to be taken as facts and appear to be the truth. It is helped by the victim remaining mute or in some circumstances agreeing to the false blame for an easier life (or even to protect the narcissist from the consequences of their behaviour).

11. **Implanting good things about themselves:** A narcissist may well try to implant good things about themselves, through the victim's words. This is a manipulation technique which involves influencing the victim to tell other people how good they are or what they have done. This serves as a method of undermining credibility later should they change what they have said.

12. **Answering on behalf of the victim:.** This could include answering for the victim, especially for controversial things. If challenged for a direct answer from the victim in front of the narcissist, the victim is highly

Section 1 – Recognising the 16 Stages of Narcissistic Abuse

likely to look to the narcissist for what to say and agree with what was said because they would be too afraid to say anything else.

How they also control the victim's friends, family, colleagues, neighbours

- Everyone around a victim is likely to be categorised into people who can be manipulated and those that cannot by a narcissist.
- Those that can be manipulated can be gradually groomed to believe the narcissist's false account of the relationship with their victim. This public image is imperative to the narcissist, so that the victim's version of events will not be believed should they ever come to light. The objective is to use charm to influence and persuasion to ensure they are as believable as possible.
- A narcissist may well publicly praise their victim partner, so that any concerns about the relationship raised from the victim would be minimised (and in the worst cases friends, families, neighbours are groomed to take the narcissist's side).
- People that aren't easy for the narcissist to manipulate, or can be considered a risk to influencing their narcissistic supply (the victim), can also be vilified, ignored, isolated and removed as quickly as possible. This can be as unsubtle as 'you will not see that person again' or creating sophisticated stories about them, e.g. false allegations and lies told to the victim to ensure that they do not want to be in contact with each other.

Example: Richard and Lisa

Richard started intensifying narcissistic control by listening into telephone calls and exerting pressure for Lisa to end calls. Richard also starts creating division between Lisa and her friends and family by emphasising and focusing on petty differences. He would question if friends and family had Lisa's best interests at heart - particularly if they questioned their relationship.

Example: Ethan and Faye

Ethan's friends had shown concern about Faye because they were witnessing a change in Ethan's behaviour. Because Ethan was a proud man and protective, he continued with the relationship and ignored outside advice.

What to watch for:

Friends and family may well get increasingly frustrated that they can observe the victim being isolated, but their words of wisdom are not being heard. This in itself can cause further isolation as friends and family walk away from the victim in exasperation.

If you find yourself in this position, please don't give up on them. They are trapped.

This is what to look out for if you suspect someone is in an abusive relationship.

1. **Character changes/mood changes/behaviour changes:** Out of character changes for someone you know might include, in the beginning of an abusive relationship:
   a. Availability to talk
   b. Defensiveness about the relationship, and refusal to talk about it
   c. Regularly making excuses to get off the phone
   d. Suddenly leaving work on time and not mingling
   e. Jumpiness
   f. Empathy changing to apathy
   g. Mood swings, e.g. anger erupting at small things, moodiness, gloominess growing
   h. Addictions starting/increasing – e.g. alcohol and cigarettes
   i. Concentration and availability to be present diminishing
   j. Smile no longer reaching the eyes
2. **Changes to plans:** This often happens last minute. Or even implausible excuses. It is likely to be extremely frustrating for friends and family, who might try over and over again to make contact and be rebuffed. This is driven by the narcissist's influence in the background.
3. **Conversationally different – Suddenly wanting to positively represent abuser:** Different from wanting to talk about a new loving relationship, in an abusive relationship the conversation may be being guided out of view. We all have a certain style and pattern of conversation. When that changes, for example suddenly heaping praise on a new partner in the middle of a conversation, this can indicate that the phone is being monitored or the other person is standing close by.
4. **Conversations being led – When the narcissist is present:** This is quite a tell-tale sign of the start of abuse, when a normally outspoken friend looks almost at all times at their partner to respond to the question. This is accompanied by subtle controlling tactics such as side-glances or scowls before the narcissist takes control of the answer. This goes

beyond a loving relationship because there is never any outward disagreement, yet the victim looks scared, quiet, surprised or withdrawn.

5. **Absolutely no contradicting the narcissist in public:** This is another sign that it could be abuse. The narcissist is reliant on compliance at all times – especially when out in public and the victim is present. You might observe the victim being uncomfortable about the topic of conversation or wanting to change the topic. In contrast the narcissist may seem upbeat, happy, confident, charming whilst the abused person is down, quiet, pursed lips, shifty or sad.

6. **Taking public blame:** Placing blame on the victim in public may also start quite early on. The victim is likely to acquiesce to the abuse in public or say nothing in response (or sometime later in the abusive relationship even take the blame). In contrast, in a healthy relationship, someone might contradict what has been said in public or say, 'We'll have a chat about that later!'

7. **Observe body language and listen to what is said before they arrive and after they leave:** If you do suspect someone is in an abusive relationship, the most telling sign is watching them together before they arrive or when they leave. This is the moment that a narcissist often has their guard down and may well be trying to:

   a. **Steer the conversation:** You might witness them menacingly telling their abused partner 'what to say' or 'what to do'. The abused person may well arrive with a downbeat expression, whilst in contrast the narcissist will be upbeat and may well publicly berate their abused partner in public for being down. They can deliberately twist facts and look to point the finger at the abused partner for being the problem.

   b. **Seem more aggressive prior to arrival/when leaving:** This is particularly telling when the abused person may have stepped out of line in some way. This might include immediately after leaving the public area being aggressive towards the abused person – punishing them for stepping out of line. The interesting thing is that the narcissist cannot wait to get the venom off their chest and so is unlikely to have the patience to wait until they are home and out of sight. However, some can use brooding silence before they get back home before the real psychological/physical assaults happen.

   c. **Subtle signs of physical control:** These might include holding the money and paying for things. Generosity towards others, but meanness to the abused person. Pinching, nipping, cold stares, kicks under tables. Instead you might expect a look of annoyance, you may observe instead fear, shoulders hunched forward, head down, eyes down or silence by the abused person.

   d.   **Answering for the abused person:** This again is quite common and a tactic to ensure the narcissist keeps their public image intact. This will include blatant lies in favour of his/her own narrative.

8. **Conversations on phone loudspeaker:** This is a method of control when you may want a personal conversation, but the narcissist makes the victim take all calls on loudspeaker so that they can interject into the conversation. The conversation becomes driven by the narcissist.

9. **Phone conversations being recorded:** There is every possibility that the phone conversations with your friends and family are being recorded and monitored. This is to ensure that the conversations do not go off topic from the narcissist's public persona and to administer control. Sometimes you can hear a distinct clicking noise in the background when this is happening.

10. **Gut feel:** Not to be trivialised. When you know a person well and despite any denials from the vicitim, you still feel things don't seem right, go with your gut and continue to observe.

11. **Bruising or scratches:** This is quite a sure sign that the victim is in an abusive relationship. They will, however, probably be programmed to cover the bruising up.

Practical advice – How to identify and help a friend or relative who is with a narcissist

Narcissistic relationships completely differ from healthy relationships or even slightly combustible, volatile relationships. Whilst the social mantra is generally don't get involved with other people's relationships, there are times when getting involved could help someone or even save their life. You don't have to be an expert, but they may need your calm help one day and these things may help that:

1. **Keep a diary/record/texts/emails of events that concern you:** This might include times you have had to support your friend/family member when upset and why they were upset. This may include the narcissist trying to have 'a private word' with you. This could form important evidence if your friend or family member ever needed it.

2. **If meeting them:** Carefully observe when the couple arrive or leave. It is often easier to witness the abuse when the narcissist believes they are 'out of earshot'.

Section 1 – Recognising the 16 Stages of Narcissistic Abuse

3. **Keep a record of 'the story':** 'The story' is what you are being told by the narcissist. It may well differ greatly from the truth. It might include why your friend or family member has changed.

4. **Confirm 'the story' with the victim:** Do not allow assumptions and what has been said by the narcissist. Ask the victim directly if 'the story' given is true. Watch for signs of relief and/or more silence/anger. Phrases like 'Help me understand why they might say that?'

5. **Tell the victim what is likely to happen next:** This is more of a shock tactic, but the words, 'If I am right in thinking that xyz is a narcissist, the next thing you can expect is ... If that should happen, promise me that you will [call me, get help, walk away].' This works in a reverse way so that the victim is focused on what could happen next and knows what to do if it does happen.

6. **Give them the telephone number of support networks that understand coercive control and abuse:** This can include:
   a.   Woman's aid: Live chat: chat.womansaid.org.uk
   b.   The National Domestic Abuse, Refuge UK: 0808 2000 247
   c.   Suzy Lamplugh Trust: 0808 802 0300
   d.   SafeLives – www.safelives.org.uk
   e.   Victim Support: free support on 0808 1689 111 or live chat
   f.   ManKind Initiative: 01823 334244
   g.   Police: 101 or 999 if you are in immediate danger

7. **Give them books/information on narcissism:** This helps to validate what they are going through.

8. **If you have evidence/witness violence, whistle-blow:** If you are certain that someone is being subjected to physical abuse, it is okay to intervene and whistle-blow. Your friend or family member may thank you one day.

9. **Don't give up trying:** Know that what your friend or family member is going through is extremely difficult and it is almost impossible for them to leave. Your support in the background will be needed to get them through one day – so don't give up.

10. **Prepare a spare room for them/funds:** Let them know that there is a safe place for them to come to if needed. It most likely will be turned down until things become desperate. Be prepared. To get out of a controlling relationship requires careful planning by the victim. It is not as straight forward as just leaving. It will also require planning from you.

Prepare a safety plan: This safety plan will need to include:

a. **Write down what has happened:** Because the victim may have been **brainwashed** or completely under the narcissist's control, it is important to write down what you are observing, objectively. Ask (if possible) and note down the following:

1. What made you leave today?
2. Have there been any times that you have felt afraid? Why?
3. Have you been asked to keep a secret you are not comfortable with?
4. Have there been any threats made to you or others? What were they?
5. Are you under any pressure in the relationship?
6. What do you think would happen if you leave?
7. Are you frightened?
8. What do you think that xyz will do?
9. Can you give me an example of something that has made you concerned?
10. What does xyz say when you want to visit me?
11. Is everything okay with finances? Who makes the decisions? Who is paying?
12. How often is xyz in contact with you normally?
13. Are you concerned that you might get punished for being here? What would that punishment entail?
14. Have you left anything behind of value?
15. Are you being blackmailed at the moment?
16. Is there anything you are ashamed of? Can you tell me or someone else?

b. **Expect the narcissist to try to charm you:** They may ask for a 'private word' or that they are 'worried about the victim'. Keep neutral because you do not know if they will get back together at this point. Listen to what they have to say.

c. **Be prepared for extra pressure on the victim:** This may well include being inundated with phone calls, turning up at your house and potentially threats to harm. Have a plan of action that:

1. The victim advises the abuser that they are safe and that they want no further contact at this time.
2. What to do/who to call/where to go if the narcissist turns up.

d. **Consider that the victim may be dependent on alcohol/drugs/cigarettes:** Provide support to help them deal with the drugs/alcohol. It may be possible that they cannot deal with leaving a narcissist and giving up addictions at the same time without extreme withdrawal symptoms.

e. **Plan for extreme emotions:** This may include shame, blame, guilt, hurt, self-loathing. The narcissist may have manipulated the victim so much that their sense of 'self' will be disappearing. Trying to rationalise is unlikely to work, just get the victim to share their feelings and validate them. It would be best to have professional help at this time.

f. **The victim may still idolise the narcissist and talk about their positive traits:** Try not to be angry with them when they explain how loving the narcissist is. This idolisation may take professional support to convince them otherwise.

g. **Agree what to do if the narcissist shows up:** Have a plan of action if the narcissist suddenly turns up. They may use charm to get in. Don't let them.

h. **Agree what to do if the victim returns to the narcissist:** Agree that you will keep the space open for them if they return. Victims typically go back to their abuser over seven times. Be prepared that they don't leave straight away or need to make a more detailed escape plan before they leave.

i. **Be aware that items/personal things may be destroyed:** This is not a normal relationship and the level of aggression can be high. Consider personal effects that are left could be destroyed.

11. **Research coercive control laws:** Spend time researching coercive control laws and understanding legal aspects. See below for this.

12. **Research non-molestation laws and safe houses:** Read the non-molestation order in advance so that you know what needs to be done.

13. **Be one step ahead:** Be aware that your communications may not be private and could be recorded.

14. **Be prepared to be let down again:** The victim may be feeling high levels of shame already, so if you can, recognise that a fear of punishment may be behind this.

15. **Learn NLP eye movements and body language:** This is rather extreme but may help you ascertain when someone is lying.

16. **Expect the facts to be twisted:** Be aware that the narcissist has few morals or boundaries, so they may deliberately twist the facts to fit their version of events.

17. **False accusations:** Be ready for false accusations from the narcissist, e.g. if the victim is being abused, the narcissist may well proclaim that they are the one being abused.

When the victim is actually ready to leave the relationship, a plan is needed. You may need to help your friend/relative step up and go to extreme measures such as installing security devices and hiring a private detective.

Leaving could lead to stalking and harassment. Seek professional help if this is the case, such as the Suzy Lamplugh Trust. Garner as much evidence as you can, which may help in the future secure a prosecution. Remember that a narcissist is very likely to appear calm and rational and may even make false accusations and lies about what is happening. You need to be able to evidence facts – so keep text messages, emails and any diaries of events.

Phase 4 - Trying To Leave - The TRAP Moment

Chapter 13 - The TRAP Moment

The TRAP moment is a moment in an abusive relationship when you may feel that the only option left open to you is to stay in the abusive relationship - even if you desperately want to leave.

The TRAP is:

> **T**errifying
> **R**ealisation the
> **A**buse won't stop and you feel
> **P**revented from leaving

The trap moment is so powerful that you are likely to be shocked and suddenly realise the seriousness of your situation. You may realise that you are trapped if you start to talk about leaving the relationship and the reaction of the narcissist.

WARNING: IF YOU ARE IN A PHYSICALLY ABUSIVE RELATIONSHIP DO NOT PRE-WARN THE NARCISSIST BEFORE YOU LEAVE - PLAN TO LEAVE CAREFULLY. Any talk of leaving the abusive relationship by the victim may give the narcissist time to consider suitable punishment and revenge.

A narcissist under threat of the victim wanting to end and leave the relationship may feel rage, contempt and disgust. Because the narcissist may believe that the victim 'belongs to them' (as an object) and it may have taken time to manipulate a victim, a sudden departure can represent a potentially distressing loss for the narcissist. Not because of love, but because sudden removal of necessary narcissistic supply (literally the supply of attention, adoration, services or money) means that they would need to put in considerable effort to find another victim replacement.

The bruising of their ego can be so severe that they might plan and inflict punishment on their victim. The punishment and revenge for daring to leave them can be administered in a calculating and vengeful way.

Revenge can be done swiftly to put a victim 'back in their place' (under control).

Leaving the relationship also risks the exposure of the narcissist's false public image and reputation, so they are likely to protect themselves and possibly go on the attack as though their whole life is in danger. This is why a narcissistic attack can be so ferocious.

Some of the methods used by a narcissist to stop a victim leaving:

- **Relationship blackmail:** Exposing secrets or exposing illegal activities the victim has been coerced or forced into.
- **Revenge:** Revenge can be swift – from false allegations, publishing information, to phoning around work colleagues, friends and family members and spreading rumours or gossip about the victim. Often this is in the guise of 'could I have a confidential word about xyz – I am worried about them.' It is used to swiftly demonstrate their power over the victim.
- **Threats of violence:** This can be against the victim, their family or wider targets, and can include threats against children or animals.
- **Actual violence:** This can be a *warning shot* such as harming animals, harm to children or harm to the victim. This can escalate to be severe physical harm or in the worst cases murder.
- **Threats of revealing private info:** The threats may include private information you have shared that might be illegal or shameful to expose.
- **Pregnancy/children:** Sometimes the victim might have children and may be afraid of leaving the relationship for their sake. Pregnancy is another factor which could result in a decision to stay in the abusive relationship (in the hope things get better).
- **Financial control:** If a victim does not have enough money to financially support themselves, they may feel unable to escape the abuse and a narcissist may take money away.
- **Not speaking the native language:** For some victims, they may be in a country with different legal, cultural or even language barriers. The ability to communicate may be taken away if they cannot understand or communicate effectively in their native language.
- **Reputational damage:** The narcissist could start to plant false accusations or information locally, in case it is needed. This can be a subtle as planting false concerns, e.g. 'I'm so worried about my wife/husband – they are acting so irrationally/have a drinking

problem at the moment. Have you noticed?' or as horrific as false claims of abuse. The purpose is to deliver a pre-emptive smear campaign and create uncertainty (which also keeps the focus away from themselves).

- **Creating a smear campaign:** This might be where a narcissist deliberately uses gossip or media campaigns to discredit the victim by making false accusations or claims. The smear campaigns very often have little 'fact' and are generalised for dramatic purposes.
- **Mental health in the victim:** Depending how bad the relationship becomes, it is common for victims to start having their own mental health problems which can also limit escape opportunities.
- **Social gaslighting:** This is where the narcissist can secretly start planting doubts in other people's mind about the **cause** of the victims mental health. They might say something along the lines of 'I love them so much, but it's hard when they are having one of their depression/anxiety/self-loathing moments, I just don't know how to help them ...' This would seem to other people that they care and the cause of the changes in the victims behaviour is nothing to do with the narcissist.
- **Being physically restrained:** This might include being prevented from working, socialising or getting out of the house.
- **Enlisting help of the narcissist's 'socially groomed' audience:** Particularly painful for a victim is when the narcissist might *deliberately lie* to their 'groomed' audience (those that completely believe the narcissists version of events). This might be for example falsely accusing the victim of something. This has the benefit of making other people turn against the victim without them knowing why. This could also include friends and family of the victim if the narcissist has been successful in charming them.
- **Financial demands and control:** This can be where the narcissist begins to demand *entitlement* to the victim's money, home, possessions as their own. In a narcissist's mind, when they go into a relationship they 'own' everything. If the victim has no money or assets, then financial control is where they threaten (or actual do) make the victim completely reliant on them.
- **Rape/sexual exploitation:** Pressure may be applied for sexual exploitation or dominance might be shown, e.g. rape (because they are entitled/because they need to assert authority).
- **Forced into illegal activities:** This could be part of the coercive control technique to prevent the victim from leaving. The threat would be to expose their activities.

- **Loss of freedom:** This could include locking the victim inside and refusing them all access to go out alone.

The TRAP moment is when the narcissist is showing their true colours and forcefully starting to exhibit their power and control over their victim. For a narcissist a threat by a victim to leave can evoke a powerful narcissistic attack. The narcissist may:

1. **Control and punish the victim:** From a narcissists point of view, only they can make decisions about ending a relationship. They have spent significant time grooming their victim and when threatened with the victim potentially leaving the relationship, a narcissist can react in an extremely hostile way. Punishment in the way of blackmail, threats, harm – any method that regains control again may well be used.
2. **Keep the relationship going on their terms:** If the narcissist has a strong public image, they may not want to completely destroy the relationship, so may put extra effort in retaining the victim.
3. **Demonstrate their power and ownership of the victim:** A narcissist may not hesitate to use blackmail as a method and demonstration of power and ownership over their victim. There may be a total lack of remorse or care about the victim. In a narcissist's mind it appears that blackmail is justified because the victim started the problem by wanting to leave the relationship.
4. **Enjoy watching another suffer:** This aspect can be quite disturbing, but seems to be that as well as the deep anger that is felt for someone having the audacity to consider leaving them, they also appear to enjoy watching their victim suffer. It appears to feed their ego that they are superior and entitled.

Through all of this a narcissist is likely to desperately want to avoid:

5. **Humiliation or damage to their public image:** The damage a relationship break-up may do to their public image and reputation would make a narcissist very angry. In their mind, they seem to have taken considerable trouble to build up their 'false' public image and a relationship break-up could seriously damage their reputation. This means that the victim must be discredited as much as possible if there is any danger of this.
6. **Anyone knowing the truth:** A narcissist may well do almost anything to cover up the truth. This can include pathological lying, fierce denials and counter-accusations to deflect from blame. There may also be

80   Section 1 – Recognising the 16 Stages of Narcissistic Abuse

'half-hearted' apologies to ensure their public image is retained and the uncomfortable truths are not believed.

7. **Having to find another source of narcissistic supply:** A narcissist is likely to be very concerned that their source of narcissistic supply may be leaving them (the victim). This may be a disastrous for them because they may require the attention of a victim to feel fulfilled.

Practical advice – How to plan for the narcissistic attack

The TRAP moment is demoralising for a victim when they realise that they are trapped in an abusive relationship. This doesn't mean that a victim cannot start planning their exit. This is where a victim needs to take every ounce of inner strength (that they may not know they even had) and use it for themselves.

When a victim finally does decide to leave (which may take more time), they will have to do so swiftly and completely. At the TRAP moment, when blackmail or other terrifying discouragements may be happening in their life, they need to survive the narcissist's attacks and use it as an opportunity to start planning their escape.

Narcissistic attack is likely to be ferocious and vengeful. It is very different to leaving a normal relationship because the victim is highly unlikely to be able to hold a rational conversation or have healthy disagreement. Whilst leaving a normal relationship may be devastating or hurtful, leaving a narcissist is likely to include behaviours such as revenge, public humiliation, blackmail, punishment and threats/real violence.

Narcissistic attack is characterised by some of the following:

(1) Ferocity
(2) Lacking any moral/legal/ethical considerations
(3) Worse than you could imagine
(4) Designed to really destroy, hurt, harm and degrade you
(5) Designed to hurt you over and over again directly and indirectly

If you are the victim, you may realise that you are trapped at the moment, but you can prepare for the worst when you decide to actually leave the relationship.

1. **Know what you are letting yourself in for:** This is a painful truth that you have to anticipate the worst possible outcomes. This may be losing everything you have - your work, business, your friends, your family, your children, your pets. Or it may be exposure of all of your deepest

darkest secrets publicly. Be aware some narcissists will go for all of it, probably at the same time. They have no morals and their objective is your total *humiliation and destruction.*

2. **Leave with planning, unless your life is in danger:** The exit strategy has to be swift and complete with support mechanisms. If you don't have support, there is a strong risk you could be charmed back. The ideal scenario is no contact after you leave and move away.

3. **Don't talk to the narcissist about leaving in advance:** Advance notice allows some narcissists to plan their narcissistic attack(s). It will be vengeful, so don't give them extra time to plan.

4. **Get a support network around you:** This is imperative. I do not believe that you can do it alone. Support will be needed outside of friends/family e.g. specialist abuse charities, psychologists.

5. **Anticipate your weaknesses/get over embarrassment:** Imagine that potentially all your deepest, darkest secrets you have shared with the narcissist could be made public. Anticipate it, plan for it. This might for example include having to advise friends/family that they could be sent explicit photos and to ignore them. You may have to leave your job or your business. Plan for it.

6. **Be ready for the unexpected:** Whatever you think a narcissist might do, they probably can think of something worse. It is going to hurt but know there are people out there to support you when the unexpected arises.

7. **Accept the pathological lies:** The narcissist is likely to ramp up the pathological lies to their network of 'groomed' audience and twist facts. You are likely to be portrayed as the problem and they can give the performance of their lives to convince others that they are the victim and not you.

8. **Have your facts ready:** Get factual evidence out to somewhere safe.

9. **Defend yourself/speak out:** Your biggest defence is starting to speak up for yourself. It might seem impossible and daunting at times. It can be especially hard when neighbours, friends and colleagues start avoiding you because the narcissist has spread false rumours. Keep talking your truth. There are good people out there that will help you. Some won't want to know or can't hear you. Talk about it anyway.

10. **Get strong enough to defend yourself through legal channels:** Get an empathetic solicitor/lawyer who specialises in narcissism. Do not be afraid to defend yourself.

11. **Be ready for legal action and attack:** Be prepared for the attack. The narcissist may put false legal claims against you as punishment. Expect it. Learn legal terminology (or get someone to help you). Know your rights. Calmly make sure you write down what is happening to you.

Phase 5 – Coercive Control Techniques

Chapter 14 – Relationship Abuse and Coercive Control

Once you are trapped in the relationship, it can escalate to coercive control. This is a pattern of acts of assault, threats, humiliation and intimidation or other types of abuse which is used to harm, punish or frighten their victim.

It can be terrifying and come as a complete shock to the victim, because what they are observing and what is happening in the relationship is in stark contrast to the person they thought they knew.

This can be such an abrupt change from who the victim thought the narcissist was. This stage has a number of common behaviours/traits:

1. **Disbelief of facts by the victim:** The victim is so confused by the seemingly overnight change in personality, that there is a denial and disbelief of the facts (cognitive dissonance). This confusion allows the narcissist to control further by switching on the good behaviour and the bad behaviour when it suits them.
2. **Increasing the intensity and types of abuse:** By this point in the relationship the narcissist may become confident that abuse will not be reported, and the victim does not have the willingness or ability to argue back. This is because the narcissist seems to further take ownership of their victim, and as their 'object' and start to mould their victim to their needs.
3. **Generic arguing:** Generic arguing is about something without facts or detail involved. Sometimes, even if the facts exist to the contrary, the narcissist may well insist repeatedly that their version of events is true until the other person backs down.
4. **Circular arguing:** Circular arguments do not allow conclusion of any particular point, giving the narcissist the opportunity to keep coming back to points already discussed or previously resolved.
5. **Superiority:** This might include phrases like 'Everyone knows that ...'

or 'I'm surprised that you don't know ...' And then blagging (making up information) if they don't know actual facts.

6. **Deprivation:** Of needs, e.g. medical aid, food, safety, home.

7. **Humiliation:** This can include the enjoyment of watching their victim humiliated in public.

8. **Threats:** Of harm to the victim, threats to harm others, threats of humiliation and safety of the victim e.g. threats to be thrown out on the street. Threats, particularly if some are carried through, help to maintain the status of power and then dominance over a victim.

9. **Actual harm:** This can include actual harm of animals, children, harm of other people as well as the victim.

10. **Monitoring:** As the control deepens, the monitoring phase may start or escalate in some instances. This might be an increase in calls, texts, emails and demands to know where their victim is at all times. This also gives the narcissist the ability to do as they please, knowing where the victim is. Because the narcissist believes everyone lies, they seem to need to continue to check up on where their victim is.

11. **Further isolation:** This is where the narcissist is likely to now try to isolate the victim further, particularly from those who might influence the victim away from the narcissist.

12. **Physical escalation:** Physical escalation can start as the abuse increases. This is likely to be a demonstration of physical control and at times may well be brought on by seemingly insignificant reasons (yet justified in the mind of the narcissist).

13. **Taunting, mocking and goading:** There may well be double standards with taunting, mocking and goading, e.g. a female narcissist hitting her male victim and then taunting him by saying no one would believe he is being abused.

14. **Financial control:** A narcissist may believe that they own and are entitled to everything that belongs to the victim. This includes money, assets, property. The financial control may be anything from complete control of all finances, to feeling completely 'entitled' to take whatever belongs to their victim as their own.

15. **Control in the home:** This can start subtly at first and include buying only the clothing that the narcissist wants the victim to wear. This may also include control over what the victim can eat, when they can eat and is likely to be especially annoying and aggravating to the narcissist if there are any special dietary requirements.

16. **Control the victim's movements:** This can include going to work, school or anywhere outside of the home. Again, this is because the narcissist is running a schema which believes that 'everyone is lying'

Section 1 – Recognising the 16 Stages of Narcissistic Abuse

and that they are 'entitled' to do exactly what they want, and if they don't 'control' their environment the victim might try to take some control back. They seemingly have a need to know where their victim might be. The victim may not be free to go where they please.

17. **Domination as well as control:** This is where the narcissist has completely taken over control of all aspects of a victim – mental, physical, emotional. A narcissist may well feel quite entitled to do this as they tend to believe that they 'own' the victim as an object in their mind.

18. **Set-ups –** Such as bait and switch. This is where a narcissist sets up an argument, knowing exactly what will make a person get angry. Once they have created the anger and reaction, they then **blame the victim** for getting angry and switch the argument so that the narcissist claims to be the **harmed party**. They have switched the argument by baiting someone

19. **Personal gaslighting:** Where the narcissist makes a victim question their own sanity or reality, e.g. deliberately telling the victim to meet at a specific time, then arriving earlier and demanding to know why the victim is late. The narcissist will vehemently insist it is the victim to blame for getting it wrong (their memory, they are too sensitive) until the victim backs down.

20. **Brainwashing/mind manipulation:** This is a technique similar to deconstruction of sanity but goes further. A victim can be 'brainwashed' entirely to respond as they have been programmed to do by the narcissist.

21. **Vague accusations:** These may start with grandiose accusations, involving hard to defend subject matters or socially sensitive subject matters. An example might be accusations of sexism without being able to give any specific examples.

22. **Programming severe consequences for speaking out:** This mind manipulation technique ensures that eventually, with just a look, a narcissist can completely control their victim. It works on the principle that minor things are punished harshly by the narcissist, so that the victim is painfully aware that stepping out of line will result in even further punishment. As such, they become compliant.

23. **Inability to de-escalate arguments continues – The set-up:** Narcissists are skilled at deliberate set-ups. There seems to be a certain enjoyment for a narcissist when they deliberately say different things to different groups of people and then observe the outcome from a distance.

24. **False accusations/put downs:** The narcissist may start to make false

accusations and put downs may well become more regular. They are likely to use words which are intended to wound and hurt the victim. Sometimes the false accusations are actually projections to cover up their own deviant thoughts and to cover up their own actions, e.g. very often accusations of cheating towards the victim are because the narcissist has or is already thinking about cheating.

25. **Threats:** This is likely to help the narcissist ensure their victim remains compliant and in fear. This is for *control*. Threats can be genuine (and carried through) or they can remain a method of intimidation. From a narcissist's point of view, they may well believe that threats would not be necessary if the victim just did what they were told to do.

26. **Freedom of movement control:** This can include anything from miniscule time keeping to tracking devices and spyware. A narcissist can want to know where their victim is because it may free time up for them to do as they please (affairs, going out).

27. **Freedom of speech control:** This method seems to be to prevent the victim from speaking out. It may also trivialise what the victim has to say both inside and outside of the relationship. This is closely linked to *recruitment of false witnesses*.

28 **Recruitment of false witnesses:** This process is designed to deepen the victim's isolation. This includes recruitment of neighbours, community leaders, work colleagues, unsuspecting counsellors, friends and family. The purpose of false witnesses for the narcissist is to help them support lies. They are likely to work extremely hard to convince these people that their lies are true because they need them to help *isolate the victim, discredit the victim or vindicate themselves.*

29. **Do as I say, not as I do:** The stark contrast between what the narcissist is saying and what they actually do can be vastly different. Whilst telling their victim (or even their false witnesses) one thing, they may well be doing the very *opposite and completely contradicting themselves.*

30. **Isolation of the victim:** The isolation of their victim increases through the various methods of control – false witnesses, monitoring movements and preventing freedom of speech.

31. **Increased deprivation of the victim:** This can include anything from food, shelter – even to asking their victim to participate in depraved acts for their *pleasure.*

32. **Humiliation:** This can include public shame to control their victim. It is used when the narcissist perceives that the victim may expose the truth about them or simply as a method of *pleasure or gratification* for the narcissist.

86   Section 1 – Recognising the 16 Stages of Narcissistic Abuse

33. **Venomous words/name calling:** The words used by a narcissist can be designed to shock and be venomous. They go beyond insults or criticism to cut to the core and create *verbal wounds.*

34. **Physical escalation:** Physical harm may start to escalate over time. A slap can become a punch or kick – even broken bones. It can also include threatening harm to other people (threats of violence) or threats and/or actual abuse to animals and children. The underlying message is *if you don't do as I say, you will be next.* The incidents may start gradually, or instantly and often show any true *lack of remorse.*

35. **Financial control:** This is highly likely to occur. Because a narcissist believes in controlling all aspects of a victim, this is likely to include finances. A narcissist seems to perceive that they are entitled to everything the victim has. If the victim has money, it will be considered the narcissist's and if the victim does not have money, it will be seen as a grand gesture to support them, or take that support away when other pre-conceived *narcissistic needs are not met.*

36. **My home, my rules:** A home may need to be kept immaculately tidy. Whatever the spoken and unspoken 'rules' might be, the victim must stick to them. The 'rules' seem to show no tolerance for another person's preferences or needs. It is almost completely one-sided and straying from the rules can have severe consequences for the victim.

Because some of this is happening, the victim is likely to start exhibiting emotional distress:

1. **Victim starts exhibiting distressed behaviour:** Because abuse is happening out of sight, it can help the narcissist validate their 'calm public image', whilst the victim can appear 'erratic' or 'emotionally distressed'. Generally, people are more likely to listen to the 'calmer' person. The erratic behaviour demonstrated by a victim can include prolonged sorrow, moodiness, sadness, withdrawal, more and more negative outlook and an unwillingness to engage in conversations.

As a victim becomes more isolated and alone, there may be added pressure from the community and outside of the relationship:

1. **May hide the victim from the community:** Considerable effort can be invested by the narcissist to change people's view and opinions to match their own. If it is not possible to change people's opinion (that the victim is at fault), a narcissist may hide the victim or remove them out of the community (e.g. by moving away from an area or

deliberately stonewalling certain groups of people). Narcissists can be very reliant on secrecy and it is likely to be too painful for a narcissist to have to face the reality of their actions – especially if it is publicly known.

2. **Society can turn a blind eye to relationship abuse:** The narcissist can be further helped in their control of their victim and ability to undermine the victim in private because society tends to:
Turn a blind eye: Whilst neighbours or others may witness distressing incidents, generally people will turn a blind eye to the situation and believe that 'it is none of my business'.
Society likes to believe the best in people: There is also an underlying belief in most of society that likes to look for the best in people.

Chapter 15 – The Domestic Abuse and Coercive Control Laws in the UK

Both domestic abuse and coercive control laws exist in the UK to help victims of abuse.

If you believe you might be in a relationship with someone who poses a risk to you, you (or a close friend or family member) have the right to make an enquiry to the police under Clare's Law. You will need to complete the Domestic Violence Disclosure Scheme application form.

Important changes to the Domestic Abuse Law 2021 are being rolled out early 2022 and preventing violence against women and girls is expected to be a policing priority early March 2022.

Coercive control is thankfully a criminal offence in the UK. The legislation came into effect from the 29 December 2015 under Section 76 of the Serious Crime Act 2015.

For a prosecution to be successful, there are a number of aspects that need to be met. I have taken this information as a layperson and it is therefore imperative that you get true professional advice, rather than rely on my interpretations.

	UK Legislation
Where to find the	http://www.legislation.gov.uk/ – search for Serious Crime Act 2015, Domestic Abuse, Section 76 https://www.cps.gov.uk/ – search for domestic abuse.
Definition of coercive behaviour	Coercive behaviour is an act or a pattern of acts of assault, threats, humiliation and intimidation or other abuse that is used to harm, punish or frighten their victim.
How do you define controlling behaviour in law	Controlling behaviour is a range of acts designed to make a person subordinate and/or dependent by isolating them from sources of support, exploiting their resources and capacities for personal gain, depriving them of the means needed for independence, resistance and escape and regulating their everyday behaviour.

The Domestic Abuse and Coercive Control Laws in the UK **89**

	What are the elements of the legislation?
Are you personally connected to the narcissist?	To be personally connected, you need to meet one of the following criteria: – In an intimate personal relationship – Live together as members of the same family – Lived together previously or been in an intimate personal relationship with each other
Was the behaviour controlling or coercive?	The following are examples of behaviour that might be considered: – Isolation from friends and family – Depriving you of your basic needs – Monitoring your time – Monitoring with online tools or spyware – Taking control over aspects of life, e.g. when you can sleep, what you wear, who you can see, where you can go – Depriving access to medical services or specialist support – Repeatedly putting you down – Enforcing rules which humiliate, degrade or dehumanise you – Forcing you to take part in criminal activity – Financial abuse, e.g. controlling finances – Controlling you going to work/school/place of study – Taking your wages, benefits or allowances – Threats to harm or kill – Threats to harm a child – Threats to publish or reveal private information – Threats to hurt of physically harm a pet – Assault – Criminal damage – Preventing access to transport – Preventing you from working – Family 'dishonour' – Reputational Damage – Disclosure of health or sexual orientation – Limiting access to family, friends or finances
Did the narcissist repeatedly and continually engage in the behaviour?	**Yes/No/Unknown – How?**

90 Section 1 – Recognising the 16 Stages of Narcissistic Abuse

	What are the elements of the legislation?
Did you suffer serious effects from the behaviour?	This means if you, on at least two occasions, feared that violence would be used against you or if the behaviour caused you serious alarm or distress which also had a substantial adverse effect on your usual day-to-day activities. **Yes/No/Unknown – How?**
What were the serious effects?	How would you define the serious effects you have suffered?
Was there intent to control or coerce you?	Did the narcissist intend to control or coerce you? How?
Did the behaviour have substantial adverse effects on your day-to-day activities?	– Stopping or changing the way you socialise? – Has your physical or mental health deteriorated? – Have you changed your routine at home such as household chores or mealtimes? – Have you put measures in place at home to safeguard yourself or children? – Have your work patterns, employment status or routes to work changed?
Did the narcissist know or ought to have known his behaviour would have a serious effect on you?	How do you know that the narcissist knew or ought to have known the consequences of their actions?

Practical advice – How to evidence coercive control

What is likely to be defined as acceptable evidence to show coercive control?

Getting out of an abusive relationship may require significant planning. Should the situation become so unbearable that the victim has to leave, then it is imperative to put together a plan of action. One of these elements is evidence – not necessarily to prosecute, but because it might be that a narcissist may well counter-attack with false accusations.

CAUTION: Some of these things come at significant risk of your harm if you are being abused and monitored. Do not underestimate your vulnerability. When you leave a narcissistic relationship, narcissists can escalate abuse when you leave. It is always better to leave swiftly if you suspect for a moment you might be at risk of violence than wait to get evidence. If this applies to you, please talk to professional charities who can get you out to a safe house.

Please anticipate that nothing is secure: emails could already be being monitored, phones monitored and recorded, and tracking devices may already be in place. This may be especially so if the narcissist suspects you are thinking of leaving them.

Again, I am just a layperson, so please let professionals (such as specialist abuse charities/lawyers/private detectives) guide you in what to do. To assist your case providing evidence can help you. This includes things such as:

(1)   Emails
(2)   Phone records
(3)   Text messages
(4)   Photographs of injuries
(5)   Your own CCTV recordings
(6)   Medical records
(7)   Witness testimony
(8)   Bank records
(9)   Evidence of threats made to others
(10) Diary kept by victim
(11) GPS tracking devices

In addition, the police, as part of their investigation, may consider evidence such as:

(12) 999 tapes or manuscripts
(13) Body-worn video footage
(14) Local enquiries with neighbours
(15) Previous criminal records or threats made
(16) Care plans
(17) Photographs of injuries
(18) Other CCTV
(19) Witness statements

How you might provide supporting evidence

The following may also help gathering evidence to protect yourself:

- **Speaking out:** Do not be ashamed to speak out to people around you. There are genuinely kind people out there who can see through things. Others may berate you (this is the hard part) because they have been recruited by the narcissist as a false witness.
- **Recording threats:** If you can record threats (on a separate device), do so. However, you may not be able to play this back to anyone unless a court allows you to.
- **CCTV recordings:** Make sure it is date and time-stamped to evidence what is actually happening within the relationship. You might want to also make sure that it is safely backed up, so that even theft of your device means that the images are protected. Check local laws and use CCTV only for your own property.
- **Report incidents:** You may be asked to record incidents – online or by phone to the police. The police take domestic abuse seriously in the UK and it helps them build up a picture of the crimes.
- **Provide evidence if you need to make a statement to the police:** Be factual and prove it, e.g. he threatened me by text – show evidence of it. He stole my money – show evidence where the money went from and to.
- **Be strong in defending yourself:** You may well get false accusations and even strongly worded solicitors' letters from the narcissist. Be ready to calmly prove each accusation incorrect with facts. This can take time and effort but is essential.
- **Mental health support:** I recommend choosing a psychotherapist (rather than a counsellor) that is familiar with the court system and is prepared to give evidence of your treatment if necessary. Choose someone who knows about narcissism (not all do).
- **Issue cease and desist letters for defamation:** If you find that the narcissist is defaming you (which may be likely) and other people are repeating those words, issue a cease and desist letter putting your facts forward.
- **Neighbours, friends, locals may berate you and accuse you of lying and malicious behaviour:** On top of leaving an abusive relationship, the narcissist may put considerable effort into charming people around the victim with false allegations and lies. This means that when the victim looks for support, they instead get falsely accused with whatever lies the narcissist has told them.

The Domestic Abuse and Coercive Control Laws in the UK **93**

- **Gather your own evidence:** Ask witnesses and people you know to write down facts. Date and sign it.
- **Vindictive behaviour:** Anticipate vindictive behaviour. This might include destruction of your property, lying to damage your reputation or to inflict embarrassment or destroy your career.
- **Get a solicitor or lawyer:** Finding a good solicitor can be hard. Anticipate that they may not understand the nuances of narcissism. Only some solicitors seem to specialise in coercive control. Those that do are often too busy to take your case. Solicitors and lawyers' costs can be financially expensive if you cannot get legal help free. It can also be an incredibly emotionally traumatic process to get someone representing you to fully understand the seriousness of your coercive control. Expect to have to do a lot of your own work to save costs.
- **Going to court for a non-molestation order:** It would be easier to help yourself through charities such as Woman's Aid/Mens Advice Line rather than rely on a solicitor (speed may be of the essence).
- **Get another cheap phone/phone number:** This can be used to make calls to safe houses if necessary and keep in contact with friends/family/support.
- **Put tracking devices in your own car and link to a friend/family member:** This ensures someone you trust knows your whereabouts (e.g. family).
- **Ask other people to watch out for the narcissist for you:** Don't just rely on yourself, ask other people to watch out if they see the narcissist in the area.
- **Change your routines:** Do not go the same route, change habits, be observant and vigilant.
- **Speak to your doctor:** Explain what you are going through and have it recorded on your notes.
- **Advise someone at work:** This is a risky strategy and can cost you your job, but if you have advised someone at work what you are going through, they will be obliged to consider your health and safety. It also helps because your work may suffer significantly.
- **Friends and family:** Support is vital as you come out of an abusive relationship. But do not expect friends and family to be equipped to give you wise counsel. Only a professionally trained therapist is able to do that or people who have been through narcissistic abuse.
- **Malicious rumours about you:** Address any malicious rumours – publicly if needed. Anticipate some disbelief and backlash.
- **Acceptance of loss:** You may well lose friends, neighbours,

colleagues, local support. People can treat you differently afterwards. It is a high price you pay (extremely unfair) but society feels uncomfortable talking about abuse openly at the moment.

- **Write down what happened straight afterwards:** It is highly likely that your memory will be influenced and writing down facts straight after you have left (or as you go along) ensures they are recorded as accurately as possible.
- **Keep a copy of your evidence somewhere else safe:** Do not just write one copy of evidence – make sure you put another copy elsewhere e.g. a safety box if required.
- **Only deal with a narcissist in writing:** This ensures that facts cannot be twisted.
- **Get pets away:** Pets can potentially be at risk of harm. Get them away – to rescue centres if necessary.
- **Children:** Ensure safety of children. Insist on implementing a co-parenting app so that all evidence is recorded.

Domestic Abuse Act 2021

A range of new protection orders are also being piloted early in 2022 under the Domestic Abuse Act 2021. These are called Domestic Abuse Protection Notice (DAPN) and Domestic Abuse Protection Order (DAPO). These give immediate protection following a domestic incident and can be issued by the police. If a perpetrator breaches the terms of these notices and orders it can result in a maximum of five years imprisonment.

The updates to this legislation, gives much greater protection to victims of domestic abuse.

To be covered by this legislation, both parties must be over the age of sixteen and must be personally connected (by means of being married, agreed to be married, in a civil partnership, living together or in an intimate personal relationship or parenting the same child).

Behaviour that is classified as abusive within this legislation includes:

- Physical and sexual abuse – including non-fatal strangulation.
- Violent or threatening behaviour – Including threat to publish intimate images.
- Controlling or coercive behaviour – even after the relationship has ended.

The Domestic Abuse and Coercive Control Laws in the UK   **95**

- Economic abuse: Where one person's behaviour exerts a substantial adverse effect on another person's ability to:
  - ✧ Obtain goods and services
  - ✧ Acquire money or other property
  - ✧ Use money or other property.
- Psychological, emotional or other abuse – If children see, hear or experience the effects of abuse, they will be recognised as a victim.

In court, crucially this new legislation ensures that victims are entitled to special measures which mean that they can have a separate waiting room. This legislation also stops the cross-examination of the victim by the perpetrator and ends the defence of 'rough sex'.

The new laws give police the powers to intervene earlier when abuse is suspected. With some trial introductions of the DAPO and DAPN early in 2022, it will be good to see this fully rolled out nationally to see greater protection for victims.

The law includes a new role of domestic abuse commissioner, Nicole Jacobs, who will have the role of holding both agencies and government to account in tackling domestic abuse.

In practice the DAPN issued by police may give a victim up to forty-eight hours protection when the perpetrator has to leave the home. Alternatively, if you are made homeless from abuse you will be given priority for housing with local authorities under a new duty to provide survivors or victims of abuse support in finding accommodation or safe accommodation.

With the DAPO, it is currently planned that this can be requested by victims of abuse or specified third parties directly to the family courts. Importantly this can be issued in civil, criminal and family courts – meaning more protection for victims. Perpetrators can be asked to attend behaviour changing programmes, be electronically tagged and asked to stay a certain distance away.

Where to find the legislation: https://www.legislation.gov.uk/ Search for Domestic Abuse Act 2021.

What else to watch out for: What a narcissist is likely to do to avoid punishment

Because a narcissist often believes that they are smarter and above the law, they are unlikely to take any legal limitations very seriously, unless they have to.

They may approach the law with contempt and arrogance and look for any loopholes or use various techniques to disprove, discredit or get any legal action thrown out.

Techniques that may be used by a narcissist

These are some of the techniques you can expect a narcissist to use if faced with any legal challenge, as they would find it incredulous and an insult that someone is not buying into their version of events. This could include:

- **Smoke screening:** This involves creating numerous versions of events to make the truth very difficult to find.
- **Pleading innocence/ignorance:** This would be used to pretend to not understand the severity of their actions or simply to state they did not know.
- **Generalised accusations without evidence:** This method typically might be completely exaggerated or even untrue. It might be a *generalised character/behaviour slur e.g. 'He is so sexist!'*
- **Recruiting false witnesses/staging:** This aspect is used by the narcissist to 'groom' witnesses to only see their version of events *e.g. deliberate self-harm by the narcissist but passing it off as assault by the victim.*
- **False accusations/false trails:** This method means that venomous false accusations are given against the victim to slow and confuse the facts.
- **Lies:** Lies are likely to be believable and may well be widely repeated (especially to false witnesses).
- **Discrediting evidence and proof:** Evidence provided by the victim is likely to be scrutinised and discredited, e.g. recruiting alternative experts.
- **Implanting false evidence:** If it is possible to implant false evidence to incriminate someone else then the narcissist may do so *e.g. if a narcissist wants to make false allegations that their partner drinks heavily, they may deliberately hide alcohol in the house, invite a friend round and pretend to be devastated when they 'accidentally' find it.*
- **Removal of evidence:** Another aspect can be removal of any incriminating evidence quickly.
- **Civil v Criminal law:** In the UK for example, the accusations can be classified under *civil and/or criminal law.* It may mean that a victim may have to defend themselves and relive the abuse in court.
- **Withholding key information:** This would be the deliberate withholding or omission of information that could implicate the narcissist.
- **Undermining credibility by remaining calm:** This method is when a

The Domestic Abuse and Coercive Control Laws in the UK **97**

narcissist stays calm, and a victim is emotionally overwhelmed because of the narcissist's behaviour.

- **Becoming friendly with witnesses/influencers:** At the same time as trying to discredit or smokescreen their own actions, a narcissist may become friendlier with their false witnesses (e.g. fake tears and part confessions).
- **Minimising what they have done:** This would typically be against any accusation to try to minimise accountability.
- **Increasing threats to victim:** This may be done to get the victim to withdraw any complaints.
- **Instigating a legal claim on the victim:** Typically, they might want to add additional pressure to the victim and instigate legal claims at their most vulnerable point (even false claims).
- **Increased work on their public image:** This could include publicly increasing charitable work locally, spearheading a local/national big cause, eliciting sympathy from others.
- **Partial admittance of lower level offences:** This technique means that a narcissist can show some accountability but *get away with* more serious allegations.
- **Acting calm:** This method can come quite naturally for a narcissist and they appear to know that acting calm gives them more credibility.
- **Acting the hurt party:** This method goes back to manipulating people with how hurt they feel (to elcite sympathy).
- **Secret vengeance:** Whilst working hard on their public image, the narcissist may be seeking vengeance on the victim, the victim's friends or family in private.
- **Questioning victim's mental state and believability:** This technique can be delivered well by a narcissist as they have an ability to stay calm and remain detached. It can shift the focus onto the victim having to defend their believability even before discussing any facts.
- **Breaking into emails/phones and deleting evidence:** This may happen in an abusive relationship. Sometimes the phone and emails are already being monitored.
- **Bugging, photographing and video recordings:** The narcissist is likely to be bugging, photographing, and recording their victims to use as evidence of bad behaviour. It can be preceded by the narcissist goading the victim and then recording the ensuring explosion. The evidence would likely be cut to only show the victims explosion and not perhaps the substantial goading beforehand.

- **Stalking and harassment:** This may be used to apply pressure on the victim to back down or withdraw any complaints/legal proceedings.

In conclusion – it is very difficult to leave an abusive relationship, which is why it can take someone up to seven attempts to get out and get free.

Phase 6 - Food and Mealtime Abuse

Chapter 16 - Food Abuse Tactics

Food abuse is not commonly defined when considering abuse, but it is where significant control can be wielded over meals and mealtimes.

Food control is another powerful way for a narcissist to control their victim. It can include:

1. **Demonstration of their superiority:** Some narcissists may believe that their cooking skills are so exceptional that they are culinary experts. The grandiose belief and confidence in their own abilities cannot be shaken. There seems to be no possibility in their mind that anyone else can possibly cook better than them.
2. **Knowing better than any experts:** The belief in their own abilities to cook are so strong that they will regularly state that they know better than any chef or expert.
3. **Punishment using food:** Punishment around food can be from serving food that their victim dislikes, not being able to leave the table or physical abuse. The punishment can be because of the narcissist's high standards, which can be unreasonable. They are likely to expect everyone to abide by their standards and rules.
4. **Food as control:** Food used as control - e.g. what you can have, when you can have it, how you eat the meal. The narcissist seems to see food as their entitlement to have what they want, when they want it, and to be treated in a special way. It does not matter about anyone else's needs.
5. **Food used to deliberately change the victims mental state:** Food that induces reactions might be used as a method to secretly punish the victim or for revenge.

Other methods of food abuse and control that may occur are:

1. **Controlling what is eaten:** The control of what can be eaten is entirely decided by the narcissist. There may be a number of ways that this can be set-up.
   a. **Pretending to care:** For example, asking 'What would you like to eat?' It is not a question as such, it is a method of superficial asking. You will get what you are given anyway.
   b. **Questioning what the victim wants to eat:** This method is used to wear the victim down. It might include repeated, 'Why would you want that?' or 'Are you sure? That's not healthy for you', 'Let's just stick with …'
   c. **Criticism to prevent change of food eaten:** Another tactic would be extensive criticism of food choices requested by the victim. For example, the narcissist may repeatedly criticise, using strong derogatory statements such as 'I'm not eating that rubbish!' or 'I hate your food choices!' The purpose is to criticise the victim so much that they 'give in', asking for what they want for an easy life.
   d. **Controlling meals outside of the home:** This method of control may be used to ensure that the victim is eating what has been prepared for them and only that. It goes beyond someone caringly preparing a packed lunch, for example, because it only allows the victim to eat what the narcissist has prepared. The narcissist may then check the lunch has been eaten.
2. **Controlling when you eat:** This might include:
   a. **Being insistent on precisely what time a meal is eaten:** This might be down to the second and minute and there may be punishment or harsh criticism for not having a meal ready on time.
   b. **Delaying food preparation:** This could include deliberate delays to having meals ready (sometimes hours). This may be combined with not 'allowing' any snacks before the meal is ready. Additionally, this can come with the demand of being present the moment the meal is ready, putting the victim on permanent standby.
3. **Punishment using food:** This may take several forms and includes:
   a. **Deliberate set-ups:** This may include promises of a certain meal that they know a victim likes and then dishing up something they know the victim hates. There is an anticipation of a meal you might be looking forward to and disappointment when this doesn't happen. This may also include phrases like 'Well why are you not happy?', 'Why do you think you are so special, I'm doing the cooking!'

b. **Food that you dislike:** Another method is deliberately cooking food for the victim that they strongly dislike. This can be as punishment because you have or have not done something. Sometimes this might include an unspoken want or need by the narcissist, so you are unable to find out what you have 'done wrong'.

c. **Not being able to leave the table:** This is punishment of not being able to leave the table until all the food is eaten. This can even be implemented when a victim is ill, for example.

d. **Food being thrown at the victim/the walls/floors:** This method of control will mean that the victim may be in fear at mealtimes, which will not be conducive to digestion. It can include a victim's face being pushed into food.

e. **Plates/crockery/cutlery:** Another fear tactic could be the deliberate breaking of plates/crockery or cutlery being used in menacing ways, such as stabbing the table with a knife. Alternatively, it might include severe psychological punishment for dropping a plate for example.

4. **Food used to harm you:** In the extreme this might include deliberately giving food that you are allergic or intolerant to. For example, deliberately giving wheat to a coeliac to make them unwell.

5. **Food used to change mental state:** This can include spiking food with drugs.

6. **Controlling the finances around food:** Either the amount of money to spend on food is controlled or what can be purchased limited.

In addition to food that may be used as punishment against the victim, a narcissist will be demanding some really high standards. There seems to be a correlation between food, mealtime abuse and narcissism.

This is what you might observe:

- **Food perfectionism:** A narcissist may truly believe that their food preparation, presentation and experience is exceptional. This might include having certain routines at the dining table, e.g. laid out precisely for all meals.
- **Food prepared the way they want:** There seems to be no tolerance for alternative methods. They may believe that their 'recipes' are so amazing that they simply cannot tolerate food being prepared any other way.
- **Take the credit:** They may also take the credit for someone else's recipes if they 'added' a little something.

- **Table manners/etiquette:** Table manners may be extremely important to some narcissists. Everyday meals may need to be eaten as if you are at a five-star restaurant. A grandiose experience.
- **Food preferences:** Because they may well believe that their palette is superior to other people's, they usually try to insist that their partner eats what they have chosen. They know what is best for them.
- **Disagreements:** There may be no room for disagreement about the food chosen because they believe that their knowledge is superior in the relationship. In fact, it seems to be an annoyance that anyone could either fail to enjoy what they have cooked or have done it in a better way.
- **Timing of food:** Because the narcissist may need to control the timing of the food, food is likely to be served to meet their own preferences above anyone else's needs.
- **Food as a punishment:** Food can be used as a punishment if they feel that they have been wounded in some way. They are likely to say 'If you had done/said ... then I wouldn't have had to do that.'
- **Important guests:** With important guests from outside the family home, concessions can be made to adjust the meals and/or timing. This would be to meet the narcissist's needs, e.g. influencing someone.
- **Restaurant/chef criticism:** Narcissists are likely to believe that their palette is exceptional. Because of this it is hard for narcissists to find somewhere perfect to eat out. Most meals out are subject to their criticism of service, food, delivery or presentation because they do not meet their exacting standards.

Practical advice – What to do – Food abuse

When talking about food and mealtime abuse, it is important to realise that everyone's body is different. It is also important to note that this is significantly different between someone cooking food for someone in a caring way and a controlling way. Etiquette and table manners differ also.

My focus therefore is on the more serious food abuse, such as deliberately serving food to harm. Here are some ways to help:

1. **Independent diagnosis:** It may be necessary to get more than one independent diagnosis. Depending on your level of freedom, you might need to do this secretly. A record of your deteriorating health may be necessary.

2. **Inviting other people over more regularly:** If you are able to invite other people over more regularly, then it is likely that you may be eating food that is good for you at a prescribed time.
3. **Making it seem the narcissist's idea:** Sometimes, you may be able to 'plant' an idea for meals. If done carefully, this method can appear to make the idea the narcissist's.
4. **Record what you think is happening:** Records of events become important. Be extremely careful how you keep records away from your abuser and if necessary have more than one copy.

Where food abuse becomes assault – such as pushing your face in food – record the assault somewhere if it does not put you in any danger.

Phase 7 - Deepening Coercive Control Methods

As the relationship with a narcissist progresses, you may find yourself subject to deepening coercive control methods. They are likely to escalate and include:

- Gaslighting and mind control
- Changing your reality - Denial of unfaithfulness
- Brainwashing, interrogation, inhumane and degrading techniques
- False witness
- Enjoyment of pathological and set-up lying

As the relationship develops, and if you experience some of these aspects of narcissistic abuse, you are highly likely to have little sense of reality any more. You may not trust yourself and rely completely on the narcissist to guide your life.

You can become a shell of your former self - unable to function. Because your reality of life is determined by the narcissist, you can get to a point where you:

- Cannot make decisions any more
- Re-write history to align with the narcissist's point of view
- Lose your job or home
- Lose friends and family
- Become depressed, anxious and nervous all the time
- Stop going out at all

It can get better and this book will show you later how to get out of this terrible situation. Somewhere inside, you will and do have the strength to end the relationship if you are experiencing these next set of deepening coercive control methods.

Chapter 17 – Gaslighting and Mind Control

Gaslighting, mind control, brainwashing, interrogation, inhuman and degrading techniques

These deepening abuse and control techniques are psychological torture and can be part of an abusive relationship with a narcissist.

These techniques can be used by a narcissist to humiliate, degrade and de-humanise someone, which seems to give the narcissist the complete feeling of power and control. Some of these techniques include:

1. **Repeated gaslighting:** When this goes on repeatedly, this is where a victim can start to question their own sanity and mind. The abuser deliberately stages and sets up the situations and then vehemently denies it. This can leave the victim questioning their memory, accepting blame for things not their fault or having their opinions, thoughts and views denied and trivialised. Examples of gaslighting techniques might include:

   a. **Questioning partner's memory of events:** For example, changing watches and clocks to make someone late. Then blaming their lateness on poor memory or their own fault.

   b. **Victim-blaming:** Blaming the victim for things that they didn't do. For example, saying that you are meeting at a certain time at a meeting point and turning up earlier to blame the victim for getting the time wrong.

   c. **Re-writing history:** This aspect of gaslighting is where history is re-written – for example the phrases used might be 'But, you said ...' or 'That never happened!'

   d. **Denial of unfaithfulness:** Vehement denial of being unfaithful, when it is blatantly happening. This goes beyond denials of unfaithfulness in other relationships (e.g. to hold onto a marriage for love). The denial from a narcissist seems to be the enjoyment of getting away with unfaithfulness, the entitlement that they can, plus the seeming enjoyment of telling the lies designed to question the victim's memory or reality.

   e. **Questioning memory:** A narcissist may repeatedly question a victim's memory as a method of questioning their own beliefs and sanity. Repeatedly done over time, the victim believes it is their memory that is the problem.

Section 1 – Recognising the 16 Stages of Narcissistic Abuse

   f.   **Turning heating on/off:** This gaslighting technique might be used to also deprive someone of heat, e.g. opening windows whilst someone is sleeping in winter to make them freeze.

   g.   **Moving objects/hiding objects:** This is another technique used to make victims question their own sanity. This might include deliberately moving objects and then blaming the victim when the object has moved. The victim is then chastised for their 'poor memory' and they start to believe that the narcissist is right and they are 'losing their mind'.

2. **Mind programming/mind control:** This can be used by narcissists. This particular mind control technique includes extensive 'seeding' of ideas along with repeated questioning of the victim's choice. Typically this might include phrases like 'If you are sure that's what you really want?', 'Are you certain you've thought that through?' or even blatant 'You don't want to do that, you want to do this.' Even when a victim clearly states their needs or wants, this technique can be repetitive and intense to undermine the victims views, and even refusal by the narcissist to accept the victim's viewpoint at all until they change their mind. There is no compromise in this tactic until the victim forms the same views as the narcissist. If the victim does challenge these approaches, they are likely to be met with phrases such as, 'Well if you didn't xyz ... I wouldn't have to do it.'

3. **Brainwashing:** This is an even more intense version of mind control. Brainwashing goes to the extreme of totally changing the victim's perception, even eradicating and minimising the victim's own beliefs and feelings and replacing them with pre-prepared answers. These answers are repeatedly drilled in, so that the victim will repeat ad verbatim what they have been programmed to say. This is even if it goes against everything the victim truly believes. It could also be brainwashing from the fear of consequences.

4. **Interrogation:** This technique can include quick fire questioning, with no chance of answering all the questions posed. The interrogation may be a series of questions and statements. The interrogation may include momentary relief with rewards for saying the 'right thing' (whatever the interrogator believes this to be) or it might get very intense by deliberately 'tying someone verbally in knots'. The purpose is to get someone to admit to something that they might not necessarily have done or create mental confusion.

5. **Sleep deprivation:** This is the deliberate act of depriving sleep, sometimes repeatedly to change a person's perspective or to alter their state of mind. It can include repeated arguments long into the

small hours of the night or waking someone repeatedly through the night.

6. **Assault during sleep:** This is when a victim is at their most vulnerable and assaults are physical, which cause the victim to wake up suddenly and disorientated.
7. **Inhumane behaviour:** This is the treatment to cause deliberate and intense physical or mental suffering. This might include blindfolding, denial of food or water or exposure to heat and cold deliberately.
8. **Degrading behaviour:** These techniques might include getting your partner to strip and humiliating them, or getting them to eat food from the floor. It appears that the narcissist treats the victim as an 'object' with no feelings at all.

Practical advice – What to do – Gaslighting

Gaslighting is serious abuse and can start to completely deconstruct and damage your mind. These are the things that you could consider doing to help yourself if you suspect gaslighting:

1. **Start making a note of when and what is happening:** You may need to be very careful, but if you can record what is happening and when, it will help to establish a timeline of events. You might also notice patterns of behaviour (e.g. only when my partner is here do things move or change).
2. **Take before and after photographs:** This is a clear demonstration of how things were before and after. It can help you be certain that objects for example have been moved.
3. **Have internal CCTV recordings in place:** This method must be done secretly so that you can observe what is actually going on.
4. **Ask other trusted people:** Friends and family if you are able to talk to them will have a better idea of your 'normality'. If you don't have any friends or family because you have been isolated, then you need photographic evidence to prove what is happening to yourself.
5. **Research historical events:** Sometimes you can go back to newspaper articles or diary notes to find out 'what was true at the time'. This may vary dramatically to what the narcissist is saying happened.
6. **Objects moving:** Control what you can control within your environment. If you move an object deliberately, photograph it and if it changes position you know that you did not do it. Another method is getting UV dye kits. If objects move and you have no UV dye on your hands, then it has to be someone else. Try www.glowtec.co.uk.

7. **Where someone has been in the house:** There are various low-tech methods such as using feathers on the tops of doors (to see if they have been opened), marking angles that doors are open with light pencil on the top of the frame, putting white powder on white tiles.

8. **Know that your memory may be affected:** If you are being severely abused, your memory may be affected. Keep writing down what you are told versus what you think is the truth.

Chapter 18 – Denial of Unfaithfulness

A narcissist may have other relationships in the background for more narcissistic supply. However, if you suspect and challenge a narcissist about their behaviour and if they have been seeing someone else, you are likely to get an extreme response of denial and indignation.

Expect aggressive phrases that deflect the argument back to you, for example:

- 'What is your problem?'
- 'You are so insecure,' or
- 'I can't believe you don't trust me!'

A narcissist seems to to feel entitled to have whatever relationships that they want.

This is because the rules of commitment and faithfulness do not seem to apply to them. They also may not believe that they will be caught out and can rely on their partner's trusting nature.

Typical techniques that may be used to cover up unfaithfulness would be:

- **Vehement denial:** A narcissist may vehemently deny any accusations very quickly and may take a question to be an accusation that has to be vehemently defended.
- **Getting angry quickly:** Getting angry quickly (i.e. when first asked) and using anger to get someone to back down.
- **Questioning their partner's faithfulness (deflection):** Another method is the deflection technique, where they turn the question around on their partner.
- **Refusal to answer:** They may be above answering the question and refuse to answer; this would be an insult to them.
- **Insulted by the question:** It can cause the narcissist to feel insulted that they dare be questioned about their behaviour.
- **Challenging you to phone someone:** Another technique might be to get their partner to back down, asking the question by saying forcefully 'Phone them, they will tell you I am telling the truth!'
- **Guilt-tripping:** This method might include statements like, 'I can't believe that you wouldn't trust me!'
- **Showing half evidence:** This could include statements like, 'Look, here's the receipt – it only shows one coffee!'

- **Having an answer ready:** A narcissist is very often a fluent liar, so is likely to use the normal pathological lies to get out of the question.

Practical advice – What to do – Unfaithfulness

Unfaithfulness happens in all types of relationships, not just in narcissistic relationships. The difference is the intention and your feelings around faithfulness (what it means to you). Before you consider unfaithfulness, in any relationship, it might be worth considering:

1. **Defining unfaithfulness for you:** Unfaithfulness means different things to different people; you need to write down what it means to you. Be specific about what it is and what it isn't for you.
2. **What are your values and expectations around faithfulness:** Defining expectations and your values is equally important. Do you expect your partner to have the same values as you?
3. **What are your deal breakers?** What would make you walk away from a relationship and what could you work through?

There are a number of methods to find out if a partner is being unfaithful, in an abusive relationship it is further complicated with the abuse that is going on. There may well be intimidation or threats to accept the situation. It may be vehemently denied and used as a method of control. If this is the case, depending on what you want to do with the information, you might consider:

1. **Accepting it:** If you are in physical danger or being intimidated, then you may have to accept the situation. This is not the same as agreeing to it, but by accepting the facts of the situation you are in, i.e. 'I am being cheated on, but I cannot leave the relationship and am being put at risk of sexual diseases,' you have the basis and acceptance of the truth of the current situation.
2. **Gaining actual evidence:** If you need to prove that your partner is being unfaithful because they are vehemently denying it, and perhaps questioning your sanity, evidence needs to be suitable for court if ever needed. In this case the options are:
   a. **Private detective:** Getting evidence that can prove that they have been unfaithful from an independent and verified source. Private detectives are also professionally trained to monitor, observe and track people without being seen. It is much harder to do this yourself. Choose someone reputable as it may be needed in court evidence.

b. **Your own low-key detective work:** This may include having to check information that you are being told independently. For example, looking at receipts. You could monitor where your partner is, but in an abusive relationship this comes with considerable risk of harm without careful planning and puts you at risk at being accused of stalking and harassment. My suggestion is always use someone independent and professional because a narcissist can be already monitoring you.

If you are wanting actual evidence, equally it is important to consider why you need the information and what you want to do with that information:

1. **Validate your gut instincts/prove your partner is lying:** Validating your gut instincts may help in an abusive relationship if you are constantly being told your gut instincts are wrong or any type of mind control that is being used to invalidate you.
2. **Leave the relationship:** If you are planning to leave the relationship, then unfaithfulness evidence may be vital to help you do that. It needs to be irrefutable and independent if possible, as a narcissist can be venomous when you leave.

Chapter 19 – Brainwashing, Interrogation, Inhumane and Torturous Treatments

On the extreme end of narcissistic abuse, you may experience even worse behaviour from the narcissist to control you. This can include:

- Brainwashing
- Interrogation
- Inhumane and torturous treatments

These techniques are akin to torture and will require professional psychological help when you leave the relationship (which you should immediately).

An abusive narcissist may use some of the following techniques:

Brainwashing
- Repeatedly telling someone what they should be thinking/feeling until the victim changes their mind.
- Slowly changing someone's core beliefs and replacing them with their own.

Interrogation techniques
- Quickfire questioning
- Accusing the victim of something they have not done.
- Creating an urgency to respond.
- Either/or questions.
- Provocative questions/statements.

Torturous techniques
- Severe pain or suffering, physical or mental, inflicted to exert pressure or control.
- Cruel or inhumane treatments to cause serious pain or suffering (physical or mental).
- Humiliation or degrading treatment.

Practical advice – What to do – Brainwashing, interrogation and torturous techniques

If you are being abused at this level, it is imperative that you get out of the relationship. Here are a number of things you can do:

1. **Seek professional help:**
   National Domestic Abuse Helpline: 0808 2000 247
2. **Write down what has happened.** It is important to write down what has happened or tell someone. Sometimes you just need to make two columns: in one write what you are being told and in the other what you truly believe.
3. **Reconnect to your own feelings/trust your own beliefs:** These techniques are so horrific that you may no longer connect to your own beliefs and feelings. You will need specialist help with this, but again you need to discern what are your own beliefs and feelings and what are someone else's.
4. **Mind reprogramming techniques:** This technique may help some people. It is a rewind technique used by some therapists. It doesn't take away that something has happened, but it does take away the emotional pain associated with the event.
5. **Trauma counselling:** Seek a specialist in trauma counselling who can help you work through the trauma, normally by talking therapies.

Chapter 20 – Creating False Witnesses and Intimidation

When the abuse gets so ingrained in a narcissistic abusive relationship, a narcissist can silence their partner with just a look or slight body movement.

This is when the victim has been trained to do as they are told.

Intimidation methods used to silence people might include:

- **Indirect threats:** A narcissist may indirectly threaten with 'You wouldn't want to say anything against me, would you?' This would be said in a way to create fear in the victim.
- **Direct threats:** Direct threats may also be a way to silence someone from speaking out. 'If you don't say what I tell you to say, then …'
- **Physical/mental punishment:** Sometimes, threats are also emphasised with physical or mental punishments anyway to make the victim know that the narcissist is serious about the threats.

At the same time, a narcissistic abuser may be creating false witnesses, who can help them validate their own version of events and minimise/trivialise anything the victim has to say.

Recruitment of a false witness may include:

- **Getting witnesses to only see/hear what they want them to:** A narcissist may quickly point out what has happened and give a 'plausible' explanation to deflect from the truth, e.g. staging broken furniture in the home to look like they have been asssaulted. The narcissist may lie and say that THEY are the victim of violence or blame the victim in some way for the incident.
- **Lying/placing blame elsewhere:** A narcissist is likely to lie and place the blame elsewhere.
- **Silencing the victim:** If the victim is in the same room, the narcissist may use indirect body language to silence the victim from speaking out.
- **Leads the conversation:** They may speak for the victim and then ask them to confirm their version of events. A victim in trauma may agree (even if it is untrue) for fear of consequences.

- **Insistence on not having prefessionals involved:** A narcissist may try not to get professionals involved. A 'false witness' may not know what to look for and take what is said by the narcissist at face value.

Practical advice – What to do – Being silenced and creation of false witnesses

When you are being silenced not to tell anyone after abuse, then I suggest that you:

1. **Write it down/take note:** Even if you ultimately make the decision you are too afraid to speak out at this point in time, at least write it down and take note – if it is safe for you to do so.
2. **Memorise:** If it is not safe for you to write anything down or make a note, then memorise what you can. Link it the date to something on the news that is memorable and different to help you memorise a timeline.
3. **Record your thoughts on a phone/recording device:** If you can, again if it is safe to do so, record your thoughts on a phone or recording device immediately afterwards.
4. **Why are you afraid?:** Establish in your mind or write down why you are afraid to speak out. What are the consequences (real or imagined)?
5. **Tell a specialist:** If you can, call a charity (abuse charity), who will record the telephone call. Although you may decide not to do anything, the voice recording is on record. Alternatively see a councillor/therapist who knows about narcissism and abuse. Please note that if they suspect that your life is in danger, they will legally have to intervene for your safety.

What to do – Someone visits after hearing domestic violence

If you are traumatised from domestic violence and abuse it may be you are too frightened to speak out against your abuser. This may be because of the direct or indirect threats that can be happening. If and only if it is safe to do so:

1. **Secretly pass a note:** Help. Call the police please.
2. **Secretly point to your injuries:** If you are unable to speak, try to point to your injuries.
3. **Ask the witness not to leave:** Offer them a cup of tea/coffee/water so that you have a moment alone to ask them for help.

Please be aware that this may be a very risky approach as the abuser may use charm, diversion tactics and pathological lies to discredit what happened. They may say anything to put the blame on you. After the witness has gone the abuse could even get worse.

Otherwise, if you need to be safe:

4. **Say nothing**: This is likely to defuse the situation with the abuser. Nod in agreement if you have to. A narcissistic abuser will likely do most of the talking anyway.
5. **Leave the house**: Take yourself to a safe house, friends, family.

As a last resort, if your abuser is trying to get you to agree to something you didn't do in front of a witness:

6. **Repetition:** 'I can't tell you'/'No comment'/'I don't remember.'
7. **Agree:** This is if you have no other choice for your safety.

After violence, it is important to get to a doctor as soon as you can.

Practical advice for anyone attending a domestic violence incident

Firstly it is better to leave domestic violence and abuse to specialists such as the police who are trained. They will also be recording what is happening and separate out the parties to ask their questions.

But, if you do decide to intervene, be aware that:

1. **Listen/observe at the door before you knock/enter:** You will establish more information if you pause first and listen/observe what is going on before knocking on the door or entering.
2. **Record from the outside first:** If you have a recording device, leave it running before you enter. If you think someone is at risk of harm, call the police.
3. **What you see may not be the whole picture:** If someone answers the door, what you see may not be the whole picture. Take care to not make assumptions.
4. **What is being said may not be the truth:** A narcissist can be a fluent liar and may spin believable lies about the domestic violence situation. They may even come to the door jolly and cheerful after you have heard arguing and screaming. They may try to put you off or pretend to be the one being abused.

5. **Do not enter:** This could put you at risk of abuse also.
6. **If you do decide to intervene (not recommended alone):**
   a. Note who is quiet/talking/loud/hysterical. Abused men/women can go silent/hysterical rather than being able to say what is happening. They are traumatised.
   b. Go with more than one person, never alone.
   c. Stay calm.
   d. Observe – neck, head, hands, face, hair, damage to clothing.
   e. Ask is everything is all right? What happened? But be aware you may be lied to.
   f. Look for signs of abuse.
7. **Record what you saw after you leave (on paper/phone/by email/text).** It may be needed.
8. **Go back five minutes later and listen** if it is safe for you to do so.

Chapter 21 – Pathological Lies and Set-Up Lying

Pathological lying is one of the things that narcissists appear to excel in. The lying is different to white lies that may be told to stop hurting someone's feelings because pathological lies are impulsive, continual and for their own gain in some way.

Whereas the glib narcissistic lies seem to be used to evaluate how people respond to lies and how easily people are manipulated, pathological lies seem to be used to gain something for the narcissist.

To understand the pathological lies, it is sometimes easier to ask the question, 'What does the narcissist want?' This appears to drive the lies. They seem to have absolutely no feelings of guilt or remorse in getting what they want by lying. It is simply a means to an end.

Types of pathological lies:

1. **Lying for advantage:** This type of pathological lie would be used to gain some sort of advantage. This might include lying to get:
    a. **Money/possessions:** This might be fraud for monetary advantage, catfishing romance scams to tax evasion and money laundering.
    b. **Relationship:** This might include trying to lie about who they are to form a relationship that will give them a social or monetary advantage.
    c. **Career:** This might go as far as lying about qualifications obtained or taking the credit for work other people have done to further their career.
    d. **Status:** This could include lying about universities they have attended, for example, even if they have never been to university.
2. **Lying to implicate another:** This might be because the narcissist wants to:
    a. **Get away with their actions or behaviour:** This can be deliberate lies and accusations about another, that would require full investigation to find out if the allegations are true or not. An example might be a false rape accusation.
    b. **Deflect the blame onto another:** This could be where the truth is twisted so that the narcissist takes partial blame for something minor, but then tries to deflect the rest of the blame on someone else.

3. **Lying to feel grandiose:**
   a. **Exaggeration:** This might include lying about how much money they earn to be boastful.
   b. **Totally made-up lies:** These lies can be quite elaborate and resemble what the narcissist would like to have had in their lives, but instead lie fluently. For example, they might say that they had a university degree and an amazing career, when in fact they had no degree and a mediocre career.
   c. **Social standing:** This could include name dropping of celebrities that they claim to know personally or only living somewhere exclusive that matches their feelings of grandiosity. They may expect entitlement of elevated social status.
   d. **Get into an organisation/club:** These lies might be used so that they can elevate their social status by gaining access to privileges offered by exclusive clubs or organisations.
4. **Lying to get attention:**
   a. **Provocation for attention:** An example might be claiming they have been the victim of abuse or some other type of victim to gain attention.
   b. **Defamation of character:** This could be where they lie to defame someone else's reputation.

Pathological lying can be prevalent with a narcissist much of the time, depending on what they are trying to 'gain' or 'avoid' and who they are trying to influence for what purpose.

Pathological lying from a narcissist may be grandiose or blatant lies, but they are likely to justify this as:

- **Necessary to get ahead in life:** In their mind, lying and deceit seems to be a necessity of survival in a 'dog eat dog' world.
- **Believe everyone does it:** They may believe that because they lie, everyone else does and therefore minimise it.
- **Vehemently believe they are entitled to any rewards or gains from lying:** They believe that if they get away with their lies, then they are entitled to any rewards or gains.
- **Enjoy the thrill of getting away with it:** A narcissist actually appears to enjoy lying. They are often thrill-seekers and the enjoyment is getting away with it
- **Gains an opportunity to practice their poker face:** Lying is likely to have been learned over a sustained period of time. Narcissists acutely watch other people's responses and have a 'poker face', i.e.

are good at hiding their emotions and true intent and can therefore appear extremely genuine and calm when lying.

The key point is that: *They rely on their lies not being challenged or checked for detail.*

The set-up type of lying comes later on in an abusive relationship, when the narcissist knows that they have almost total control over their victim's mind and what they say.

The narcissist is confident at this point that they can:

- **Silence their victim:** A narcissist at this point is likely to have already used aggressive mind control, violence and/or threats/blackmail to silence their victim.
- **Getting the victim to admit to things they have not done:** This technique is used under extreme coercion and control in a relationship to exonerate themselves from blame.
- **Throw enough lies and some will stick:** They can also be aware that, socially, if they consistently throw out lies, that some will stick in the wider social context. This method can socially isolate a victim further.

They may also have a certain pleasure and enjoyment of lying to others. Lies may be:

- **Forceful and persuasive but lack detail:** A narcissist may get aggressive or agitated and very defensive if their version of events is challenged. They could use vague phrases like 'She abused me' and 'Don't you believe me?' and 'I can't remember exactly when' if asked for detail.
- **Elaborate detail in stories:** At the opposite end of the scale a narcissist may devise a complete 'lie plan' in their minds from start to finish. This may be very detailed and convincing.
- **Well-practiced:** A narcissist may well have been brought up in an abusive environment and their need to lie may have been borne from necessity of survival to evade harsh punishments. Because of this they can be well practiced in lying (far more than most people).
- **Difficult to tell on face/body language:** This aspect also goes along with their history of practicing lying. They may have honed the art of deception very well and it can be difficult to tell if they are lying or not.
- **Insistent on their lies:** Once a narcissist has thought through their

defence, they will be very insistent on their version of events and lies. They rarely deviate/back down or change their story.

- **Effortlessly explains differences in story:** Even if you do find differences in their story, they may deny it, minimise it, say that you are mistaken, misheard or find a plausible excuse.
- **Often lead the conversation:** This technique makes sure that they get 'their version of events' out quickly. This is normally done in front of the victim, with the subconscious suggestion that the victim must 'follow what is said'.
- **Extremely offended/vocal in any accusations/vigorous denials of the truth:** Because a narcissist is expecting everyone else to be lying, they know to act *extremely offended and vocal* in any accusations to try to deflect blame. They may also vehemently deny accusations over and over again and often state 'legal' threats in a bid to get someone to 'back down'.
- **Deflection/admittance:** This technique is used to admit a lower level of guilt in return for deflection of a higher level of guilt to someone else. In this way they can appear to placate the need to admit something but try to place the blame on someone else.
- **Cold or uncaring if found out with facts:** Faced with hard evidence, they may say 'So what?', or 'Prove it' or go silent.

Practical advice – What to do – Pathological lies and set-up lies

When talking pathological lying and set-up lies, it may be important to determine the truth. This may be because you need to know if you partner is lying to you or may be because you need to understand the subtle nuances of people who lie.

There are a few techniques that may help you (it can be extremely empowering to learn these techniques):

1. **NLP and eye movements:** It is a misconception that if someone can look you straight in the eye that they are telling the truth. NLP and the study of eye movements is far more insightful to establish if someone is telling the truth or not. It is not failsafe, and you will need to practice on yourself first, but generally:

    a. **Looking 'right' you are lying:** If you try to construct a lie in your mind you will note that if you try to imagine it visually, you look up to the right. If you try to construct what you heard as a lie, you look to the right middle. This means if you ask a question that they don't know in advance about details of the lie, it is difficult for a narcissist to answer without looking to the right because this is the part of the brain that is used to make up a lie.

b. **Looking 'left' you are remembering:** When someone looks to the left when asked to remember visual things, they will look up to the left. They will look left also for auditory remembering of events.

2. **Body language:** You will need to research and practice this further, but the basics are that you have to establish when someone is telling the truth or not. It may be necessary to find out what people do when telling the truth first. They will have a set of ways that their arms, hands and face move. When someone tells a lie, however, the following might change:

a. **Face movements:** Covering the lips (subconsciously I don't want to say) or ears (I don't like what I am hearing).

b. **Hands:** Hands will have gestures after what is being said rather than at the time. They might repeat words and gesture with their hands (repetition to buy time).

c. **Eye contact:** Most seasoned liars will look you straight in the eyes. This is therefore not a good indicator of lying. NLP can be very useful if you use the right questions.

d. **Tone/volume of voice:** The voice may become higher pitched or become more forceful.

e. **Pursing the lips:** This may be when someone is holding information back and trying not to say something.

f. **Protecting the body:** Instinctively hands may move to cover the throat, chest or abdomen.

3. **Tell the lie backwards:** This technique is good for when someone has lied to you (and practised it). They are very unlikely to have practised it backwards and will make mistakes if asked to do so.

4. **Have hard evidence of the facts:** Irrefutable independent facts can help to establish lies. This is particularly true when asking for detail. Detail will be vague when someone is lying or so detailed that it seems convincing.

5. **Get what is being said down in writing/recorded:** A narcissist will deny that they said things, so it is important to get what is being said written down or recorded. A narcissist will be conscious not to put anything down in writing, particularly if it is independently witnessed, as this may incriminate them later.

6. **Leave it to the professionals:** The police are excellent at determining facts, as are accounting forensics. It is a sad reality, however, that despite good evidence, some court cases are lost because a narcissist is

a master manipulator and liar, and may even use charm, deflection and outright lies in court to influence judges and juries. This is why it is so important to have your own facts independently verified and to be emotionally balanced before going to court. Otherwise you can be seen as over emotional, which does not help your case – particularly when a narcissist can be extremely calm under pressure.

7. **Micro-expressions:** If an interview with a narcissist is recorded, there are micro-expressions that can help establish lying. This is a specialist area but will show subtle signs of contempt and anger, for example. They are the same micro-expressions that you will be aware of before a narcissist is violent (the way the face or a muscle in the face moves).

8. **Kinesiology/muscle testing:** This technique is very subtle and powerful and relies on the body being able to tell a lie when a lie is being spoken. With good training, you can tell when someone is lying by their muscle movements and if you perfect it you can use it to find if someone is telling the truth or not very quickly. A good demonstration of this is locking your finger and thumb together and trying to prise them apart with your other hand. If you say the truth, for example 'My name is ...' You will notice that it is easy to keep the finger and thumb together. If, however you tell a lie 'my name is [a lie]' and try to hold your fingers together, it is much harder and often the fingers come apart. It requires practice.

Phase 8 – Normalising Coercive Control and Narcissistic Abuse

Chapter 22 – No Place Like a Home from Hell

As abuse continues in toxic narcissistic relationships, the victim becomes desensitised to abuse and even higher levels of torment/control and abuse are required for the narcissist to get a reaction from the victim.

Periods of harmony can even appear to be 'dull' in comparison to the extreme emotional rollercoaster inflicted by a narcissist. Small things can be blown out of all proportion deliberately by the narcissist because they want 'attention'.

In response the victim may start alcohol or drug dependencies to try to 'numb' the extreme feelings or try to continually placate the dramas believing that this will change things. They may start to become of a shell of their former self and even minimise or 'normalise' the abuse.

The victim may well be in a state of traumatisation and shock and may well justify the abuse or keep believing that 'Mr Nice' or 'Mrs Nice' will come back. Of course the love-bombing stage was not the real person and the abuse they are experiencing in this stage of an abusive relationship is the 'real self' of the narcissist.

At this point in a narcissistic relationship, there may also be a real or perceived power struggle, whereby the victim may try to establish some boundaries, assert themselves, try to leave the relationship or rebel in some way. This is unlikely to be tolerated by the narcissist and the *techniques of control may well increase and be escalated.*

These escalating techniques are likely to include:

- **Humiliation:** This can include public humiliation (e.g. revenge porn) or private humiliation.
- **Deprivation:** This may be of food, sleep, clothing, warmth, safety, medical treatments. These techniques can be used to create mental anguish in the victim, ill health or used as a method to 'prove' to people outside the relationship that the victim has mental health

issues for some reason (e.g. if they want to divorce them, discard them or leave the victim).

- **Further loss of freedom/isolation:** Should a narcissist consider outside influences to be a threat, further loss of freedom is likely to be implemented. This can include ultimatums.
- **Embarrassment:** This technique might include deliberately causing a situation of embarrassment for pleasure or punishment, e.g. deliberately getting someone to over-dress for an event, knowing full well it is casual. Then publicly admonishing them.
- **Extreme arguing/narcissistic rages:** The relationship can be extremely volatile and include extreme arguing and rages. These are arguments that can go on for extended periods of time, the purpose of which is to de-stabilise the victim in some way. Narcissists seem to deliberately 'set-up' an argument with extreme goading, accusations, contentious subjects and then enjoy watching a victim become enraged or destabilised.
- **Recording the abuse for blackmail and enjoyment:** A narcissist may even record the **outcome** of their goading, accusations and arguments to look like the victim is unstable, volatile, abusive or angry. For example picking a fight for two hours, then recording the two minutes when the victim explodes in anger to share as blackmail and evidence of the victim's mental health.
- **Monitoring and controlling movement and what the victims say:** There are various technological advances used, such as spyware, CCTV, tracker devices, hacking emails, phones, texts. This might also include insistence on knowing all passwords in the guise of openness in the relationship. The purpose, however, is to ensure contact outside of the relationship is monitored and controlled if the victim is stepping out of line. This can include insistence in responding to certain people as the victim is told to do.
- **Escalating rages/intense questioning:** This technique is used to get people to back down and regain control and respect.
- **Sexual abuse:** This is where the victim is sexually abused in the relationship. They conform from fear of retribution. This may also include, for example, performing degrading or subservient sex acts. Alternatively, they may set up sexual encounters, record it, and use it as a method of blackmail.
- **Cruelty/physical abuse/torture:** The escalation of cruelty to more and more extreme physical abuse or torture (children, animals, you) may continue the longer the victim is in the relationship.
- **Animal cruelty**: Animal cruelty, including torture and killing them,

may be used as another control method to keep a victim of narcissistic abuse in line. The display of power is to demonstrate 'you will be next' or 'this is what will happen to you'.

- **Threats to harm or kill:** These may be often seeded into the victim's mind – they know that if they step out of line they will be harmed, killed or their friends or family will be harmed or killed without their compliance to the narcissist.
- **Blackmail:** This may be for money/property, reward, sexual gratification or revenge.
- **Brainwashing:** These techniques might include trying to repeatedly change the victim's memories by repeatedly arguing that they have 'forgotten' the facts. Brainwashing pressurises the victim to change their own beliefs and can be reinforced, for example, with violence, deprivation and gaslighting.
- **Complete isolation:** This may be implemented by a narcissist to help minimise outside influences and gain complete control.
- **Controlling socialising – Dramas to prevent attending:** Another technique used is creating sudden dramas to prevent socialising by the victim. This is often last minute and it doubly acts as a way to alienate friendships a victim may still have.

Practical advice – What to do – Escalating abuse

As the abuse begins to escalate with the narcissist, it is important to realise the seriousness of the situation and try to leave the relationship as soon as possible. This is easier said than done for a victim of abuse.

However, it can be done the first time. This is where planning ahead can help you get out very quickly. Once away from the abusive relationship, the best option is to go no-contact.

If you are in the UK, go back to the chapter on coercive control laws in the UK and work through the criteria. Get help from professionals.

Read section 76 of the Serious Crime Act 2015, 'Non-Molestation Orders, Injunctions and Going to Court' so you start to know HOW to get out of the situation.

Phase 9 - Assaults, Cruelty and Violence

Chapter 23 - Assaults and Breaking Point Moments

Assaults and threats of violence can be terrifying for a victim. They can happen behind closed doors and it may feel like there are no options to leave. But there are. Confronting the behaviour with a narcissist is likely to result in very strong denials of facts (or violence for asking), which is why evidence is so important.

This is what is happening at these break point moments:

1. **Assault and violence in the moment:** When you experience assault or threats to harm or kill, it may feel terrifying. Depending on the type of violence or threat, we all react differently. Some of the things you may experience are:
   a. **Fear:** Depending on the ferociousness of the assault or threat to harm, the fear can be paralysing.
   b. **Powerlessness/vulnerability:** This aspect is really if you are physically overpowered, physically vulnerable or not confident in your abilities to fight back. The overwhelming feeling may be 'I can't fight back,' or 'I am not strong enough to stop this.'
   c. **Out of body experience/numb:** This is where you seem to be so numbed by the event, you almost observe the trauma from outside of yourself because it is too painful to be present in the moment.
   d. **Shock:** Shock can mean that your response is frozen, whilst you process what is happening. As you process the information, which can be real threats or perceived threats, your responses slow down.
   e. **Reaction - Freeze or fight back:** Once your unconscious mind decides that you are in a dangerous situation, you may decide to freeze or fight back. Depending on your own capabilities and thought processes, this reaction can be almost automatic.

128 Section 1 – Recognising the 16 Stages of Narcissistic Abuse

2. **Survival mode:** At this moment, you may be filled with feelings of:
    a. **Rage:** 'How dare you!'
    b. **Hatred/revenge:** 'You will be sorry.'
    c. **Extreme fear:** 'Get me out of here.'
        And reactions of:
    d. **Assertiveness:** 'I am going to do something.'
    e. **Passiveness:** 'I am going to stand still/do nothing.'

Violence may be threatened and used when a victim tries to leave the relationship or cannot be controlled in other more subtle ways.

The narcissist expects their needs to be met and has little tolerance if the victim no longer can or is prepared to meet those needs.

Possible methods used:

- **Private threat of violence/blackmail:** This ensures maximum intimidation.
- **Private real violence:** This may be done in private to eliminate any risk of their public image being damaged in any way.

For these to be effective control methods, the narcissist must be quite certain that:

- **The victim will not report them:** To ensure this, it is likely that further violence may well be threatened or actual violence perpetrated against the victim.
- **The victim will go back to being compliant:** It is imperative that their actions mean the victim becomes compliant again and starts meeting their needs.
- **The victim will cover up bruises/wounds:** This may include brainwashing the victim to deny what happened and cover up any bruises/wounds for the narcissist. This will be classified as loyalty.

A narcissist is also likely to be of the belief that the victim:

- 'Brought it on themselves/had to be brought in line,' and
- 'If they had done what they were told, then it would never have had to happen.'

Assaults and Breaking Point Moments **129**

If a narcissist does, however, apologise after physical altercations, it may well be generalised rather than specific and again blame the victim for causing them to lose control.

Practical advice – What to do – Violence

When it gets to actual violence or threats of violence a victim can be in a very dangerous position.

Whilst you may not know what the triggers are or see it coming, there are things that you can do to protect yourself as much as possible. It is important to report this crime to the police.

You might need to consider the following options:

1. **Self-defence:** Under the UK law self-defence still needs to be reasonable and honestly and instinctively what was necessary in the heat of the moment. Be aware you could be prosecuted if the self-defence was pre-meditated or had a degree of excessive force, and the way in which the force was applied will be investigated.
2. **Recording the assault:** Make a doctor's appointment (hospital appointment) and get a doctor to record the assault. It is important that you receive treatment and an independent record is made of your injuries or the incident.
3. **Look for the warning signs and get away:** If you know certain triggers (e.g. alcohol) and you are aware of the 'brooding period', then you have the option to get out and away to maintain your safety. Even if it is just out for a walk.

Chapter 24 – Cruelty Begins

There are many types of cruelty in an abusive relationship, but they all have the impact of making a victim suffer needlessly. Cruelty can include:

- Child abuse
- Animal abuse
- Your abuse

This might be, for example hitting a pregnant partner to cause a miscarriage or tormenting a partner with the sole intent of harming them.

There are also different levels and types of cruelty which can begin in an abusive relationship.

A victim subjected to cruelty may start numbing and dissociating. This can include:

1. **Starting to internalise:** The emotional/physical pain of cruelty may be such a shock to a victims normality, that they may find that they cannot find the words to express internal grief. Emotions may be so strong and words ineffective at expressing the pain felt, that there appears to be a 'closing down' of painful emotions and 'putting them away/distancing from them'.
2. **Extreme emotional/physical pain suppressed:** It is not that a victim cannot feel the pain or that there is no reaction inside, but they seem to have to minimise acknowledgement of it for fear it would engulf them or the reaction would be so extreme as to scare them. Victims might start to suppress feeliing of:
   a. **Hatred**
   b. **Anger**
   c. **Fear**
   d. **Rage**
   e. **Revenge**
   f. **Retaliation**
   g. **Anxiety**
   h. **Confusion**
   i. **Isolation**
   j. **Depression**
   k. **Embarrassment and shame**
   l. **Numb**
3. **No longer yourself:** At this point in the relationship you may start to become just a fragment of yourself. You may find it hard to smile, get happy about things and become resigned to your situation.

Cruelty does not appear to have the same impact on a narcissist as it does to other people. It is likely to be:

1. **Minimised/trivialised:** If you speak to a narcissist about cruelty, they are likely to have a neutral response (as though they are talking about an innate object). It is not necessarily that they don't know mentally the difference between right and wrong legally or morally, but it is more that it does not apply to them.
2. **Lacking any normal reactions or feelings:** Sometimes, they don't even appear to know which emotional response most people in society have to traumatic events. They might even need to research the reactions of other people to get a visual sense of how other people react to be able to replicate it and enable them to fit in.
3. **Forgotten quickly:** After a traumatic event, narcissists appear to be able to compartmentalise or forget about the incident relatively quickly. Whilst the same event could traumatise other people.
4. **Oblivious or unaware of the impact on others:** Chillingly, a narcissist seems to be quite oblivious to the reaction their behaviour creates in other people or not particularly care how others' feel as long as they can get away with it.
5. **Sadistic and calm:** They could even enjoy watching the pain and suffering of others in a very calm manner. This might be because in their mind the other person deserves the treatment for some particular reason within their own internal code of conduct.
6. **Thrill seeking at not getting caught:** This is another aspect which seems to be enjoyable to a narcissist the thrill is being clever enough not to get caught.

Practical Advice – Cruelty

With cruelty and any lack of remorse from the narcissist, it is important to be get professional help and support.

132 Section 1 – Recognising the 16 Stages of Narcissistic Abuse

The risks of further cruelty or escalation could happen, but there are professionals that are able to assist you. This includes:

1. **Children (UK):**
   NSPCC – 0808 800 5000
   Children's social care team – local council
   Police – call 101 or 999 if the child is at immediate risk
   Crimestoppers – 0800 555 111
   Victim Support – 0845 30 30 900
2. **Yourself:**
   Police – call 101 or 999 if you are in immediate danger. Translator services are available.
   Crimestoppers – 0800 555 111
   Victim Support – 0845 30 30 900
3. **Animals (UK):**
   The RSPCA – 0300 123 4999
   League against cruel sports – 01483 361108

Phase 10 - The On/Off Cycle of Abuse

On average it takes seven attempts to leave an abusive relationship. SEVEN. Seven times that you may go back to have the same abuse. It is traumatising and traumatic and is called the cycle of abuse for a reason.

Why is that? Only someone who has been in an abusive relationship (and trauma therapists and experts) are able to answer that question.

There could be a number of reasons. Put simply these are:

- Fear of the narcissist and retaliation.
- Fear of being alone and isolated.
- Fear of losing job/work.
- Fear of where to live.
- Fear of not being believed.
- Fear of being victim blamed.
- Not wanting to relive the abuse.
- Shame of being abused.
- Lack of confidence in the ability to survive.

Put in this way, it is a huge barrier to overcome to actually be able to safely leave - which is why you would be better off with professional help from abuse charities (who can for example suddenly get you out and into a safe house). But it does require PLANNING.

I therefore have dedicated Section 2 to the pre-leaving stage and ask if you are ready to leave. This is an important step.

Chapter 25 - Withdrawal Symptoms/Trauma Bonded

When a victim leaves a narcissist or a narcissist suddenly abandons the relationship, victims can experience sudden withdrawal symptoms. A victim may be so accustomed to the extreme emotional highs and lows that victims experience separation anxiety.

Emotions can be so overwhelming and painful that the only perceived solution is to return to the abusive relationship, where there is temporary 'relief' from the emotional pain.

Narcissists can trigger feelings of rejection, abandonment, deep hurt and betrayal when they are seemingly able to get on with their lives as if nothing ever happened – even having a new relationship within days.

Why you may go back to your abuser

There are many reasons why you might go back to your abuser after successfully managing to leave. There are some very strong emotions and painful withdrawal symptoms. This might include:

1. **Desperate loneliness:** Because you may have isolated yourself from friends and family, the desperate loneliness is two-fold. Firstly, because you have been programmed to be attentive to the narcissist's every whim you are therefore on high alert at all times. This means you have neglected yourself so much that you don't know what else to do with the spare time available. Secondly, because you may feel like there is no one to turn to you and you do not have a communication outlet to help you through. Victims may feel disorientated.
2. **No support mechanisms around you:** Who is looking after you? Who is supporting your needs? Very often the answer to these two questions is no one. In those first twenty-four hours particularly, you need emotional support, but realistically for the next few months. Without it, you may have only your own unsupportive thoughts going round in your mind, which will continue to go round in circles. It is very difficult to see the truth, without help from professionals.
3. **Inability to suddenly act on your own/think for yourself:** This can be because of the brainwashing techniques used by narcissists. You may be convinced that your views are somehow wrong. This means that

when you try to make a decision, you can become indecisive because you have been so used to someone else making decisions for you.

4. **Money for survival:** It could be that escaping a narcissist puts you in extreme poverty and you need their financial support to survive.

5. **Jealousy/abandonment:** You may be emotionally traumatised if a narcissist moves on extremely quickly to someone new. It could happen within hours (because they already have someone as a relationship back-up). Victims may feel completely worthless when a narcissist moves on this quickly. They may also want to goad and flaunt their new partner in the victims' face deliberately to hurt them further.

6. **Cannot let go:** You may want to keep watching out for them, searching for them online or asking people about the narcissist. This doesn't help you move on.

7. **Inability to be your own wise counsel:** Because you have come out of a traumatic experience, you may have some erratic thought patterns. Making decisions may be hard for a time and you may seek advice from everyone other than yourself. It takes time, practice and patience to become your own wise counsel.

8. **Thinking your abuser is the only one to understand you:** When you remember the 'pedestalled' moments above the abuse, you may think that your abuser is the only one that understands you.

9. **Frightened of speaking out:** You may also be terrified for your health and safety and be in fear. You may be afraid of punishment for speaking out, so you remain silent and internalise the emotional pain.

The narcissist moves quickly on to replace you

In addition to your overwhelming feelings, the narcissist may very quickly move on – as if you meant absolutely nothing to them.

From a narcissist's point of view, you meant nothing to them except for what you could provide for them. Their NEEDS are the most important to them. For this reason, a narcissist may:

1. **Suddenly and quickly replace you:** A narcissist does not appear to function well on their own and needs people/someone around who can admire them. For this reason, they are likely to seek to move on to another person as quickly as possible. This can include calling up ex-acquaintances, online dating sites or already having a second supply ready to go in the background.

2. **Use punishment to make them feel happy about themselves:** Because a narcissist would not like being rejected, they may need to

do things that make them happy and punish their ex-partner. This could include:

   a.   Goading

   b.   Flaunting new relationship(s)

3. **Feel that they are the victim:** They may believe firmly that they are the victim and are likely to talk widely about how they have been wronged to prevent reputational damage.
4. **Consider taking the victim back:** A narcissist may take the victim back, if they are unable to find an adequate alternative source of narcissistic supply and the victim is apologetic enough for wounding their ego.
5. **Enjoy making their victim suffer publicly:** Because it may seem inconceivable to them that someone should leave them, they could make their victim suffer. This could include:

   a.   False accusations

   b.   Smear campaigns

When a narcissist is on their own, the narcissist is left with a void to fill. There may be feelings of anger and hurt, but these are mostly from a *bruised ego*.

Instead of using more humane behaviours that might be used in a healthy relationship break-up, the narcissist is likely to see a break-up in a different way:

- **Surprise:** They may be genuinely surprised that their victim has left them as they would consider the victim under their control.
- **Brutal:** Unlike a healthier break-up, the exchange of words can include severe threats and be brutal. They may well feel like they are the "victims" themselves and apportion all the blame onto the real victim for leaving them.
- **An insult to them:** Because it is such an insult to their ego, they may consider enacting revenge and possibly look at ways to vindictively degrade the ex-partner.
- **Will need to look for other source(s) of supply as soon as possible:** This could be literally a few minutes after the victim has left. The narcissist may not tolerate having to wait.
- **Cut off quickly emotionally:** They seem to have the capacity to switch off any feelings for their ex-partner quickly. This can feel very cold and calculating as if the ex-partner is a stranger.
- **No accountability:** The narcissist is unlikely to have any accountability for the reason why their partner may have left them. It is unimportant. If asked, they may try to convince others that they in fact were the one who was the "victim".

- **Keep on the backburner:** Another tactic is to keep the ex-partner on the backburner with laments of missing them and how special they were. This is in case they cannot find someone to replace them quickly enough.

Practical advice – What to do – Withdrawal

The first time you leave an abusive relationship may not be the last. The withdrawal can be very painful without support.

One way to help is to treat the withdrawal process like an unhealthy addiction. In this case, you might consider:

1. **Appropriate support network 24/7:** Having a support network there 24/7 will be very important. Going from an intense relationship to isolation can create a very unnerving vacuum and having other people available who understand the problem is important. It may not be enough to use the help of friends or family who are unqualified in the intensity of this withdrawal.
2. **Preparation:** Anticipate to be made jealous and for the response in some cases to be brutal. You can plan for this.
3. **Off social media:** It can be a source of torment to yourself to see your ex-partner on social media. It is better to come off it completely at this time.
4. **Limit triggers/over-sensitised:** Your emotions and senses may well be in overdrive when you leave an abusive relationship. The intensity has meant that you have been 100% focused on survival and will not have been paying attention to your own needs. You may be hypersensitive about some things (e.g. looking out of windows repeatedly, fear of some situations, not relating to other people).
5. **Pamper yourself:** It is important to pamper yourself. Turn the caring you had for the narcissist towards yourself. It may feel extremely uncomfortable and you may feel numb, but you need to turn inwards and start working out what makes you smile again. It can be as simple as sand under your feet, a candle or bath or doing your favourite hobby (or having the TV remote to watch what you want).
6. **Get a recovery plan in place:** This means starting to write down what makes you happy and understanding yourself more. Please see the recovery steps later on.

Phase 11 – Effects of Abuse on Mind and Wellbeing

Chapter 26 – Effects of Trauma and Abuse – Mental Wellbeing, Addictions and Specialist Help

There are likely to be some adverse mental wellbeing affects for you from living in an abusive relationship (depending how abusive it got). If you are in this situation, be gentle on yourself because what you are going through is very difficult. Please don't think that you can do it alone; it is almost impossible to. Get specialist help and only get help from specialists that understand fully about trauma and abuse.

After you leave, there is relief, but once out of an abusive relationship, it can also trigger more psychological traumas.

Whilst in the relationship, because of the abuse you may have been subjected to, it may be that you experience a decline in your own mental health and physical health. I am not an expert, but this could include:

1. **Depression/self-harm/suicidal thoughts:** This may include continual low mood and sadness, tearfulness, low self-esteem, feelings of being hopeless and helpless. This can also include being intolerant of others and can also include anxiety, suicidal thoughts or self-harm.
2. **Fear of everyday things:** If your mind is being controlled and you are being abused, you may start to have a very acute fear of doing the 'right thing'. The fear can extend to things that you would never have been afraid of before the relationship started and finding it hard to make decisions.
3. **Borderline personality disorder (BPD):** There may be a link between ongoing traumatic abuse and showing symptoms of BPD including fear of abandonment, volatile emotions which are difficult to control, feelings of emptiness, explosive anger, unstable relationships and self-destructive behaviours.

4. **Dissociation:** This is when the abuse has been going on for some time and it becomes so bad that you simply cannot acknowledge what is going on. It may be that you 'step outside' of yourself and observe the abuse as if it were happening to someone else, or 'forget it' entirely as a way to cope.
5. **Addictions:** Additions to drugs, alcohol, prescription medication may be ways to cope in the abusive relationship and 'numb' the emotional pain.
6. **Moodiness:** It is of little surprise that your moods will fluctuate in an abusive relationship. If your survival is based on how your abuser is feeling/acting, then you will have learned to adapt your own moods.
7. **Lack of belief in yourself/confidence:** Lack of confidence and belief in yourself declines the more the abuse continues. As the abuser uses gaslighting techniques, refusal to allow you your own views or opinions and ongoing abuse and torment, you are likely to start to lack confidence and belief in yourself.
8. **Feelings of guilt/shame/worthlessness/hopelessness:** These feelings may surface because you don't know how you managed to get into the abusive situation in the first place and how you get out of the relationship safely. It can be reinforced by the abuser because when you feel these emotions, the narcissist is often telling you repeatedly how terrible you are.
9. **Declining physical health:** As a natural outcome of all the stress and abuse, you may be experiencing declining physical health. From headaches and migraines, broken bones and bruising up to more serious illnesses.

When you leave an abusive relationship the mental health challenges may not stop there.

After escaping, you will have to learn to focus your attention back on your own needs. This may be difficult. At this point it is absolutely necessary to have specialist support (psychotherapy for trauma for example). You may be experiencing:

1. **Declining mental health:**
    a. **PTSD:** Post-traumatic stress disorder can happen after you have left the relationship. Reliving the traumatic events and being hypervigilant. There are some excellent treatments for PTSD including psychological therapies such as cognitive behavioural therapy, rewind techniques and NLP.
    b. **Depression:** Depression can increase temporarily when you leave

an abusive relationship as you come to terms with what happened. With time happiness does return.

   c. **Anxiety:** If there were threats and abuse, you may be very frightened doing things that you could previously have done. You may feel frightened of doing certain things by yourself, because you were accustomed to being told what to do.

2. **Memory loss:** As your mind and body adapt, it may be that you experience some memory loss. This would not be surprising given the level of stress experienced in an abusive relationship. You might even find that memories start re-appearing when you are safely able to do so.

3. **Emotional rollercoaster:** Emotions may be all over the place when you leave. The anger and hurt has to be channelled constructively (e.g. punching pillows). There are methods to help with anger, hurt, guilt, shame. All these emotions are likely to surface and need to be constructively dealt with. It can be a big change from supressing emotions to letting them out. Acknowledgement is the start because in the beginning you may be so numb you don't know what emotions you have actually been suppressing.

4. **Nightmares:** Nightmares can happen after leaving the abusive relationship. These things will get better as the emotions are expressed and the trauma spoken about.

5. **Addictions:** Addictions may continue as you leave. Once you have left, however, you can get support networks around you to start to relieve addictions.

6. **Lack of trust:** Your trust can turn into distrust of others (almost everyone). From being overly trusting you might have to learn to trust again very slowly. You learn to trust actions over words.

7. **Hypervigilant:** You may be triggered by unrelated events. You might be extremely fearful and watching everything for a while, particularly if you consider yourself at risk of harm.

8. **Self-isolation and withdrawal:** Sometimes you may feel so alone with your experience that you self-isolate and withdraw from social contact. You actually need people around you, even if this is online groups that have been through the same as you, but you may be feeling unable to socialise.

9. **Numb to normal conversations:** You might become numb about everyday conversational topics. You may find them trivial in comparison to what you have been through, and it may even annoy you.

10. **Critical of others:** Because you have been on the receiving end of

abuse for so long, you may pick up some of the abusive traits, for example being critical of others. This will fade with time as you get back to being more like yourself.

11. **Finding likeminded people:** You may be driven to seek out people who have had the same experiences as you to help you validate what happened and move on with your life.

A narcissist, however, seems to see the effects on a victim's wellbeing entirely differently

A narcissist on the other hand is likely to have little or no regard for their partners declining wellbeing. This could be for a number of reasons:

1. **It's their own fault/nothing to do with them:** A narcissist may well believe that their partner's declining mental wellbeing or health is a nuisance, annoyance and probably in their mind. They may well be of the belief that it is their own fault.

2. **Minimise ill health/expect a quick recovery/no external help:** Because a narcissist needs to be the centre of attention, they are likely to minimise any ill health or mental illness in their partner because it distracts from their needs. Even if diagnosed by a professional, a narcissist may think that they know better than the specialist.

3. **Part of the plan:** Depending on what a narcissist is wanting out of the relationship; the declining mental wellbeing or health of the victim may be part of their plan. This might include wanting to get someone out of the way, as an excuse for them to find another partner or just punishment because they did or did not do something the narcissist wanted.

4. **Drugs and alcohol to manipulate:** The use of drugs or alcohol can be another way to manipulate their partner. The narcissist may see this as a method to get their own way.

5. **A source of annoyance:** A narcissist does not seem particularly interested in their partner's health. In fact, it can be a source of annoyance because it prevents them being of service to the narcissist.

6. **Encouraged for personal gain:** A narcissist may be encouraging declining health or mental wellbeing for self-gain, e.g. obtaining money from an insurance policy or getting a partner sanctioned to get rid of them.

142 Section 1 – Recognising the 16 Stages of Narcissistic Abuse

They may be preventing medical care anyway, at times with such grandiosity believing themselves to be specialists even if they have had little or no training.

This means that they appear to:

- **Know better than trained psychologists:** A narcissist may believe that they know better than any expert. They may try to question their expertise or find a therapist they are certain they can manipulate.
- **Know better than experts** A narcissist is likely to research the subject area and use this to question the integrity of any experts – including medical doctors.
- **May try to evade their own mental heath diagnosis:** A narcissist may use deflection to the victim's 'problems' as a way to evade their own diagnosis. A narcissist is unlikely to see that they have any reason to be assessed. They are likely to be of the belief that 'There is nothing wrong with me'.
- **Can use online psychology tools to harm their victim:** The online psychology tools may well serve as evidence to themselves that they are not a narcissist or they may use the tools to misdiagnose and torment their victim.

Practical advice – What to do – Effects of trauma and abuse – Mental wellbeing, addictions and specialist help

When you are in the midst of an abusive relationship, it may be extremely difficult to change your environment. Addictions may progress but when you are ready, specialist help is available. Here are some ideas for when you are still in the relationship or have left and need addiction help.

What to do – When you are still in the abusive relationship

1. **Secretly drink less:** One method if you are being coerced regularly into drinking is to sip slowly, take drinks into the toilet and top up with water or secretly tip away when you can.
2. **Do not take things offered to you.**

What to do – When you leave an abusive relationship

The real help comes when you are out of the abusive relationship and can start to address your triggers and reasons for substance use or abuse.

1. **Find the best therapist:** Do not settle for anyone who has not been specifically trained in trauma and abuse. If you don't like your therapist, you do not have to continue to see them. Finding the best therapist is critical to your recovery.
2. **Work out your triggers and how you react to them:** A trigger is when you have an extreme emotional reaction to something. It is important to start to work out what your triggers are and what you can do to help yourself. A trigger might be anything from what someone has said to you, getting something wrong or even a song. Working this out gives you the opportunity to make different choices:
   a. **Write down what triggers you:** This helps identify what is causing the emotional pain.
   b. **Work out your response:** If it's alcohol, try alcohol-free, low-alcohol or small bottles of wine for example.
   c. **Forgive yourself:** Whilst other people may judge you, only you know what you are going through.
   d. **Change what you do:** If your triggers are boredom – find something else to do, e.g. exercise instead.
3. **Hypnotherapy:** Hypnotherapy can work for some people.
4. **Stop-drinking apps:** Online support from other people and goals can be very helpful to stop drinking.
5. **Professional help:**
   a. **The AA:** The AA have a number of meetings and their twelve-step process. Call 0800 9177650. They have local AA meetings where you can also meet people who will help. See also https://www.alcoholics-anonymous.org.uk.
   b. **Rehab for addiction:** These people can help support with drugs and counselling and therapy. Call them on 0800 140 4690 or www.rehab4addiction.co.uk.
   c. **Doctors:** Your GP may have a number of remedies to help you.
   d. **Clinics:** This may be an option for you. Clinics such as Priory hospitals – telephone 0808 274 3409. Or see here: https://www.priorygroup.com.

Phase 12 - Preparing to Leave - Evidence

Chapter 27 - Planning Required

When looking at preparing to leave and evidence, it is important to balance safety first versus evidence. When you do leave, it can be extremely dangerous; you can probably expect a hate/smear campaign against you. The evidence-collecting can help protect you from this as well as false allegations that you may receive.

Please remember that your safety comes first every time. A narcissist is suspicious by nature and may try to stop you if they find out what you are trying to do. Caution is therefore warranted. My advice is:

1. **Only get evidence if it is safe for you to do so:** It is imperative that you get out if you are in immediate danger. Evidence can come later if needed.
2. **Did it happen? Prove it!** If you want to fully defend yourself, you will need the right evidence. It is not enough to just say something happened. Evidence will need to demonstrate your point. If you say 'He/she/they threatened to harm me,' that is not enough. You could, however, demonstrate this by having:
   a. A recording of the threat
   b. The threat in writing (e.g. email/text)
   c. A witness of the threat being made

   If you state that they are monitoring you, evidence might include someone independent and professionally trained proving this, e.g. a private detective or IT specialist.

   If you state you have been financially abused, evidence might be that you show receipts and money coming out of your account and into the narcissist's.

   If you have had private information published, screenshots of the publication, a link or where it has been published might be needed.

   If you have been assaulted, GP or hospital records may show this.

   It is up to you to prove it. If you work on the assumption that you will be severely challenged when you leave, evidence is the best form of defence.

3. **You may need to store evidence elsewhere:** This might include safety deposit boxes, for example.

4. **Get professional help:** If you need to, hire a private detective to obtain the evidence you need, for example photographs of cheating, make sure that they are professional enough to stand up in court. Get help with recording devices in your own home if needed or get someone with expertise to search for evidence that you are being watched/recorded/monitored.

5. **Know for certain you are being monitored and recorded also:** You may also need to assume that you are being monitored and recorded.

What a narcissist may be thinking

A narcissist is likely to want to be in control of the relationship at all times. With regard to evidence gathering, a narcissist is likely to:

(1) **Know the law:** A narcissist is likely to know the law well enough to know what they can or cannot do. They may well also know loopholes, from what they admit to, to how to deny anything.

(2) **Be naturally suspicious:** Because narcissists are naturally suspicious, they are likely to also be acutely aware of what other people are up to. In their minds, they are anticipating other people's motives and therefore can be highly observant.

(3) **Making up evidence of their own:** This may include setting up a victim, for example goading someone to react before recording a victim's anger as 'evidence' the victim is the angry one. Or presenting with self-sustained injuries to a doctor and proclaiming they have been assaulted by the victim. They are additionally not above breaking the law to get evidence they need, e.g. breaking and entering.

(4) **Stalk because they are entitled to know:** A narcissist appears to be of the belief that they are entitled to know what their partner is doing. For this reason, they may consider monitoring and stalking their partner acceptable.

(4) **Be enraged if they think they are being monitored:** A narcissist would be extremely angry and enraged if they knew that they were themselves being monitored in any way. They expect their own freedom.

146 Section 1 – Recognising the 16 Stages of Narcissistic Abuse

What's going on? Preparing to leave – Evidence

How Might a Narcissist Think, Behave & Respond?

Evidence being collected against a narcissist

A narcissist who is aware that evidence is being collected against them is likely to:

- **Destroy the evidence:** A narcissist may go about to destroy any evidence as quickly as possible when they think someone might be incriminating them.
- **Cover their tracks:** They may start to cover their tracks, e.g. breaking into emails to remove the victim's evidence.
- **Set traps:** They may try to set deliberate traps to see how far they are being monitored. This, for example, might include deliberately saying they are going out and then turn up unexpectedly to see what is going on at home.
- **Start testing their victim:** They may start testing their victim more, e.g. asking questions about their whereabouts.
- **Start false accusations:** A form of defence is attack and they may start spreading false accusations to increase the victim's isolation.
- **Start a smear campaign/false witness:** A narcissist may believe it necessary to start a smear campaign or groom a false witness as a diversion tactic.
- **Be enraged:** A narcissist is likely to be extremely angry that someone would be trying to collect evidence against them. They are likely to consider themselves smarter and may wait before acting. Inside, however, they are probably enraged.
- **Punishment:** If the victim is caught, a narcissist may not hesitate to consider punishment. Evidence being collected would be something they would want to control.
- **Start monitoring the victim more:** This could include starting to put recording/tracking devices in place, e.g. Apple AirTags.
- **Get legal help:** The other option may be to start getting legal help and stating that they are the victim. Another deflection technique.

A narcissist who is aware that they are being monitored is unlikely to say anything about it straight away, but instead simply start plotting their revenge.

Planning Required **147**

Practical Advice – What to do – Preparing to Leave – Evidence

When you are ready to leave the abusive relationship, you need to know that it is not going to be easy, but there are people out there who will support and help you. Do not think that your abuser can't or won't do some of the things described – they certainly can. And it is safer to assume they might and plan for it.

As soon as you leave it may turn particularly nasty, so be prepared to defend, defend, defend.

Gathering evidence may be crucial in proving you have been abused, defending against false accusations that may be put against you and to stop the possible smear campaigns on your character.

When you leave, do it once and completely. Have everything ready to defend yourself fully. You may well need it.

What to do – Preparing to leave – Evidence

1. **Decide what it is safe to do to gather evidence:** Caution is warranted. Only you will know the details of your abusive relationship and if you have any spare time, places you can go that are not under the control of your abuser. You also need to decide what is safe evidence gathering and what is not.
2. **Hire professionals:**
   a. **Forensic accountants:** Might be necessary where a lot of money is involved. You have to be prepared that financial accounts will be closed immediately and your access to them denied overnight.
   b. **Private detectives:** Only choose private detectives that are above the law. Ex-police officers are excellent for example.
3. **Do not assume your secret hiding places are safe – have new ones:** You must assume that your 'secret hiding place' is not safe at all. You will need a new one as well as continuing using your existing secret hiding place. Ideally your new safe place is away from the home.
4. **Store evidence in more than one place:** One way to make sure you can get away with evidence is to store copies in more than one place.
5. **Expect evidence to disappear and get destroyed:** You need to anticipate that your evidence is not safe. Emails may get deleted, phones destroyed, text messages deleted. Have a back-up plan to ensure there is more than one copy available.

6. **Know that you could be assaulted if you are found out:** This is the risk of leaving an abusive relationship. It could get worse. That is why discretion is required and your safety is the most important thing.

7. **Phones can be tracked:** Your phone may well be tracked. You may need to turn it off or leave it at home when depositing evidence elsewhere.

8. **Cars can be tracked:** Your car may be tracked. You may need to take public transport or find another way to deposit evidence safely.

9. **Go to a safe house/police if in danger:** If at all in danger of violence, be ready to go to the police or a safe house. Have the number memorised.

10. **Don't be afraid if you are being blackmailed:** Even if you are being blackmailed and are likely to still be blackmailed, do not be afraid. People can help you.

11. **Don't be afraid if you have committed crime yourself through coercion:** Do not let your own crimes potentially stop you from gaining evidence and leaving. The law is aware that you can be coerced into criminal activity.

Phase 13 - Snap Leaving Moment

Chapter 28 - The SNAP Leaving Moment

We all have a different tolerance for a SNAP leaving moment. That moment could be when you know you have to get out of the abusive relationship for your own safety, or the safety of your children. It is a moment when:

1. **You suddenly realise the truth of the situation:** You suddenly realise that the words and the actions just do not match and that you don't want to be with the other person.
2. **You believe that it cannot get any worse than it has:** Anything is better than the current situation you are in, including any fear about being on your own.
3. **Your sanity and/or your life depend on it:** You know that you are going down emotionally, psychologically and physically and you have to act. It may be when the abuse gets too much, broken bones for example or threats to kill.
4. **You have to protect children/animals:** You have to act to protect children and animals.
5. **You no longer fear the consequences of loneliness/no money/no job/no home as much as you do the abuse and violence:** Anything is better than the abuse you are currently suffering, even being homeless and penniless.
6. **You do not care about the consequences of blackmail:** You no longer care about the threats that kept you in the relationship. The shame of blackmail is replaced with a need to protect yourself at all costs.
7. **You fear for your life:** You fear that the abuse could get worse or that they might try to harm you.

If the narcissist knows that you are about to leave the relationship, this is likely be an affront to their need to control. A narcissist may well:

1. **Increase control tactics:** It is possible that abuse strategies will be increased to stop the person leaving. This can include violence, threats and blackmail. They may start carrying some of the threats out.

150   Section 1 – Recognising the 16 Stages of Narcissistic Abuse

2. **May try to win you back (be nice strategy) at first:** If the narcissist does not suspect this is the last time you are leaving, they may try charm and fake apologies to win you back round.
3. **May seek revenge and punishment:** However, they are more than likely to be planning revenge for the humiliation you may cause them.
4. **May start to plan smear campaigns:** A narcissist may start preparing the ground for a smear campaign, e.g. starting to text/email/talk to people to put out a 'sad story' or try to 'discredit' their partner. They may do this in the guise of 'I am so worried about him/her/they,' or 'Have you noticed that they are acting strangely?' It is unlikely to be direct communication and will rely on gossip.
5. **May be calm initially, but enraged reaction:** There may be a delayed reaction to being rejected. A narcissist is likely to feel entitled to the relationship and have an expectation that it continues solely on their terms. In their mind they have put considerable effort into *manipulating and making the victim conform to their ways*. It would take effort to replace them.
6. **Disgust and contempt:** A narcissist is likely to feel disgusted that their partner might be trying to end the relationship.
7. **If I can't have you, no one can:** Some narcissists might have a thought process of either/or in their mind. For example, if they can't have you, no one can. This is particularly dangerous and could result in assault or even murder attempts.

Practical advice – What to do – The SNAP leaving moment

When you are ready to leave the abusive relationship, there will be a SNAP leaving moment in your mind, when no matter what your partner says, you want out of the relationship.

- **S**udden realisation that
- **N**arcissistic
- **A**buse is real, continuing, and you have to
- **P**rotect yourself by leaving

If it is safe to leave immediately, do so. But most likely if you are with a narcissist, you will need to prepare and plan carefully until you are ready to do so.

At this point, you may have already tried to leave several times before. You may already know that leaving is not going to be easy, but there are people out there who will support and help you.

With the SNAP leaving moment:

1. **You will have weighed up the likely consequences:** You already know the depths that your partner may well go to. Expect it, however, to get worse initially, before it gets better.
2. **Better to remain internalised:** For your safety, it is better to make this decision in your mind. If you do tell anyone, make sure it is someone like an abuse helpline rather than friends/family.
3. **Trust your intuition/gut feelings:** You will have to get your intuition back on track when you leave. It may help your recovery. You will also need it because a narcissist is sensitive to you leaving and may try anything from charm to threats.
4. **Protect yourself – your life may depend on it:** Leaving a narcissist may be extremely dangerous, so after you've made your decision to leave, don't do anything rash until you have planned your escape. Unless your life is in immediate danger – in which case get away.

If not, start planning your escape and exit.

The ONLY way that you can do this is with other people's help and support. It can be done, but you may need to start reading up about HOW to escape and talk to experts such as domestic abuse charities.

Start reading up on non-molestation orders, coercive control laws, injunctions and what to expect if you need to defend yourself (which is possible if you leave a narcissist).

Chapter 29 – Non-Molestation Orders, Injunctions and Going to Court

When you need to leave, it is likely that you will enrage a narcissist. So, it is best to know what your options are – who can help you escape. These are:

- Getting an injunction
- Non-molestation orders
- Reporting to the police

At this point start COLLATING and UNDERSTANDING what you need to do to leave safely.

When violence is involved, you may need help with the following options:

1. **Get an injunction – Family Law Act 1996, Section 62: Non-Molestation Order at a local family court:** You may need to act quickly, so research what to do in advance. Please think carefully if the narcissist is very dangerous – for some narcissists this will be no deterrent at all (as the law and rules do not apply to them) and in fact can inflame the narcissistic rage further and their entitlement. Only you will know this. If you do proceed, I suggest you will need help from someone who understands the intricacies and can support you through it:
   a. **Woman's Aid –** Online at www.womansaid.org.uk
   b. **National Centre for Domestic Violence –** 0800 970 2070 or www.ncdc.org.uk
   c. **Mankind Initiative –** https://www.mankind.org.uk

   A non-molestation order means that you will have to attend your local court, where you will have to present three copies of the non-molestation order FL401.

   Don't worry, whilst it can be very daunting, the courts are likely to be very kind to you if they know it is about domestic violence. You will have to telephone in advance to book a hearing. This can happen within a few days.

   When you arrive at court you will be searched, with all the contents of any belongings searched, and you will go through an x-ray scanner.

   You will then be led to the office area, where you will be required to submit three copies of your application, with supporting evidence.

You will then be asked to wait in another area to be called by a judge to the court room. At this time, the judge will have read through your application and will call you. He or she will ask you a number of questions. Be mindful of what to call the judge, e.g. sir/madam. The judge will then make their ruling.

You can request two things at the hearing:

a.   Non-molestation order

b   An occupation order

The judge will be making a decision about 'with or without notice' to the respondent. You will be termed as the applicant and the respondent is who the injunction is against (i.e. the abusive partner).

You can find this document to download at www.gov.uk under publications (or search for FL401). ALWAYS GET HELP FILLING IT IN. I suggest here: https://www.advicenow.org.uk/statement-injunction

These are some of the terms and what you need to expect:

Terms you need to be aware of	Meaning and key information
Non-molestation order	This seeks to prohibit a person from carrying out certain actions, e.g. threatening violence, approaching, damaging property.
An occupation order	This is occupation of a named property if you have legal/'home rights' (through marriage) to occupy the house.
Applicant	You.
Respondent	Your alleged abuser.
With or without notice	Without notice (i.e. when the respondent is not in attendance) can only be made if: • There is a significant risk of harm.Where you may be deterred or prevented from pursuing an application if it is not made immediately. • Where the respondent is deliberately evading service. If you do not fulfil these criteria the application will be made with notice, which means that the respondent will need to attend the court also.

154 Section 1 – Recognising the 16 Stages of Narcissistic Abuse

Terms you need to be aware of	Meaning and key information
Relationship to the respondent	E.g. Married, civil partnership, cohabiting, were cohabiting, intimate personal relationship which was of significant duration. Some of the definitions: • Cohabiting means people who are living together as if they are married. • An agreement to marry – this would need to be formally agreed. • Intimate personal relationship – the relationship needs to be sexual. Significant duration is not defined in case law.
Non-molestation order	This can be broken down into health, safety and wellbeing affected under Family Law Act 1996: Section 42, subsection 5. **Physical harm** • Direct threats, physical abuse. • Threats to harm other people. **Emotional harm** • This could be stalking. • Intimidating and harassing behaviour. • How it has affected wellbeing. • Isolation. **Financial harm** • This could include pressure regarding money. • Theft of goods. **Reputational harm** • The courts would only be concerned with direct threats which are of such a degree to justify intervention by he court.
Non-molestation order	Terms that you can request are: • Cannot use violence against you, nor instruct, encourage or in any way suggest that any other person should do so. • Cannot threaten violence against you, nor instruct, encourage or in any way suggest that any other person should do so. • Must not intimidate, harass or pester and must not instruct, encourage or in any way suggest that any other person should do so.

Non-Molestation Orders, Injunctions and Going to Court **155**

Terms you need to be aware of	Meaning and key information
	• Must not damage, attempt to damage, tamper with or threaten to damage or tamper with any property owned by or in possession or control of [you] and must not instruct, encourage or in any way suggest that any other person should do so. • Must not go to, enter or attempt to enter [property] or any property where the respondent knows or believes [you] are living and must not go within 50 meters of the address.
Duration	Routinely orders are made for a duration of one year.
Occupation order	Stating the address and why you are entitled to occupy the property and why the respondent is entitled to occupy.
Interpreter at court	You have the option to ask for an interpreter at court and the language.
Evidence	All accusations will need to be evidenced.
Witness statement – Get help filling this in	This will need to state the facts. You can download a template from https://www.advicenow.org.uk/statement-injunction. It will have to include things like: • Written in your own words in the first person, e.g. 'I' statements. • State facts and specify the source of the information. • Relevant dates and times of incidents. • Supporting evidence e.g. from police/health workers/hospital. • A timeline – chronological order of events. • Use numbered paragraphs. • Statement of truth. Follow a template so you don't go wrong.
Service on the respondent	You will need a process server to serve the respondent personally with a copy of the application notice.

2. **Solicitor:** It is likely to be difficult to find a solicitor that can help within short timescales. That is why it would be better to contact someone more specialist like the National Centre for Domestic Violence who can help you within twenty-four hours.

156   Section 1 – Recognising the 16 Stages of Narcissistic Abuse

If you are lucky enough to find a solicitor who can help you, they will need:
- A timeline of events (what happened, when)
- Evidence of any abuse/threats/harm

3. **Safe houses/somewhere to stay:** This option can move you and your children within a few days/weeks if you need somewhere in the UK. This is an option to get away somewhere safe if you are being abused. You will likely have to share kitchens and bathrooms, but the address will be kept secret and you may have to move from the area completely. People who can help you include charities such as:
   a. Woman's Aid – www.womansaid.org.uk
   b. Refuge – www.refuge.org.uk
   c. Unseen – www.unseenuk.org (anti-trafficking)
   d. National Domestic Abuse Helpline – 0808 2000 247
   e. Local Authorities – see
      https://domesticabusecommissioner.uk/resources/

4. **Getting pets Out:** My suggestions are
   a. **Dogs Trust Freedom Project –**
      https://www.moretodogstrust.org.uk/about-freedom/
      about-freedom
   b. **Endeavour** – https://www.endeavourproject.org.uk
   c. **Cats Protection Paws Protect –**
      https://www.cats.org.uk/what-we-do/paws-protect
   If they are unable to help, I suggest that you ask your vet or last resort give them up to an animal charity and state that it is because you are in an abusive relationship and would like the option to have your pet(s) back when it is safe to do so.

5. **Police:** My opinion is that the police have an excellent support system in place in the UK and will recognise your situation. They will go through a DASH risk check list with you or will be able to support you if you are in any danger. The DASH risk check list questions will include things like:
   a. If you have been injured
   b. If you are frightened
   c. What you are afraid of
   d. If you are depressed or feeling suicidal
   e. If you have tried to leave before
   f. Harassing behaviours
   g. Details of the domestic violence
   h. Details of the abuser(s)

Non-Molestation Orders, Injunctions and Going to Court **157**

From this you will be assessed as standard, medium or high risk.

As well as dealing with the abuser(s), they will put you in contact with people who can support you (e.g. victim support).

You may also need psychological support:

1. **Counsellor/psychotherapist:** Choose a counsellor and psychotherapist carefully. Not all are trained in domestic abuse and narcissism. If you are finding it does not work for you, you have the right to change therapists.

Some of the practical steps you can take when you leave includes thinking about:

1. **New phone/telephone number:** Even a pay-as-you-go. If needed, pay cash for a cheap pay-as-you-go in the interim, so that it does not show on joint finances.
2. **Bank accounts:** You may need to write to your bank if you are a joint bank account holder and state that they need to check with you before any cash withdrawal. If you explain the situation, they may be able to help.
3. **Address – The post office:** The post office is quite powerful and can help you with redirection and also assist if your home is being used for fraud (e.g. ex-partner setting up loans against the property).
4. **Not being listed on council tax/voting:** You have a right to be anonymous and can ask not to be listed on the council tax/voting so that it is difficult to find you.
5. **Change all passwords:** You may need to do this overnight and quickly because you must assume that your ex-partner will have knowledge and access. **Do this immediately.**
6. **Change vehicle:** It is daunting to have to change things but changing to another vehicle can empower you to be less visible if needed.
7. **Get a tracking device installed on your vehicle:** The tracking device is helpful to let friends/family know where you are at all times.
8. **Get CCTV installed:** This can be anything from Ring devices or full-blown security. Make sure they have date and time stamps that can be used in evidence. Please make sure that the camera is only focused on protecting your address and does not overlook someone else's.
9. **Get an app/recording device to record all telephone conversations:** Some apps will allow you to record your telephone conversations. Whilst you cannot play these back to anyone, you can make them evidence in court if required.

10. **Get a private detective:** Get a legitimate one whose evidence can be used in court. Ex-police officers are perfect and know how to stay within the law. This may be needed to protect yourself and gather factual evidence for court. Please note that the GDPR rules mean that it can be difficult to gather some evidence. A private detective will be able to advise you.

Phase 14 - Leaving and The Leaving Dangers

Chapter 30 - Be Prepared for the Worst When You Leave (Danger!)

Leaving an abusive relationship can be very dangerous and create rage in the abusive partner. When leaving, if it is safe to do so, think through carefully how you are going to do it.

Remember that a narcissist:

'Is likely to say anything and do anything to make themselves attractive to you in the beginning of forming a relationship and say anything and do anything to destroy you at the end of a relationship,' AM Buck

I would strongly recommend leaving completely, with absolutely no contact unless/until you are legally required to do so. Here are some tips:

1. **Your abuser does not deserve a final goodbye:** It is absolutely okay to just up and leave without any forewarning. In fact, it is likely to be safer than having any final 'I am leaving you' conversation. If you can move a long way away or take refuge in a shelter, this may be a good option.
2. **State your decision calmly in a public place:** If you choose to tell your abuser you are leaving, do so in a public place after you have packed your belongings and have somewhere else safe to go. This method can help prevent a narcissistic rage at the time. You might consider recording the conversation if it is safe for you to do so.
3. **Be fully prepared to defend yourself by stating facts:** This will require every strength you have but being prepared to defend yourself fully is very important. This may require:
   a. **Legal help:** Getting legal help in place. Sometimes this can inflame the situation, but even having a legal defence team in the background can help you to understand your rights. This is particularly helpful because the narcissistic attack after you leave

can be ferocious. You need someone calm behind you. To do this you are going to have to present the legal team with the facts in chronological order.

b. **Professional help:** Get help from charities specialising in abuse.

c. **Recording all false allegations and refuting them:** It is important to record all false allegations and refute them strongly. The law will expect you to do so.

d. **Be prepared to state in writing any blackmail threats:** Be prepared to write down the blackmail threats against you or to tell a solicitor. If you have to send a solicitor's letter have it well documented.

e. **Be prepared to state in writing any physical/psychological harm and threats:** Again, be prepared to state what physical and psychological harm you have experienced. Doctors or psycho-therapy notes may be needed.

4. **Be prepared for false allegations:**

a. You might have to consider what to do if the narcissist makes up false allegations. If the law protects you, get that protection. If it doesn't, do not sit suffering false allegations alone, tell someone/ write it down/have it recorded.

b. False allegations or exaggerated allegations should be anticipated. This is a strong method used by narcissists to deflect blame. Just state that it is untrue, a false allegation and the facts are xyz. They are likely to be consistent in making the allegations, you need to be equally consistent denying it. Be strong. Where you can prove that the allegation is malicious and wrong, do so.

5. **Be fully prepared for the abuser to pull at your heart strings:** At any point, the narcissist may use the 'let's talk', 'for old time's sake' or 'I really love you, can't we work this out' manipulations. In these vulnerable moments, stop. Think what you have gone through. Abuse does not change without full admittance and full professional support. Saying they will get support is not enough – it has to be demonstrated. These words are just a tactic to make you stay. Your response could be 'I will see you again when you have gone through an abuse programme and can demonstrate you have improved.'

6. **Be prepared for narcissistic attacks:**

a. **Legal letters:** You may well receive legal letters. They can be vicious and at a time when you are emotionally depleted. See the chapter in Section 2 for how you respond in full, giving a narcissist no room for further threats. Ask someone else to look through any legal letters you receive calmly (who also understands legal jargon). When you are in a heightened state you may misread or misinterpret what is being said. Legal letters are written very specifically and in some instances, where there is lack of evidence or some doubt by the other solicitor, there are some key words to watch out for such as 'we allege' (this does not mean that they have evidence and 'know' this to be 'fact').

b. **Further threats of violence**

c. **Further threats of false allegations**

d. **The narcissistic rage:** The anger over the perceived betrayal may be too much for a narcissist and invoke a narcissistic rage.

e. **Stalking/harassment:** Make the assumption that this could happen and be prepared. Putting up subtle CCTV cameras (such as a Ring doorbell) will give you a lot of security and knowledge. Installing CCTV cameras in your car (if you are followed) and adding a car tracking device to your own vehicle will also make sure your movements in the vehicle are recorded. Be aware of GDPR and data laws and make sure you are recording just your own property.

f. **Damage of property:** A narcissist can be very vengeful. Expect the unexpected.

g. **Harm to pets:** Keep pets safe and inside for a while. A narcissist is not above harming pets to get to you. If need be temporarily house them somewhere safe for a while.

h. **No agreement – making everything difficult (finances, childcare):** Narcissists may use emotional blackmail to stop the other parent seeing their children or make it impossible/difficult. This is where using an app that tracks visiting rights becomes very important e.g. Our Family Wizard. Some countries make this a legal requirement, currently that is not the case in the UK.

i. **Expect that they may want to take everything you own:** Even if it does not belong to them, a narcissist may well expect to take everything you own for leaving them. For this reason, do not give any concessions at the beginning of negotiations.

j. **Revenge plotting** is also likely. This might include illegal activities if they can get away with it. Revenge threats and actual revenge may be used to intimidate, hurt, harm or devalue their victim, so that they can feel a sense of catharsis.

k. **Loss of job/finances/credit:** A narcissist may consider how to damage anything the victim values such as their credit history, their job, finances, career.

l. **Smear campaigns:** This can include smear campaigns to discredit you in the community/locally/nationally.

162   Section 1 – Recognising the 16 Stages of Narcissistic Abuse

7. **Be prepared, it is likely that they replace you with another person swiftly:** This may be done secretly, because a narcissist requires constant attention. Be mindful that they may already have someone else on the sideline (even someone you know). A narcissist would find it very difficult to be on their own, so this may be a priority for them. Hire a private detective to prove infidelity if you need evidence.

8. **Be prepared that children can be used as bargaining chips:** If this is the case, and you are a father, you are advised to take help from charities such as Families Need Fathers or Fathers for Justice. What you need to work out is what the narcissist wants. This may be maintenance money or the house, for example. There is unlikely to be any compromise because they are likely to feel entitled to take what they want. Expect that you may be goaded, visiting rights may be taken away or changed at short notice. This needs to be documented and recorded. You may have to go to court to get your rights established.

9. **Be prepared to move a long way away:** Be prepared that you might have to move (or your children can be moved a long way away from you). These are all things to consider.

10. **Be prepared for your safety and wellbeing:** The most important aspect is your safety and wellbeing. At the leaving stage, make a safety plan as well as a leaving plan.

11. **Be prepared for their calm, calculating approach:** This may involve a lot of questioning or secretly going through your things.

12. **The 'I want you back' charm approach:** This approach may be used to try to maintain the relationship. Punishment for trying to leave would be given later once the victim is securely back in the relationship.

13. **Planting or removing evidence:** This may be required to deflect detection or avoid detection.

Practical advice – What to do – Prepare for the worst

This is a hard challenge, but it can be helpful to work out the following:

1. **Prepare a SWOT abuse analysis:** to work out Strengths, Weaknesses, Opportunities and Threats. See example below.
2. **Who can you trust? Prepare a social/environment/character analysis:** Make a note of who believes in you (advocates), who believes the narcissist, who has neutral views and who is likely to gossip.
3. **Work out possible influencing/defending options:** Work out what you could do to influence and defend yourself locally, socially, national or internationally if required.
4. **Work out financial implications:** Work out how you can support yourself/get help.
5. **Work out how you will defend yourself from narcissistic attack:** How will you defend against:
    a. Demands for money/property
    b. Stalking/harassment
    c. Smear campaigns
    d. False allegations
    e. Property damage
    f. Threats
    g. Violence/threats of violence
6. **Prepare a timeline of events:** Start to write down the timeline of events. When the relationship started, when the abuse started, what is was, what happened. Have evidence ready. See example below.
7. **Get ready for legal defence (or attack):** Get prepared to defend yourself strongly and include everything that has happened.

164   Section 1 – Recognising the 16 Stages of Narcissistic Abuse

SWOT abuse analysis – Example

Victim strengths: What I have/support	Weaknesses: What they have over me, they could use against me
Finances: • [What financial means do you have?] **Illness/injuries/medical/counselling:** • [Have you had your injuries recorded, diagnosed or have you seen a counsellor?] **Home:** • [Are you able to find somewhere safe to stay or do you need the abuser to leave?] **Children:** • [Are children safe and protected?] **Pets/animals:** • [Are animals safe and protected?] **The law – Legal:** • [What laws are on your side? Who can advise you?] **Friends/family:** • [Are there friends and family who are aware of what has happened?] **Work:** • [Is work aware of what has happened?] **Neighbours:** • [What have neighbours observed?]	**Finances:** • [What finances does the abuser have to challenge me?] **Illness/injuries/medical/counselling:** • [Has the abuser faked any injuries?] **Home:** • [Has the abuser got somewhere else to go? Will they take your home?] **Children:** • [Are children safe and protected from harm from abuse?] **Pets/animals:** • [What animals and pets could they take from you?] **The law – Legal:** • [Has the abuser made false allegations?] • [Are there any threats?] **Friends/family:** • [Has the abuser charmed friends and family to lie for them?] **Neighbours:** • [Has the abuser manipulated neighbours?]

Victim opportunities: What can be done to protect yourself?	Following through on threats: What they might try to do:
The best opportunities to protect yourself is never seeing the narcissist again and going no-contact.	**What is your biggest fear?** Whatever your biggest fear(s) are, a narcissist may have no hesitation in going for this.
Speaking out:	**Doing their worst:**
• **Abuse charities:** [Speak to abuse charities for support.]	**Threats:** • [What might they threaten you with?]
• **Legal:** [Take legal advice.]	**False allegations:**
• **Speak to counsellor to advise the truth:** [Speak with a counsellor to work through the emotions and one who is able to provide evidence.]	• [What possible false allegations will they use against you?] **Humiliation:** • [How could they humiliate you?
• **Speak to hospital/doctors:** [Record the abuse with doctors or at a hospital.]	**Taking things/damage to property:** • [Anticipate that they might keep property and/or steal items.]
• **Speak to neighbours:** [Talk to neighbours to say you are being harassed or stalked and ask for their help watching out for the abuser.]	**Harming/stalking/harassment:** • [Start thinking about safety. Change routes. Take advice on protective equipment/CCTV.]
Defending:	**No agreements:**
• Legal letters: [e.g. send a cease and desist letter for false allegations or smear campaigns.]	• [A narcissist may use every possible tactic, including prolonging legal matters as punishment, e.g. to increase costs and/or not agreeing to anything. You may need to be prepared to simply walk away without anything.]
Threats: • Let other people know of the threats.	
Work:	**Financial compensation:**
• [Tell employers (although you could lose promotions and jobs through this).]	• [A narcissist may want full compensation and expect to take everything you have/own/have built up. Assume they want it all.]

166   Section 1 – Recognising the 16 Stages of Narcissistic Abuse

Victim opportunities: What can be done to protect yourself?	Following through on threats: What they might try to do:
CCTV/recording devices: • [Get surveillance in place – CCTV – on your property only.] **Move away quickly:** • [Move to a different area as quickly as possible.] **Pets:** • [Move them with you or put them somewhere safe.] **Children:** • [Take them with you if you legally can.]	**Reputational damage:** • [Assume that a narcissist may attempt reputational damage. This could mean isolating you from your own social circles, local area or public humiliation.]

Who can you trust? Social environment/character analysis – Example

Believe the truth about my abuse	Believe my abuser's story
Who are the people in my life who believe me and are prepared to back me up? My *positive advocates* are:	Who are the people who will believe the abuser's story? Who are the **advocates of my abuser?**
People who may believe the truth if I tell them	**People who do not want to know the truth/believe what they are told**
Who is neutral and/or has no fixed opinion? Can I trust telling them anything?	Who is likely to gossip and not want to know the truth?

Influencing/defending options:

An abuser can only abuse you if no one knows about it. Who can you influence or defend yourself against by telling the truth?

Local	Social
• Shopkeepers • Neighbours • Local people	• Clubs • Social media
What could you say? [Note, if you talk about abuse most people will likely recoil and not want to talk about it directly. Also, if you have to continue living in the area, narcissists can be very charming and believable, making it even more difficult.]	**What could you say? To which clubs or social media?** Again, be careful what you say because people may isolate you further when you mention what has happened. Clubs and social media are often about talking about the **positive** aspects of life. You may instead need specialist groups and support who understand what you are going through.
National	**International**
• Papers • Internet	• Internet
Why might you need this approach? It may be needed depending on how vindictive the narcissist is. It may be just a curt denial of accusations required. You may need help from PR/legal representatives.	**Why you might need this?** This again is only to set the record straight or deny false allegations. Again, help from PR/legal representatives may be necessary.

168 Section 1 – Recognising the 16 Stages of Narcissistic Abuse

How you defend yourself: Types of narcissistic attack

Type of narcissistic attack	Options to defend yourself
Stalking/harassment	<ul><li>Speak to helplines that can give you advice and support.</li><li>Install CCTV at home and recording devices – check current laws.</li><li>Have a tracking device installed on your car.</li><li>Change routes regularly.</li><li>Get legal/court help but think carefully as this can sometimes make it worse.</li></ul>
Smear campaigns	<ul><li>Be brave, speak out and ask people what is being said about you. Get it in writing if possible.</li><li>Issue a cease and desist letter to people repeating untrue gossip.</li></ul>
False allegations	<ul><li>Defend yourself fully. State it is a false allegation amounting to defamation of character. You refute it entirely and then give an explanation of the truth.</li><li>Issue a cease and desist letter.</li></ul>
Property damage/theft	<ul><li>Take photographs, report property damage/theft.</li></ul>
Threats	<ul><li>Speak out about the threats and make sure other people know what they are. Write them down and record them so that they are specific, e.g. 'On the [date] [Name] threatened that they would [the threat] if I did/or did not [xyz].' Or, 'On [xyz date] [name] threatened to [kill me/harm me by ...]'</li><li>If anything happens then this is recorded.</li></ul>
Violence/threat of violence	This should be a police matter and be on record.<ul><li>Avoid confrontation if possible.</li><li>Get CCTV installed outside and inside as required.</li><li>Get rape alarms.</li><li>Train yourself in self-defence.</li><li>Tell people locally you fear of violence from your ex-partner.</li></ul>

Legal aspects – Legal 'covering'

You may also need to go down the legal route, the best way to prevent narcissistic attacks is legal 'covering'. This means that you need to find a good solicitor/lawyer who can articulate the whole problem, threats including putting in writing anticipated actions and reserving all rights.

For example, ask your solicitor to write a letter which covers all the abusive elements – which gives courts a fuller picture of what is going on. It may be necessary to take out civil proceedings against your abuser as another option.

So, for example, include subsections for:

Possible subsections	Things to cover
Physical abuse	• State the time period when the physical abuse was suffered, when it started, what happened. • State specific dates of abuse (noting if evidence of abuse is available from doctors). • State that the abuse must cease and desist.
Psychological abuse	• State the type of psychological abuse, when it started, how long it went on for and what happened. • State evidence if available (e.g. texts, emails). • What made your frightened? Why? • Has the abuse had a serious effect on health? What? Is there independent psychological evidence?
General abusive behaviour	• What were the threats made? • Have they been followed through? • Did the abuse cause you alarm or distress? • Have you had to change your everyday activities? Why? What happened?
Agreed under duress	• Have you agreed to anything under duress? • What was it? What happened? Why did you agree to it?
False allegations:	• What are the false allegations? • Refute them entirely or correct what is alleged.

170   Section 1 – Recognising the 16 Stages of Narcissistic Abuse

Possible subsections	Things to cover
Threats – Disclosing information	• Has anyone made threats against you? • What were the threats? • Has anyone threatened to disclose information about you? • What would disclosing that information do to you? • Does anyone gain from these threats? Or what do you lose? • State that the threats must cease and desist.
Defamation of character	• State that you have been defamed, how and to whom. • Request cease and desist of untruthful and disparaging remarks that would amount to defamation.
Harassment and stalking	• When did the harassment and stalking occur? • What actions have been taken? • Did the abuser break legal requirements, e.g. bail terms/molestation orders? • How often is the person in contact? Why? • Request the person keeps distance as it is deemed harassment.
Money	• State any financial arrangements. • Was there any control over money/possessions? • State financial agreements.

Prepare a timeline of events

A timeline of events in date order: If you are able to list the key points in date order, this will help a solicitor/lawyer and yourself to understand the extent and patterns of abusive behaviour:

This is what a timeline of events might look like (see page 256):

Date	What happened	Consequence(s)	Evidence
On or around the [date] /Between [dates]	• [What happened]	• [How this impacted you]	• [What evidence you have, e.g. email, text, recording]

Police/police statements

If you need to make a police statement, having a timeline and some evidence will help. They will do their own investigations and may need phone records, emails etc. Photographs or recordings are best with 'meta-data', i.e. it has evidence of dates and times.

The police are best placed to help with domestic violence, will ask appropriate questions using the DASH risk identification model for abuse and protect you.

Filing charges can enrage an abuser further. Only you will know how dangerous the situation is. If the police do protect you they are not there all the time, so you need to also consider restraining orders to protect yourself.

Phase 15 – After The Relationship Breaks Up – Narcisstic Attacks May Increase – Protect Yourself

I describe leaving a narcissist as being in a 'war, not of your own making'. You may have to learn to protect and defend yourself fully. This may include if necessary:

1. **Speaking out:** A narcissist is reliant on a victim's silence or acquiesce. If you no longer do this and speak out about the situation, other people will be able to help.
2. **Legal:** Do not be afraid to protect yourself by having legal representation.
3. **Your safety:** You have to put your safety, and that of any children, first.
4. **Evidence:** Evidence becomes crucial to avoid the denials, lies and false allegations.
5. **Non-molestation/possession order:** Go to court if needed.

If you are dealing with a truly vengeful narcissist (which some are), you will not be able to get away lightly and the leaving could enrage them further. You will need to protect yourself. It may be a dangerous time and you need to know all the ways in which you can defend yourself. Anticipate narcissistic attacks may start.

Remember:

'Not all rule and boundary breakers are narcissists, but narcissists will nearly always break boundaries and rules.' A M Buck

This means that you are not likely to be on a level playing field and you MUST ANTICIPATE that they may play dirty to seek their REVENGE.

Even if other people are involved to help you, they may not be there all the time. You have to learn to protect, protect, protect yourself.

Chapter 31 – Protect, Protect, Protect Yourself

Protecting yourself after you have left an abusive relationship is just as, if not more, important. At the point when you may be physically and emotionally depleted, a narcissist may well increase their various methods of attack. These are the ways that you can help protect yourself:

1. **When you leave, that's it:** End the relationship for good, don't go back on your decision. This is normally only possible after the SNAP leaving moment.
2. **Don't do it alone – seek professional advice:** From abuse charities to online support forums to psychotherapists.
3. **Be more vigilant:** A narcissist may want to track your movements after leaving, so be very vigilant. This is the reason why it is better to move away.
4. **Change locks:** Copies of keys could easily have been made, so do not miss this step. Changing locks gives you more peace of mind. Also add spy holes to doors or chains to stop someone coming in.
5. **Change the way people enter your home:** Never just open the door to someone – have a chain on at a minimum. Change the way you allow people access. Check all badges, including officials, by independently ringing to check they are genuine. Make people wait outside, no matter the weather. Do your own checks. Ways that a narcissist might try to gain access include being disguised as delivery drivers, utilities, property agents or the council.
6. **Change your route to work:** If you go by public transport, change the times. Change to cycling or go by car. If you go by car, work out what other route options you might have and change them regularly. If you are unexpectedly followed, record it. If you need to get someone from work to walk with you, do so.
7. **Change jobs:** Even better is to change your job and move away completely. Start again. If you are a director, use an accountant's address to make sure you cannot be found that way.
8. **Move away:** If you do move away, make sure you are not listed on the council tax bill or voting (so you cannot be found easily). Make sure you receive and then destroy the post redirection letter, so it cannot be accidentally found. Make sure estate agents are aware of your situation, so that they don't accidentally give out information (explain

the reasons you are moving if necessary). Ask any companies where you change your address to confirm that they don't send a confirmation to the old address just in case.

9. **Change your name:** If you want to, consider changing your name by deed poll so that it is harder to find you as well.

10. **Get security devices installed:** These can range from CCTV (such as Ring doorbells that record anyone who approaches and show it on your phone). Consider other security devices to record and save the recordings to cloud. Make sure that the security cameras you install (especially in homes) are not easy for someone to hack into and watch you.

11. **Safety for phones/laptops:** Cover up cameras on phones and laptops if you are not using them.

12. **Go round your home to see where there are security risks and fix them:** Put yourself in the mind of a burglar, or someone who wants to watch you. Work out where there may be weak points. Make protecting your home more secure.

13. **Who overlooks you?:** Check which properties and windows overlook you. This may be important because it would not be beyond a narcissist to move close to you. They may even consider moving next door to you because this doesn't break any laws but does mean that they can watch you.

14. **Get a rape alarm:** They can be put on a keyring. It is a very loud warning and gives you a couple of seconds shock factor to get away or alert others.

15. **Record conversations:** If the narcissist insists on trying to keep in touch (which they may do), record the conversations. You cannot legally play the recordings to anyone, but it does help evidence threats and abuse if needed to in court. A court may allow the release of the recordings if deemed necessary. Make a physical transcript somewhere else.

16. **Save all abusive and threatening messages and texts:** Make more than one copy. Do screenshots of the text messages as photos. Upload them to computers and print them out. Do not have just one copy.

17. **Tell a solicitor what has happened:** Use the timeline of events example to pull together your own key facts and evidence of what has happened.

18. **Tell work if you are being stalked/harassed:** In the UK, tell your boss. It may affect your career, but your safety and support is more important. Going through the aftermath of abuse can affect your work performance and ability to earn.

Protect, Protect, Protect Yourself **175**

19. **Move things to a safety store:** Another option is to keep valuables in a safety store for a time. This can be from safety deposit boxes to container storage.
20. **Protect animals – Move them away if needed:** Helpful organisations who may be able to help including Dogs Trust Freedom Project, Endeavour and Cats Protection Paws Protect.
21. **Speak to school if children are in danger:** This option may be necessary if you think your children may be in danger.
22. **Change your phone and telephone number:** Either change your phone number (which will be deleted overnight if you explain you are in an abusive relationship) or have a second phone available (for example a cheap pay-as-you-go).
23. **Burn information you don't want found:** This might include receipts or information such as changing your address that you don't want found by your abuser.
24. **Don't put personal items in the bin:** Bins can be gone through and so can rubbish bags. Take them personally to waste recycling or make sure nothing personal goes into them.
25. **Get your mail redirected:** Royal Mail will redirect your post for a period of time, but they do send out letters to your previous address to advise of the redirection. This will not be forwarded, so will indicate that there is a redirection in place.
26. **Write to banks/joint accounts to put on hold or get money out:** Make sure that joint accounts are moved to joint signature or ask if the account can go on hold.
27. **Have an exit plan/strategy if there is a break-in:** Have a plan in mind if there is a break-in to your home. Where will you exit?
28. **Go out with another person rather than alone:** When you go out and about, be with someone else if possible.
29. **Security-assess your home:** Or get someone professional to security-assess it. Where are the weak points?
30. **Watch online information and practice self-defence:** Watch self-defence online information or read in books. Practice how you might respond. Go to classes if it is safe to do so.
31. **Don't be too quick to let your guard down:** It is important to keep your guard up for a time, especially entering/leaving home, work, school and also when you are out and about. Stay away from remote areas if you can.
32. **Start speaking out:** It may be that a narcissist has told you to keep secrets. You do not have to hide their secrets.
33. **Keep talking:** It is really important to keep talking about what is

176 Section 1 – Recognising the 16 Stages of Narcissistic Abuse

happening and reaching out to the right people. It can be very easy to isolate yourself. Keep the talk about the abuse to specialists rather than rely too heavily on friends and family.

34. **Protect your mental wellbeing:** Get a good counsellor/therapist/psychologist. This is really important. Only choose someone who has experience of abuse. Some may say they have, but their experience may be very limited.

35. **Don't be put off by other people's negative judgements:** You do not need to be victim shamed on top of it all. Tell people firmly if required, 'I will not be victim shamed by you!'

36. **Read about narcissism:** Reading about abuse and narcissism will help you validate what you might have gone through. It is an important part of the recovery, but it is important not to get stuck in this stage.

Phase 16 – The End of Narcissistic Abuse

The final stage is when you are finally away safely, you have dealt with all the narcissistic attacks and the abuse in the relationship has finally ended. This can take considerable time (weeks, months, years).

Congratulations – this is the END OF ABUSE, but unfortunately, due to the nature of narcissist abuse, the start of the RECOVERY STAGE. I want you to know you can get through this and that what I will share with you will SPEED up your recovery.

In conclusion, I hope that you have found this first section helpful and practical to help you get away from a narcissistic abusive relationship.

Remember that as you move through the next sections – which helped my recovery and I hope so for you too – that:

One day this will be behind you, and you will be a wiser, stronger and empowered version of yourself again

Section 2 – The Pre-Leaving Stage – Are You Really Ready To Leave?

It may take several attempts to leave an abusive relationship. This is understandable given the level of fear and emotional manipulation being used. Negative reasons to stay might include fear of physical punishment, social isolation or even threats. More positive manipulations might include charm, humour or sexuality and a return to the highs that you had in the beginning of the relationship.

The pre-leaving stage can be an extremely frustrating cycle because you know that the relationship is not good for you, but you cannot or are not quite ready yet to separate. Something has to snap before you make that final decision. For this reason, the pre-leaving stage can go on for some time – even years.

In my opinion, there are two **pre-leaving stages** and after you have left eight recovery phases that you go through. The **pre-leaving stages** are:

> Phase 1 – Am I really ready to do this?
>
> Phase 2 – Why I am leaving?

It looks fairly simple at first glance, but it isn't. There are a set of fears that you have to overcome to be able to move forward and a lot of things that may pull you back into the relationship.

In the pre-leaving Phase 1 you may well be describing leaving the relationship with phrases such as 'I can't' or 'If only ...' This is putting the decision to leave out of your own hands. You may start getting stronger by asking for what you need such as 'Only if' (see table below). This is a sign that you are starting to take your own needs more seriously.

Pre-leaving – wanting others to change (NOT READY)	Pre-leaving – empowering yourself (READY)
'IF ONLY' I were closer to him and love him more, he will realise he doesn't need to be bad.	'ONLY IF' his behaviour changes and he will agree to independent help, will I give our relationship another chance.
'IF ONLY' she could see how good she can be, I am sure I can help make her realise.	'ONLY IF' he accepts responsibility for his bad behaviour will I consider reconciliation.
'IF ONLY' I show them my love, they will get better.	'ONLY IF' she genuinely demonstrates positive behaviour changes will I allow her closer.
'IF ONLY' I try not to annoy him, he won't get so cross with me.	'ONLY IF' they get professional help for their temper.
'IF ONLY' he didn't hurt me/hit me, the relationship would be fine.	

When you realise that you do have the power to leave, you start using 'I am' statements:

'I AM leaving' is when the victim is empowered to find a way to leave

This is when you might say something to yourself such as 'I AM leaving and NEVER having him/her/they back in my life because I AM worth more than this.' **It is the moment you realise that the only thing you can change is YOU.**

Phase 1 - Am I Really Ready To Do This?

You will be ready to leave an abusive relationship when the fear of leaving is less than the fear of staying.

The Cycle of Excuse – Leaving an abusive relationship

Decide I AM leaving
Find people to help
Safe home
Financial support
Not being
Afraid

What pressure is on me to stay?

Charm
Abuse
Threats
Jealousy

What I need to do to leave?

Why I feel trapped?

Finances
Protect others
Fear

Can I survive on my own?
I am unsure?

What are the consequences

What I am afraid of?

Isolation
Separation anxiety
Heartbreak
Being alone
Financial ruin

182 Section 2 – The Pre-Leaving Stage – Are you Really Ready to Leave?

When you can fill out and totally commit to the section 'Why I am leaving', you are ready to become accountable to yourself and are ready to leave the relationship. The first box is an example, complete the second box with your own answers.

WHY I AM LEAVING – 'I AM' leaving because I believe ...	WHY I STAY – 'IF ONLY', then ...
I am leaving this relationship because EXAMPLES:	If only they would ... the relationship ... EXAMPLE:
• Physical, *e.g. I am leaving this relationship because they have hit me, and I am worried they will get worse.*	• Physical, *e.g. If only he would not hit me, the relationship could work out.*
• Long term *e.g. I am leaving this relationship because I expect the assaults to get worse and I fear for my safety.*	
I CAN'T LEAVE BECAUSE ...	I WILL STAY – 'ONLY IF', then ...
I can't leave because I am afraid of ... (EXAMPLE):	Only if they ... then the relationship ... (EXAMPLES):
• Physical *e.g. I can't leave because I am afraid that they will try to harm me.*	**Positive:** *e.g. Only if they ... respect my needs, then the relationship can survive.* **Negative:** *e.g. Only if they ... stop harming me, then the relationship can survive.*

Complete the sections below that are relevant to you:

WHY I AM LEAVING – 'I AM' leaving because I believe ... (be specific)	WHY I STAY – 'IF ONLY', then ...
I am leaving this relationship because:	If only they would ... the relationship ...
I CAN'T LEAVE BECAUSE ...	**I WILL STAY – 'ONLY IF', then ...**
I can't leave because I am afraid of:	Only if they ... then the relationship ...

Phase 2 – Why I Am Leaving

When you can definitely complete the 'I AM leaving the relationship because' statement you are ready to make a declaration to yourself of the reasons why you are leaving in more detail.

You will need to write this down to protect yourself from being drawn back into the relationship and will need to refer to it often in the leaving stages of recovery.

Next is a series of questions to fill in about your relationship. There are no right or wrong answers, but it will help you make up your mind. These are:

1. **'I am valuable because' matrix:**. This will determine how validated and loved you feel in your relationship.
2. **My values and beliefs are:** This table will help you determine what is really important to you regarding your values and beliefs.
3. **The compromise table:** This will help you establish what you have compromised in the relationship.
4. **The bottom line:** This helps you realise if you have broken your own boundaries and expectations from a relationship.
5. **My expectations versus reality:** This helps you focus on what your expectations from a relationship actually are and if these are being met.
6. **Why I always go back:** This will define the areas you need to focus on to be able to stay strong if you are intent on leaving.
7. **What does a loving, respectful relationship look like:** This helps you define what it is that you actually want in a relationship and compare it with the relationship you are in.

When you have completed these exercises, you will have a better idea if the statement still holds true.

'I AM leaving my partner because ...'

Section 2 – The Pre-Leaving Stage – Why I Am Leaving? 185

'I am valuable because' matrix:

I AM valuable because ...	My partner tells me that I am valuable because ...
My good points/qualities are (I describe myself as):	My partner praises me and tells me that: What % of the time is this?
I feel worthless sometimes because ...	**A person who knows me well and whose opinion I trust would say ...**
My partner criticises and insults me about: What % of the time is this?	What would someone who you trust say your good qualities are? What would they say about your partner's criticisms? How do these answers differ from what your partner says about you?

What did you learn from this exercise?

_____

_____

186   Section 2 – The Pre-Leaving Stage – Are you Really Ready to Leave?

My values and beliefs are:

My values/beliefs (examples)	Does my partner treat me that way?	How my partner treats me (examples)
Trust – I am looking for a relationship where I can trust my partner and they can trust me.	Yes/No/Sometimes/ I don't know	E.g. *trust – My partner doesn't trust me and checks up on me.*
Respect – My partner respects my views, even if they do not agree.	Yes/No/Sometimes/I don't know	
Being valued – I am valued for who I am.	Yes/No/Sometimes/I don't know	
Faithfulness – I expect my partner to be faithful, this means that ...	Yes/No/Sometimes /I don't know	
Kindness – My partner is kind to me..	Yes/No/Sometimes/ I don't know	
Listening to me – My partner listens to what I have to say	Yes/No/Sometimes/I don't know	
Honest – My partner is always honest with me.	Yes/No/Sometimes/I don't know	
Security – My partner makes me feel secure in the relationship.	Yes/No/Sometimes/I don't know	
Physical – My partner has never hit me.	Yes/No/Sometimes/I don't know	
Mental – My partner never tells me what to do.	Yes/No/Sometimes/I don't know	
Fear – I live without fear in my relationship.	Yes/No/Sometimes/I don't know	
Health – My partner looks after my health and wellbeing.	Yes/No/Sometimes/I don't know	
Takes care of me – My partner takes care of me	Yes/No/Sometimes/I don't know	
Does what they say – My partner is reliable and does what they say	Yes/No/Sometimes/I don't know	

Section 2 – The Pre-Leaving Stage – Why I Am Leaving? **187**

My values/beliefs (examples)	Does my partner treat me that way?	How my partner treats me (examples)
Laughter: We have a lot of laughter in our relationship.	Yes/No/Sometimes/I don't know	
Criticism – My partner has never criticised me.	Yes/No/Sometimes/I don't know	
Your examples		

What did you learn from this exercise?

188 Section 2 – The Pre-Leaving Stage – Are you Really Ready to Leave?

The compromise table:

What are the compromises you have accepted in your relationship	As a consequence ...	How has this affected your needs in the relationship?
E.g. XYZ controls the finances for food.	*E.g. I cannot eat what I need for my health.*	*E.g. My needs are neglected in the relationship. I must eat what I am given even if it hurts my health.*
E.g. XYZ controls me through fear.	*E.g. I am frightened to leave.*	*E.g. My basic needs and rights of safety and security have not been met.*
Your compromises	**As a consequence ...**	**How has this affected your needs in the relationship?**

What did you learn from this exercise?

The bottom line – you always said you would leave your relationship if:

You always said that you would leave your relationship if (EXAMPLES):	Why did you stay?
He/she/they hit me.	E.g. I stayed because I was afraid to leave.
I didn't feel safe.	
I was ever assaulted.	
He/she/they threatened to harm me.	
He/she/they hurt my pet.	
He/she/they hurt my children.	
He/she/they disrespected me or tried to stop my opinions.	
Your examples – you always said you would leave a relationship if ...	Why did you stay?

What did you learn from this exercise?

_____

_____

190   Section 2 – The Pre-Leaving Stage – Are you Really Ready to Leave?

How low is your REAL bottom line?

What are your real bottom line(s) EXAMPLE	What can you do about it
Hit me more than once	*E.g. get a non-molestation order.*
Unfaithfulness	*E.g. gain evidence.*
Your bottom line	**What will you do about it**

What did you learn from this exercise?

My expectations versus reality

Your expectations [Examples]	What actually happened [Examples]
I expected things to get better and for [name] to change their ways, like they said they would.	E.g. [Name] didn't change and the abuse got worse.
I expected [name] to be faithful.	E.g. [Name] betrayed my trust but minimised it and got angry if I tried to talk about it.
I expected to be able to go out with friends.	E.g. [Name] became angry and tried to isolate me.
Your expectations in your relationship	**What is likely to happen if you stay? ...**

What did you learn from this exercise?

Why I always go back to the relationship

Complete the following sentence. I always go back to my relationship because ...

What did you learn from this exercise?

192 Section 2 – The Pre-Leaving Stage – Are you Really Ready to Leave?

What does a loving, respectful relationship look like versus yours?

Loving, respectful relationship	How does this compare with your relationship?
I feel loved and appreciated.	
I feel safe.	
We might disagree, but it is safe for me to express what I am thinking.	
I feel respected.	
I know I can trust my partner.	
I know my partner would never hurt me.	
I know my partner would never be unfaithful to me.	
I know that my partner loves my/our children.	
I know that my partner would take care of me if I were ill.	
I have friends of my own in our relationship.	
I have free time to enjoy my own hobbies and past times.	
My partner has the same outlook as me in life.	
I know that my partner is looking for a long-term commitment.	
Other things that are important to you in a loving, respectful relationship ...	**How this compares with your relationship ...**

What did you learn from this exercise?

Section 3 – Now You Have Left – The Recovery Begins

You are out of the abusive relationship. Congratulations. That is a huge positive step forward. This is the part of the recovery process where the narcissist may step up their attempts to control you and get you back (known as Hoovering) or discard you completely. If their initial attempts do not work, they may well move onto narcissistic attack. This can include false allegations and smear campaigns or simply painfully moving onto another partner very swiftly, stonewalling you or flaunting their new partner in front of you.

Nearly all advice after an abusive relationship is to go no-contact and this is certainly crucial. However, you may not be able to do that straight away, so in the meantime you will need to modify your contact and learn very quickly to:

(1) Protect yourself
(2) Defend yourself
(3) Change your old patterns and beliefs

You need to know that it is almost impossible to do recovery on your own. You can read self-help books (like this), but you are going to need support around you from people who understand what you are going through.

You are very likely to be traumatised and may not be making decisions from a calm, rational perspective just yet. You may be numb, disassociated from the experience, depressed or many other feelings and emotions around what has happened. It is a shock.

After such a traumatic experience it can be difficult to shake off wanting to talk about the trauma and reacting/overreacting to things. You may be feeling raw and sensitive. This is normal after the abuse. You also need to know that you cannot rationally think your way out of this – there is so much going on unconsciously, that if you don't address the raw emotions, the triggers and unconscious belief systems, you may get stuck in a cycle of being emotionally wounded and not being able to get out of that.

I want you to know that there is a way out and you can recover from abuse in either a relatively short timeframe (weeks/months) or a longer timeframe (years), depending on what therapy and treatment you chose. It really depends on how much you are willing to acknowledge and deal with the painful emotions and the willingness to look inside yourself for the answers.

There were eight recovery phases that I observed in the post-leaving stage. This is not a linear progression from Phase 1 through to Phase 8 – you may find yourself going back through different phases, or just jump straight to the one you need in the moment. The **eight recovery phases** are:

Phase 1 – I'm out of the relationship, now what?
Phase 2 – What went wrong?
Phase 3 – Getting the help you need and your support network
Phase 4 – Ready to speak up and defend myself
Phase 5 – Remind me, what are my needs exactly?
Phase 6 – Have I changed and recovered enough?
Phase 7 – Do I accept what has happened?
Phase 8 – I am ready to move on with my life

Phase 1 - I'm Out! Now What?

Phase 1 is the crucial practical aspect of leaving an abusive relationship. This is the stage when you have left the relationship but may be emotionally raw and bruised. At this point, if you have not been ruthlessly discarded, the narcissist may try to get back in touch. This is sometimes called Hoovering. In either case, you need to:

(1) Protect yourself
(2) Defend yourself
(3) Validate yourself

At this stage, the narcissist is going to be trying six main tactics of control to get you back into the relationship. They may try to manipulate you with:

(1) Jealousy
(2) Charm/humour/false apologies/Hoovering
(3) Retaliation/threats
(4) Goading/provocation
(5) Stonewalling
(6) Guilt-tripping

Chapter 32 – Protecting Yourself

The first step has to be the physical safety of protecting you, children and pets. This means that you are now in control of protecting your wellbeing and is the first step in the recovery process. This stage may mean that you have to relocate suddenly with the help of a shelter/friend's house or get a protection order/occupation order to stay in your home. You have a right to protect yourself.

As well as your physical safety, you will also have to protect yourself from:

(1) Emotional safety and triggers such as jealousy
(2) Hoovering – attempts to get back with you
(3) The shock of being alone

Protecting yourself – physical safety

This includes making sure that you utilise all resources available to you – e.g. abuse charities. This part may be difficult because you may have been isolated and may be very frightened. More than ever now you need to protect yourself. This includes making sure you have contacted those who can help you:

a. **The National Domestic Abuse, Refuge UK**: 0808 2000 247
b. **Mankind Initiative** – https://www.mankind.org.uk
c. **Woman's Aid –** Online at www.womansaid.org.uk
d. **National Centre for Domestic Violence –** 0800 970 2070 or www.ncdc.org.uk
e. **National LGBT Domestic Abuse Helpline –** 0300 999 5428
f. **Domestic Abuse Commissioner –** www.domesticabusecommissioner.uk

If you need to get a non-molestation order or occupation order – this is form FL401 – get someone to help you fill it in. This company can help you within twenty-four hours:

a. **National Centre for Domestic Violence –** 0800 970 2070 or www.ncdc.org.uk

If you fear for your safety, have programmed into your phone:

a. **Police** – 101 for less urgent matters and 999 in an emergency. Remember to press 55 if you cannot talk.

If you have contacted the UK police regarding domestic violence in the past, they may have already put a 'flag' on their computer systems at your address which gives you another way to protect yourself. This is very important if you have been assaulted or are being physically threatened in any way.

Protecting yourself – Emotional safety – Jealousy and other extreme emotions

Your emotional safety may also be under attack the moment you leave a narcissist, or a narcissist discards you. So, you need to prepare yourself and how you are going to deal with some powerful emotions.

These powerful emotions can pull you back to a narcissist, along with all and any false promises, so it is imperative you are aware of them and have a way to handle the strong responses you may encounter.

The extreme emotions are normal in response to something a narcissist does or does not do. It is very important to acknowledge and address these because they are the emotional triggers that give a narcissist an opportunity to hook you right back in. They are looking for a reaction from you – good or bad. The narcissist will likely seek attention. A narcissist is an expert in creating the emotional reactions and seems to <u>rely on them</u> to feed their own ego. They are likely to try anything to goad you, bait you and get a response.

It is therefore imperative that you do not respond or do not respond in the way a narcissist expects.

This is where you need to find out your emotional triggers and protect yourself from reacting to them.

Emotional triggers

With emotional triggers you may be shocked how quickly they appear, but they will always:

(1) Feel intense
(2) Hurt you in some way
(3) Be in reaction to something the narcissist has or has not done, or sometimes, totally unexpected reactions from something that is SIMILAR to what a narcissist has done to you

One of the aims of a narcissist can be to take anything that is **the greatest value** to you. This can be from children, social connections to your property and self-worth. They are likely to use all methods possible – so you need to know what is of most value to you and **prepare yourself**.

What you need to prepare yourself for

When a narcissist prepares their narcissistic attack or abandonment, you need to be prepared to protect and defend yourself fully. Their techniques can be callous, heartless, inhumane and degrading, leaving you feeling in the depths of despair. This is not of your doing and you have done nothing to deserve this. You may well experience:

- Feelings of hopelessness and worthlessness
- Shame and mortification
- Loss of sanity, through confusion
- Reliance on others for your wellbeing rather than self, through undermining your worth
- Loss of job/career/income
- Alienation from social connections, leading to ostracisation, isolation and abandonment
- Loss of hope
- Loss of home/security
- Fear for your safety and those of your family
- Feeling inadequate and worthless
- Feeling devastation, ridiculed and ruined
- Outrage and fury
- Illness/ill health, through all techniques

The only way to get through this trauma is:

Speak up – Speak out – Protect yourself – Defend yourself

How to overcome these extreme emotional triggers – change YOUR reaction

You need to plan and **prevent yourself from reacting to them**, there are a few methods:

1. **No contact:** No contact at all ensures they get no response and gives you an opportunity to start recovery. It can be easier said than done.

Instead of focusing on what they are doing, focus on stabilising your emotions and what you need to do for yourself. If there is no other reason to be in contact with the narcissist:

a. Block their telephone number on your phone, change telephone number
b. Take them off social media
c. Block them on your email
d. Do not open your front door, especially if they turn up
e. Ask someone else to turn them away if they turn up at work
f. Do not go looking for them locally

If you feel that you must respond, it will need to be specific, brief and direct without emotions. 'Your [emails/texts] have been received. I do not want any further contact from you. Any further contact will be deemed as harassment.'

If you see them out in the community:

g. Leave the shop/area, walk away without any acknowledgement – note down time, place.

If they approach you in the community in public and try to engage (even if goading or baiting with other people around for humiliation):

h. No reaction – leave and note down the time/place. You may need it for your defence.

If they contact you on social media/phone make sure you have clearly stated the relationship has ended and you want no further contact:

i. Put the phone down without saying anything. Every time they ring. If they persist, send a text which states: 'I do not want any further contact from you. Any further attempts to get in touch will be classed as harassment.'
j. Do not respond in any way to emails unless there are threats, in which case you state, 'Your threats have been received and noted. I do not want any further contact with you. All attempts at further contact will be referred to the authorities.'

Do not respond to any further texts, emails and phone calls. You have to be able to defend yourself and follow through with your no-contact request.

2. **Necessity of contact:** This might be the situation when you take care of children or are having necessary conversations regarding joint property, finances and business.

Pause before any reaction or responding. This gives yourself time to make a more considered/rational response.

The tactics that a narcissist may try:

a. **Turning up uninvited:** Do not open the door. State simply 'Please go. We have not agreed to meet – send me a [text/email] to arrange a place/time.' .

b. **Sending communications with time pressure to respond 'now':** 'Your [email/text] has been received. I will respond by [date] with a response,' then no further contact.

c. **Goading –** No response.

d. **Baiting/Provocation –** No response.

e. **Insults –** No response.

f. **Threats –** No response.

g. **Harm/attempt to harm –** Report to the police.

Dealing with these emotions internally

We all deal with emotions internally in different ways. To overcome strong emotions when leaving a narcissist I found the most effective ways to take the heat out of the emotions is getting help and regularly using:

1. **Practical:** Helplines/chatrooms to talk through the emotions.
2. **Practical:** Supportive and knowledgeable friends and/or family who know about the abuse.
3. **Practical:** Psychotherapy for trauma/NLP.
4. **Practical:** Twele-stage healing trauma programme – *Healing Trauma* © 2008 Peter A Levine, published by Sounds True Inc.
5. **Alternative:** Rewind technique (counselling).
6. **Alternative:** The Narcissistic Abuse Recovery Programme (NARP)– Melanie Tonia Evans.
7. **Practical:** The Intensive Recovery Programme – Domestic and Narcissistic Abuse – www.i-recovered.co.uk

Emotion	What a narcissist may do	How to overcome this
Jealousy	• Find another partner quickly and deliberately try to make you jealous. • Flaunt another partner in front of you. • Deliberately leave evidence of seeing another person around. • Use social media to 'praise' their new partner, as if you didn't exist. • Baiting such as sending you dual messages such as 'my new partner is so lovely, but not as ... as you' – leaving a door open for you to contact them.	**Go back to your answers in Part 2.** Specifically, what you wrote for:'I am leaving my partner because ...' 'My partner criticises and insults me about ...' 'My values and beliefs are ...' 'The compromises I have made are ...' 'I always said I would leave a relationship when ...' 'My expectations versus reality are ...' Ask yourself, what is the probability of abuse happening again? So, what are you jealous about? What exactly are you losing that is worth fighting for? **If they have a new partner.** As painful as this is, it is actually a blessing in disguise. It allows you to get away from the relationship more safely.

Emotion	What a narcissist may do	How to overcome this
Humiliation/embarrassment/ shame	This may include parading a new lover or threatening to tell embarrassing secrets or send round explicit intimate photos.	**Go back to your answers to what a loving, respectful relationship looks like in Part 2.** You have nothing to be ashamed of or humiliated about. E.g. you are protected under the law: Criminal Justice and Courts Act 2015 which has up to a two-year jail sentence for revenge porn.
Anger/fury	Your narcissist may well want to trigger your anger . and rage	Whilst you need to express your emotions, you have to do so safely. Effective methods can be exercise (e.g. the gym kick boxing a punch bag) or even hitting your pillow, or listening to loud music. Other methods are anger management courses, or an alternative holographic kinetics. Anger is a natural emotion that you may have had to supress to survive.

Protecting Yourself 203

Emotion	What a narcissist may do	How to overcome this
Despair/hopeless/helpless	A narcissist may well threaten to take everything you have or destroy you.	This is where you have to learn to defend yourself – from legal aspects to the ability to calmly articulate what is happening. You may need to talk to psychologists or call an abuse helpline to get you through.
Hysterical/crying/overwhelmed	A narcissist may enjoy harming and hurting you to regain power and control. What they may well consider or do is beyond anything normal.	This is where it is imperative to have trained support. This can be a very lonely and terrifying experience. This is where you need abuse helplines, victim support, Samaritans. In addition, you may need to consider medication (ask your GP).
Suicidal/self-harm	The pain of their cruelty may be so unbearable that you consider suicide and self-harm.	Call for specialist help. Speak to a helpline – Samaritans are confidential. Call 116 123. Get some help from psychologists/mental health practitioners. Talking will help. Don't try to cope alone.
Worthlessness/rejection	The pain of being rejected by a narcissist and stonewalled.	Go back to your answers to what a loving, respectful relationship looks like in Part 2. Stonewalling, ignoring or discarding are painful methods of control. Call for specialist help to stay strong.

Protecting yourself – Hoovering

Hoovering – where a narcissist tries to get back in touch – is when the narcissist is likely to use charm, idolisation, future dreams or attraction to try to get back with you. This is only to stop you leaving. The abuse is likely to only get worse if you go back. It is again imperative to go through what you have written in Part 2 and keep looking at the reasons you are leaving.

Focus on the fact that the narcissist has probably used this method before to get you back. Focus only on why you have to leave.

Hoovering technique	What a narcissist is likely to do	How to overcome this
Charm, flattery and idealisation	Techniques might include phrases like: 'I miss you so much.' 'Don't throw away all we have.' 'Do you remember when we ... [favourable memory]' 'I was just at ... and thought of all the good times we had.'	**Go back to your answers in Part 2.** Specifically, what you wrote for: 'I am leaving my partner because ...' 'My partner criticises and insults me about ...' 'My values and beliefs are ...' 'The compromises I have made are ...' 'I always said I would leave a relationship when ...' 'My expectations versus reality are ...' Ask yourself, what is the probability of abuse happening again? Go no-contact (which is the best way). Ignore what is said. Resist the urge to respond, because this is what a narcissist wants. They can easily manipulate the conversation. So, don't respond.

Hoovering technique	What a narcissist is likely to do	How to overcome this
Sexual attraction	This might include temptations, using sex to get you back. A narcissist is likely to know that you find them attractive. 'One last time.' 'Go on, you know you can't resist me.' Or flirtation, provocation.	*Resist this*. What you don't know is if they are plotting revenge, e.g. things could get much worse, such as a discard. Again, go back to your reasons for leaving in Part 2.
Future dreams/ illusions	The narcissist may well try to apply all the emotional triggers of the future dream. These are all the promises for the 'blissfully happy' future. This might be: 'You are my soulmate – how can I live without our dream of ...'	Remember ACTIONS speak louder than WORDS. Go back to the likelihood of the future dreams happening from past behaviour. A narcissist may well have promised you the dream future. This might be anything from love, security, children. They are likely to be very convincing in their lies. It isjust a false dream that they are painting – an illusion – and you have to painfully acknowledge this. Get professional help.

Protecting yourself from the shock of being alone

This can be another dangerous aspect when you leave an abusive relationship. The sudden shock between excessive and controlling contact to silence can feel quite desolate and isolating.

You may have a lot of difficult emotions to cope with – on top of everything else – so I recommend that you try to surround yourself with people at this time. This again is a very difficult point in recovery because in an abusive relationship you may have put your needs last and therefore supressed them. It means you have to work out what you actually need and like doing and begin to enjoy your own company. The good news is that the answer to this is all inside you, however, there is an initial shock of being alone that causes a temptation to go back to the abuse. Be gentle on yourself as you are changing from being told what to do to making your own decisions. This is a big step.

Shock of being alone	What you might be feeling/doing	How to overcome this
Fear of not knowing what to do with all the free time.	Overwhelmed, bored, lonely, trapped inside. Not knowing what to do to make the hours go faster.	Write a list of all the things you used to do to enjoy yourself (even years ago). Start to do one small thing. It cannot be too difficult at this time because you are recovering. Even colouring in books will help. Read about narcissism. Read about the laws in your country. Write a journal of how you are feeling and what happened. Join a trauma/abuse membership forum.
Checking emails, texts, social media constantly.	Justifying your decisions, seeing what they are doing.	Temporarily close down social media because it will stop you taking care of yourself. Replace the urge to check emails and texts with another activity. E.g. every time you check your text/email – walk to another room. Switch to silent.
Not being able to talk to someone about your day.	Sadness, isolation, loneliness.	Live with someone else (not romantic) for a while. Start to reconnect with friends and particularly those who can talk about what happened.

Shock of being alone	What you might be feeling/doing	How to overcome this
Remembering what you 'used to do' at this time.	Sadness, loss of routine, uncomfortable silence.	You need to create a new routine for yourself. This could be exercise, watching programmes you like, cooking, having a bath, scented candles. Whatever it is that makes you happy.
Getting stuck researching narcissism.	Trying to validate what you have gone through.	Have thing you enjoy to give you a better balance.

Chapter 33 – Defending Yourself

Being able to defend yourself, whilst dealing with extreme emotions, is particularly hard. This is why it is so important to get professional support whilst you are going through this. The risk is that if you remain mute, silent and do not speak up against the abuse, that the narcissist is likely to be more persuasive with their charm and you risk not being believed or heard.

I believe it is therefore critical to get out of your comfort zone and speak up and speak out.

On a practical level you need to immediately put yourself in a position of strength and be ready to defend yourself. It is highly likely that your resolution is going to be tested, so you need to be ready and prepared. This is also going to be difficult when you may feel consumed by the relationship and still under their power and control.

A narcissist may be looking to:

1. **Cause you loss of hope:** Through isolation, negating you, destroying your faith in yourself and your opinions, taking your money.
2. **Cause you isolation and ostracisation:** This is likely to be done extremely quickly by the narcissist to start to ostracise you from your friends, family and your community.
3. **Cause you loss of belief in yourself:** Depending on how long this has been going on, the narcissist may have implanted all sorts of 'you are helpless'/'you can't work without me' belief systems. You may have been devalued, criticised and your opinions ignored. Know right now that **your opinions/beliefs are valid.** They belong to you – no one else and no one has a right to try to manipulate them.
4. **Cause you despair and desperation:** From isolating you to creating dependency on them.
5. **Cause you humiliation and shame:** From the way you look to any threats they have against you.
6. **Cause you terror and fear:** From exposing secrets to taking your home and security away from you.
7. **Causing jealousy and mistrust:** From being unfaithful to dumping you as if you never mattered.
8. **Causing you to fear for your security:** From threats to harm you to stalking and harassment.

9. **Causing your health to decline:** As a natural consequence of the above tactics, your health may decline until you defend and protect yourself.

This is a painful list to read but can be anticipated if you are leaving an abusive narcissistic relationship.

So, you need to start being ready to defend yourself against the following:

(1) How to prepare to defend against ostracisation from friends, family and community.
(2) How to prepare to defend yourself against losing your home.
(3) How to prepare to defend yourself against losing your finances/career/business.
(4) How to prepare for legal action.

How to defend yourself against ostracisation from friends, family and community using smear campaigns and false accusations

This can be particularly painful to go through. On top of the abuse, a narcissist may calmly start smear campaigns and false allegations. These are designed to punish you and hurt you further. They aim to portray the narcissist as the victim and you are likely to be accused of being the cause of this. Alternatively, the accusations may be used to provoke you, so that you have an extreme emotional reaction and appear to be emotional whilst they are calm.

When a narcissist plays the victim role, they rely on people's naturally tendency to have sympathy. This tactic is used as soon as possible after the relationship break-up to gain sympathy from anyone who listens to them – and try to quickly ostracise the victim. The provocation route could be used whilst they remain calmly spreading rumours that they are concerned about your mental wellbeing. When you have a natural emotional reaction (caused by the narcissist), people around the narcissist are prepped to see you overreacting. This is called a set-up.

Some people advise to ignore smear campaigns and false allegations and that people will 'figure out' the truth in the end. You may disagree with that approach and instead decide you will fight for justice and inform people of the truth.

210   Section 3 – Now You Have Left – The Recovery Begins

What you might observe is that you are likely to experience four types of responses to your situation:

(1) Those who believe you and support you.
(2) Those who are not really sure who to believe and ask questions.
(3) Those who do not want to get involved.
(4) Those who believe the narcissist and further spread rumours and lies about you.

This is an overview of how to handle social situations with people in these groups:

Believes you – Supports you 100%	Not really sure who to believe – asks you questions
Truth – Emotional, full story • Tell them the truth, let them help you. • If needed, ask them if they have any evidence that shows the abuse/ manipulation. • Ask them to support you. • Show true emotions to friends/trusted others. • This group is likely to include friends/ family/counsellors/therapists/abuse support/chatrooms.	**Minimum factual – Social** • Just tell them the minimum facts, in a neutral way. • May conduct their own 'trial' of you. • Will say things like they are 'Friends with you both,' 'Want to stay neutral' or 'Don't know what to think.' • May pass on information to the narcissist.

May believe you – Doesn't want to get involved/'no fire without matches' belief	Believes the narcissist – Repeats lies and false information about you
• Whilst they may believe you, they will not want to be involved and state things like 'It's none of my business,' or 'You need to sort things out yourself,' or 'I don't want to get involved.' • This group are limited in what they want to know or hear. • This group will only hear brief, factual information in an emotionless way. Response if required: e.g. 'Okay, I understand you don't want to get involved. [Domestic abuse/coercive control] is a difficult subject.'	• Ensure that you deny any lies and false information they are repeating. *You would be expected to in UK law if it ever gets that far.* • If it continues, defend yourself – this means making them personally accountable for any lies they repeat by the narcissist as defamation of character. • Keep facts to the absolute minimum if there is contact, better to have no contact. • Do not tell them what you are really planning – they cannot be trusted.

Note that the justice system (courts, solicitors, lawyers) operate from a factual perspective with evidence. They will require the factual truth, presented without too much emotion.

Section 3 – Now You Have Left – The Recovery Begins

The way the different people in your life may respond to you and either help you or not is dependent on their understanding of narcissim, availability and belief systems.

Believes you – Supports you 100%	Not really sure who to believe – asks you questions
'PROTECTS YOU – WALL OF DEFENCE' What you need from this group: • Support – emotional and practical. • Reassurance. How friends/family/therapists can best help you: • Help you maintain no contact with the narcissist. • No contact themselves – become a wall of defence around you. • Show you how to recover and protect yourself. **'KEEP IN YOUR LIFE.'**	**'QUESTIONS YOU'** How to deal with this group: • Neutral response at first. • Minimal contact/direct brief facts. • Respond with facts. How these people help you:. • They generally don't. • They may come back into your life when they realise the truth **'KEEP AWAY.'**
May Believe you – Doesn't want to get involved/'no fire without matches' belief	**Believes the narcissist – Repeats lies and false information about you**
'DOESN'T WANT TO KNOW' How to deal with this group: • Acknowledge that they do not want to get involved in difficult subjects like abuse or coercive control. **'REMOVE THEM/MINIMISE THEM FROM YOUR LIFE.'**	**'NARCISSIST ALLY'** How to deal with this group: • It is best to remove yourself entirely from this group of people as your truth is unlikely to be believed. • Do make them accountable for repeating false allegations and defamation of character if needed. **'NO CONTACT/MAKE THEM ACCOUNTABLE.'**

These are my suggestions for defending yourself, depending on the type of people you are in communication with:

1. **Friends/support network who support you 100%:** Tell them simply the truth. 'I have left xyz because of the abuse. They are likely to try to get in contact with you – please protect me by not responding.' True friends will support you and believe you when you tell them the truth. In fact, if they didn't know they may have already guessed. Ask for their help. Your friends will want to protect you. Sometimes to the point of wanting to berate the narcissist. This plays into the narcissist's hands and is definitely not advised. Ask them instead:

   a. **Not to contact the narcissist/or respond:** This is important because it will be a tactic they may try. If they do, ask them to just advise you and **not respond**. The narcissist is looking for a way to get to you and influence you/your support network. They no doubt may be crafty enough to say something like 'Could I have a confidential word ... I'm worried about ...' Or 'I am so concerned about them ... just let me know that they are safe ... Where are they?' The point is, they are likely to keep up the charming false self to elicit information about you.

2. **Friends/acquaintances who insist on keeping in contact with the narcissist:** This will be perhaps along the lines of 'I don't want to be rude,' 'I am neutral,' 'They are my friend too,' or 'I don't know what to believe.' This may all be true, but you have to find out who you can trust quickly and protect yourself. If they are not in your friends or support network, then you must protect yourself by not disclosing information.

   Protecting yourself also may mean removing them out of your life (temporarily or permanently) or minimising contact. This is imperative because the narcissist is likely to be using them to find information about what you are doing and where you are going. Just say simply to your friends/acquaintances. 'I fear you are just being manipulated to obtain information about me. You really do not know this person or the lies they tell. Unfortunately, whilst you are staying in contact with them I am afraid it is better we are no longer in contact at this time so I can better protect myself from [further abuse]. I hope that you will not disclose my personal information.'

   Said calmly (or written calmly). This is unhelpful to a narcissist – withdrawal of information through other people and the ability to punish you through them too. They eventually become 'unhelpful' to the narcissist as a source and they too may be 'discarded'.

   However, in the meantime, it can be very hard. They may repeat false

214 Section 3 – Now You Have Left – The Recovery Begins

allegations the narcissist has told them about you. They may admonish you for hurting the narcissist and they may fully support the narcissist. Remember, that *they have been manipulated too.* To respond to that you can factually state, 'I deny completely that [whatever lie was told]. Whatever lies have been told about me, the facts remain that I have had to leave to protect myself. Whilst I fear [for my safety/more lies/they may try to take my money/home/children], I will fully defend myself from any defamation of character, lies or further attempts to [xyx]. Are you prepared to [put in writing/share what you've told me] and protect me by not sharing information?'

This is a shock tactic that means that they are being asked to 'be accountable':

a.   You are now making the person repeating the gossip/lies accountable for what they say. This means if they continue to repeat lies, you can minimise harm to yourself by not being in contact. Harsh, but necessary to protect yourself. It also makes them aware of the seriousness of the matter.

b.   After this, people tend to either want facts to conduct a 'trial by themselves' about you; back down and stop repeating lies; are shocked into supporting you (although, you may not be able to fully trust them at this point) or will firmly stop contacting you and go back to the narcissist.

Because you have mentioned the lies and actions you will take to protect yourself – friends, acquaintances may start to look for lies from the narcissist and take more care in what they say.

The narcissist always slips up with their lies at some point – but this takes time.

3.   **Community/neighbours:** Whilst this is very difficult because people simply do not understand abuse – speak up and speak out. Keep talking. Silence allows their lies to grow and can cause ostracisation. The sooner you are brave enough to speak out the better because a narcissist will quickly use charm and may well put out false information about you or outright lies to harm you. It is imperative that you calmly state the facts without giving any details where you can, because a narcissist can then start suggesting you are 'emotional' or conversely ask neighbours to 'watch for you because I am worried about them' and may try to illicit information. I suggest that you use something like this:

a.   'I had to leave them. They were so nice in public and so charming and believable when telling lies. Thankfully I am away safely. They had said they would watch me and get information about me through the neighbours, so I am asking for people to just watch out for me please.'

b.   'I will have to get a good lawyer who knows about abuse and coercive control – do you know one?'

How to defend against losing your home

This is where you may need to use the non-molestation order or possession order in Chapter 29. Here is where you get someone to help you:

a.   **National Centre for Domestic Violence** – 0800 970 2070 or www.ncdc.org.uk

Make sure you have evidence of any agreements you made between you. A narcissist is more than likely going to assume that they are entitled to your money, possessions, or home. You will have to prove that there was any agreement or arrangement (e.g. emails, texts, receipts, house deeds or rental agreement).

How to defend yourself against losing your finances/career/business – Urgent

A narcissist can destroy everything – including taking your business, your career, your finances. To defend yourself against this, you will need evidence as proof that you are entitled to your business, or financial arrangements. You may need to consider:

1.   **All verbal and/or written agreements.**
2.   **Print out all relevant emails proving agreements.**
3.   **If none of these exist, write down your understanding of the agreement**, sign it, make a copy of it and give it to someone who can keep the information safe. You may need it later.
4.   **If you have not protected your trademarks, business website passwords or any legal aspects**, do this right away. A narcissist may go straight for it.
5.   **For joint bank accounts, assume money could go unless you do something:** Set up your own bank account and be responsible only for what you are responsible for. Alternatively, you can cancel the mandate and freeze the joint account. If agreement cannot be reached between how the money is split, the bank account will be

216   Section 3 – Now You Have Left – The Recovery Begins

frozen (so you cannot use it at all) until a court decides who gets what. Assume responsibility and make sure any joint payments – such as rent, mortgages are still paid until sorted out legally. Ask for a payment holiday for mortgages if you need some time.

6. **Wills:** Write/phone immediately and advise that you want to revoke all previous wills because you are out of an abusive relationship. Ask them how you can update it. Simple wills could be done online. You will have to have it independently witnessed by two people.

7. **Pensions:** Get in contact with any pension providers and ask that any joint pensions are suspended until you gain legal agreement. Ask how they can help with an abusive relationship.

8. **Bank account passwords:** Change them right away.

9. **Savings accounts passwords:** Change them right away.

10. **Cancel/put on hold credit and debit cards and ask for a replacement to be forward to a safe address:** The banks may not allow you to do this, but advise them you are in an abusive relationship so that they can put a record of this on the account and see what they can do.

11. **Put a record option by your telephone:** E.g. a narcissist who finds out that your money is being moved, closed or out of reach could threaten you. Record any threats as evidence.

12. **How can debts be run up against you:** Think about anywhere where debts could be run up against you and affect your credit rating. Resolve it. Contact CIFAS for Protrective Registration.

13. **Insurance:** Is your life insured? The house? Business interruption? Keep insurance going. If there is an insurance policy on your life, ask the company what you could do. Depending on their policies, they may flag the account if they consider there is any malicious intent and your conversation will be recorded.

How to prepare for legal action

Do not be surprised if a narcissist very quickly sends legal documentation and threats. Stay calm.

1. **Get legal help:** Speak to Refuge or Woman's Aid and advise them if you feel anxious or threatened. They can be contacted on 0808 2000 24 to help guide you or Men's Advice Line on 0808 801 0327.

2. **Forensic accounting:** If you are dealing with large sums of money you may need to consider enlisting the help of forensic accountant. Assume that any money may start to be moved around.

3. **Legal responses:** In any legal responses, your solicitor may well ask

for 'full disclosure' of all funds and accounts. A narcissist may not want to disclose everything and may hide accounts – so have details of what they are if you can.

The other important aspect is to understand what evidence is and is not.

It is not enough to be just innocent, to be mute, not to defend yourself with the truth.

Narcissists could make compelling and believable lies and stories up. The only way to defend yourself is with evidence and facts.

Evidence of Facts are not assumptions of Facts:

Let me give you an example. Consider a receipt which shows a transaction on a date and is from the narcissist's credit card (or joint account) showing two meals at an expensive restaurant. It is the same night that they told you they were elsewhere. It does not prove and give evidence that they were being unfaithful. However, a diary note from you which shows who they said they were with that night (or an email from them), along with the receipt AND a snapshot showing your narcissist kissing someone else from a private detective would be factual evidence.

Facts will simply, quietly and forcefully say 'this is the truth'.

Knowing how solicitors/courts work:

Getting the right support with a solicitor and how to go to court is crucial. I therefore completely recommend using professionals specialising in narcissistic abuse who can guide you through the process.

Chapter 34 – Validate Yourself

Validation of what you have gone through is an imperative part of the recovery process. Because you may well have had to minimise the extent of the abuse that you have gone through – it is important to hear other people's thoughts on what you have been through and for your abuse to be understood. You need to be heard, listened to and your feelings validated.

This is where support forums, books and self-help books like this one can help you put the abuse in context. It is almost a relief when someone says, 'You have been through a terrible time.'

Abuse support helplines will also be able to validate what you have been through.

One word of warning, however, is that friends and family may find it difficult hearing about your emotional pain and suffering. It is therefore critical to increase the number of people who can help your validation. My recommendation would be to use professional psychological practitioners and helplines to really get the emotional support you need. This ensures your important friends and family aren't the only people supporting you.

Keep talking – but validate yourself with the right group of people

Within your network of people around you, my suggestion would be to minimise talk of the abuse to acquaintances and new groups (and work):

Validate Yourself with the Right Group of People		
Friends and Family can Validate you	Professional Help/ Narcissistic Abuse Survivors to Validate you	Acquaintances/Others
Friends and family may be there to support you, but they cannot always help with some of the professional support you may need.	Use the professional help (psychologists) and Narcissistic Abuse recovery groups to help you work through difficult emotions.	Talk with caution acquaintances or others that may not have not experienced abuse and may not know how to respond.
✓	✓✓	?

Phase 2 – What Went Wrong?

Chapter 35 – The Search for Meaning and Courage to Change Yourself

When you first leave a narcissistic relationship – and for some time afterwards – you may find yourself asking questions like:

(1)   Where did I go wrong?
(2)   Why didn't I see that coming?
(3)   What is wrong with me?
(4)   Why can't I just get over this?
(5)   Why did I have to go through this?
(6)   What did I do to deserve that?
(7)   How could it end like this?

All of these questions (and more) are completely valid. **The answer is very simple – you did nothing wrong, it's almost impossible to spot a narcissist, there is nothing wrong with you, it will take time to get over something that horrific, it wasn't fair or nice and you did not deserve this.**

> I can say this again.
> And again.
> And again.

Does that make your feel better? Can you suddenly get up, say that's alright then and carry on as if nothing ever happened? Probably not.
What happened to you may have completely shattered your world.

Shattered your world completely,
Took away all your hopes and dreams,
Took away your trust and faith,
Hurt you more than you could ever know was possible.

Let me say:

I hear you,
I am so sorry you went through what you did,
It was horrific, but I know
One day this will be behind you, and you can be yourself again.

With my own journey, I understood my experience was horrific from a logical mindset and knew it wasn't fair or deserved, but I spent months and years asking myself **what went wrong**?

I looked at blaming myself. I looked at spiritual meanings. I looked at logical reasonings. It all came back to only one thing:

I had to change the way I was.
I had the power to do that.
I was willing to do that.
I did it.

I will share that with you. It simply means that instead of looking outside of yourself for an answer you have to start inside. Those are the parts of you experiencing all the emotional (and physical) pain that you perhaps would rather avoid, numb or pretend aren't there.

What I hope to give you are options of resources available to you and the courage to go inside and change yourself. This does not mean that you are in any way 'bad', in fact the very reason you attracted a narcissist in the first place was probably that you have some of these nicest human qualities:

(1) Kindness
(2) Honesty
(3) Selflessness
(4) Empathic
(5) Generous
(6) Strong-willed/confident
(7) Good at what you do
(8) Give more than you receive
(9) Really care when someone is hurting
(10) High levels of trust
(11) Tolerant
(12) Loyal
(13) Responsible
(14) Emotionally mature
(15) You believe the best in people/bad people don't exist

How you decide to make any changes is entirely up to you. Professional help is advised. For me, as one example, I believed 'I trusted people until proven otherwise'. Now I would 'trust people only when they demonstrate I can'. This is a subtle shift in belief systems that means the onus is now on another person to show by actions that I can trust them. Say what they mean and do what they say. I had to shift from *overly trusting to trusting by discernment and actions.*

The only way forward is the courage to change yourself.

If you don't change yourself, you can go round and round in Phase 2 wanting to understand what went wrong from a logical perspective and spending weeks, months or even years possibly becoming hurt, feeling victimised and in emotional pain. I don't want that for anyone, so I hope when you are ready, you will move onto Phase 3 – getting the help you need and a support network.

Phase 3 – The Help You Need And Getting Your Support Network In Place

Getting the help you need and your support network in place is imperative on your recovery journey. Without it there is a risk that you stay perpetually in Phase 2.

Chapter 36 – Your Support Network

When putting together your support network, you need to establish a team of people who can help you get over the abuse.

Here is the start of a list to help you establish your support network. Don't worry if it is not very big when you first leave an abusive relationship – even if you just have yourself, you will see below there are teams of people that can help you. You support network will also grow over time.

Your Support Network 223

Type of support needed	How they will help	Who can support you
People who understand abusive relationships.	Validation of what you have gone through, emotional and practical support.	**National Centre for Domestic Violence** – 0800 970 2070 or www.ncdc.org.uk **Refuge** – www.refuge.org.uk **National Domestic Abuse Helpline:** 0808 2000 247 **Other Resources** www.domesticabusecommissioner .uk
People who can support you emotionally 24/7.	Getting you through your feelings in a non-judgemental way twenty-four hours a day seven days a week.	**Samaritans – call 116 123** from any phone
Non-molestation and possession orders and injunctions.	See Chapter 29 of what is involved, what happens when you go to court (FL 401).	**National Centre for Domestic Violence** – 0800 970 2070 or www.ncdc.org.uk
For women.	Woman who can help you with housing, safety planning and dealing with domestic abuse.	**Woman's Aid** – Online at www.womansaid.org.uk
For men.	Advice for men going through domestic abuse.	**Mankind Initiative** Online https://www.mankind.org.uk
Alcohol and drug dependencies.	If you need help with addictions.	**The AA:** 0800 9177650. **Rehab for addiction:** 0800 140 4690
Emergencies for physical harm.	Treat threats and physical harm seriosly.	**Police:** 101 to make a statement and 999 in an emergency. If you can't speak press 55.
Friends you can trust.	Those who are 100% behind you and support you.	My trusted friends are:
Therapists/treatments.	Those who can help you get through the overwhelming emotions.	My therapist(s) are:

Chapter 37 – Therapy/Treatment Types

I tried many different therapies and treatments when trying to recover – which took several years. Some methods were much faster and less painful than others. The one thing that effective treatments had was the ability to tap into the **unconscious mind** and deal with the painful emotions.

These are the methods I and others tried and what worked well. Choose whatevere support you need. Recommendations may not be suitable for your needs, so always consult a qualified medical professional or go through reputable counselling organisations, such as:

- BACP – www.bacp.co.uk
- UKCP – www.psychotherapy.org.uk
- Counselling Directory – www. counselling-directory.org.uk

Therapy/Treatment Types **225**

Therapy/treatment type	What I loved/didn't like about it	Results (for me)	Cost*
Traditional: Relationship/couple counselling – Talk based therapy UK help: www.professionalstandards.org.uk	• The counsellor that was chosen was not a narcissistic abuse specialist, was not registered under the Professional Standards Authority (professionalstandards.org.uk) • Counselling was done as a couple. • The therapist was not aware that I felt manipulated and coached on my responses.	• The therapist chosen did not recognise a narcissist and focussed on communication skills/love language/communication colours. • Would have been effective for a 'normal' relationship, but not suitable for narcissistic abuse. • Preferred 1:2:1 counselling.	££
Traditional: Talking therapies/counselling – Cognitive behavioural therapy (CBT) One-to-one sessions, group sessions or free through IAPT on the NHS.	• These therapies encourage you to 'talk' about your situation, break problems down into smaller parts and is structured to guide you to come to your own conclusions. • Could sometimes bring up painful emotions.	• One-to-one sessions effective. • Required commitment to regular weekly sessions.	£££ for one-to-one

226 Section 3 – Now You Have Left – The Recovery Begins

Therapy/treatment type	What I loved/didn't like about it	Results (for me)	Cost*
Traditional: Psychotherapy for (trauma specialists only) EMDR – Eye movement desensitisation and reprocessing. Search on UKCP websites – www.psychotherapy.org.uk.	• Guided meditations and breathing techniques where you visualise distressing memories and use eye movements to desensitise the emotions.	• Relatively effective with a skilled practitioner.	££
Alternative: NLP trauma process, rewind technique, visual kinaesthetic dissociation (V-KD) – visualisation/hypnotherapy.	• Excellent deep relaxation technique which helps reprogramme the original distressing moment(s). • Guided visualisation process of 'going back' in time in your memory to the painful emotions and then reframing what happened (e.g. being able to disassociate from the memory or change the outcome). • Done well means you do not even have to state what happened. • Before a treatment you may feel distressed, afterwards you feel uplifted.	• Very fast and effective. • No need to state what happened.	££

Therapy/Treatment Types 227

Therapy/treatment type	What I loved/didn't like about it	Results (for me)	Cost*
Alternative: Book and CD Healing Trauma © 2008 Peter A Levine, published by Sounds True Inc. (stress consultant for NASA)	• Uses body awareness and the body as a tool in resolving trauma. Using a twelve-stage healing trauma programme. • Shows you how to locate the emotions in your body as a physical sensation. • Excellent methods for settling yourself with self-soothing poses.	• Effective at getting feeling back into your body, sensations, observing posture and settling yourself.	£
Alternative:: Holographic kinetics.	• Alternative Aboriginal-based healing which looks at the body holistically and targets the causes that are creating the traumatic/emotional effects in the body. Works with 'cellular memories' that store trauma and releases them.	• Extremely fast and effective. Works on a subconscious level, which may not be suitable for some people.	££
Alternative: Quanta Freedom – Melanie Tonia Evans.	• Developed the NARP (Narcissistic Abuse Recovery Programme). Uses a set of visualisation audio recordings to help identify emotions in the body, find the original trauma and release them.	• Extremely effective. • Modules allow you to access the meditations at any time.	££

228 Section 3 – Now You Have Left – The Recovery Begins

Therapy/treatment type	What I loved/didn't like about it	Results (for me)	Cost*
Practical/Alternative: Practical Narcissistic Abuse Intensive Recovery Programme. www.i-recovered.co.uk	• UK-based training course based on this book. A practical online course available 24/7 to help you with practical UK advice visualisations. • Free or paid version at I-recovered.co.uk	• Very effective. • Using practical examples. • Visualisations.	££

*£ lower cost; ££ medium cost; £££ higher costs

Please choose whichever route you feel comfortable with and take professional advice. Start getting treatments straight away to relieve any immediate overwhelming feelings and emotional pain.

The treatments that worked the best for me all have one thing in common – *emotions held within the body.* This is not as farfetched as some might imagine as we do this on a daily basis but may not consciously recognise it. We have common sayings such as 'gut feeling', 'it was in the back of my mind', 'it was heart-wrenching'. These are all emotions that you feel in your body – sometimes very strongly.

Therapy/Treatment Types **229**

Try this – Emotions held in your body

I would like you to imagine that you have just been shopping. You are in a queue and people are behind you. You have had to wait to be served and you have to be back home shortly.

As you go to pay for your item, you suddenly realise that you have no means to pay for the goods. The cashier looks at you expectantly, as do the people waiting in the queue.

What emotion(s) do you feel? Where do you feel it in your body?

_____

_____

You suddenly find your payment card and can now purchase the goods.

What happens to your body? How do the feelings in your body change?

_____

_____

_____

The concept therefore is that if you can feel emotions in your body – just by thinking about things – you can also release stored emotions from your body. As such you can also release traumatic feelings/emotions and change them from negative experiences to neutral experience.

The way you answer questions to yourself will also tell you a lot about what you might need to reflect on emotionally. For example, ask yourself 'Why am I jealous?' There are several ways that this could be answered:

Always seek professional advice.

230 Section 3 – Now You Have Left – The Recovery Begins

Question – Why do I feel jealousy?	How you answer this question	Insights
Types of response – a verb	If your answer included verbs as a description about someone else, such as: Should Must Can't Typically, this might be because they should not do that to me!	You are trying to control something out of your control, which will always frustrate you. You cannot be responsible for how people act or respond; the only thing you can be responsible for is your own thoughts, actions and reactions. With a should, must or can't answer it shows your *values and beliefs* and that your partner is not aligned to them.
Type of response – I am ...	Because I am ... For example ... hurt, rejected	You need to then ask the question of why you are hurt or why you are rejected. This is likely to come down to an unconscious belief.
Types of response – It is	Because it is ... ... Disrespectful, unkind, unfair	This type of response means that you know your values. And these values have been broken. In this case – respect, kindness and being fair.

Question – Why do I feel jealousy?	How you answer this question	Insights
Types of response – Expectations	Because I ... Expected better of xyz	This type of response means that you have unmet expectations, which have caused disappointment or hurt for example. In this example you are 'expecting' someone to think and act the same way, e.g. with integrity, with the expectation that your partner has the same values and beliefs as you. Look back at Section 2 on this.

Healing Trauma – The twelve-phase Healing Trauma programme – *Healing Trauma* © 2008 Peter Levine, published by Sounds True Inc.

An alternative route to releasing traumatic emotions stored in the body has been developed by Dr Peter A Levine who has written a pioneering twelve-phase programme for restoring the wisdom of your body in a book called *Healing Trauma*. He has a PhD in medical and biological physics. He holds a doctorate in psychology and has over forty-five years in studying stress and trauma. He has also been a consultant to NASA. The basis of the twelve-step programme helps identify emotions in the body along with effective methods of self-comforting.

What I love is a series of self-comforting postures, which really do help settle yourself. The one that gives me immediate relief is putting one hand on my heart area (the place you would naturally hold when you have had a fright) and the other hand on your solar plexus area (the place you would naturally put your hand as a sign of relief). Both together are very powerful.

Boundaries – Abuse Circles

Boundaries are extremely important in the recovery process after abuse, particularly because your boundaries will more than likely have been violated. This means that you might need to build them up again and learn to enforce them.

I would like you to draw two circles in the box below. One relates to you and the other to the person you have just come out of the abusive relationship from.

> Boundaries – Now

Now that you have done that. Take a look at how far they are apart, where they are in relation to one another, if one is larger or smaller than the other, if they overlap in any way.

> Boundaries – How you want them to be

How does this differ? Why?

Take a look at the following example of boundary circles before and after recovery from abuse:

Boundary Circle – Examples Before and After Abuse	
In this example the black dot (the victim) is a small and completely surrounded by the grey eclipse (the narcissist).	In the after the abuse example, the grey eclipse (the narcissist) is no-where in the picture. The black dot (the victim) has grown in size

A victim may feed surrounded and engulfed by the relationship.	This is likely to represent the victim being more empowered on their own.

Boundaries – Defining your personal space

This is another visual representation to remind you of your personal space and boundaries.

Get a long piece of string.

Sit in a chair in the middle of a room. Now imagine someone you like. The string represents your boundaries, your personal space. In that space no one can come into that space without your explicit permission.

Where in your imagination is a comfortable boundary for this person?

Now consider the narcissist. Where is your boundary now? Where would you like it to be.

Physically move the string if you need to, to represent where you are comfortable.

This is an exercise that your therapist may explore with you. It can be helpful recognising if anyone is overstepping their boundaries with you. Whilst it is helpful, it is also your responsibility to enforce your own boundaries. This can take some time and work with a therapist.

Early anger displacement

You may also find that along with other strong emotions, you experience bouts of anger after leaving an abusive relationship. It is normal to feel anger and a natural expression of hurt. There is no shame in feeling anger, it does need to be recognised and expressed.

Forgive yourself if this happens, after the powerlessness of an abusive relationship and not speaking out, this can happen. Spend some time asking yourself why you felt so angry and what triggered it.

Rather than stewing about it, trying to suppress anger, work out what you can do constructively – what is in your power to change. Can you take time out? Can you be assertive of your needs without getting angry? Can you count to ten before responding? Note down how you want to respond next time.

One way to stop anger building up and express anger constructively is finding an outlet. Sport can be excellent (kick boxing for example), punching pillows or even listening and jumping around the room to heavy rock music – whatever allows you to get those angry feelings out in a constructive way after the event.

Specialist professional support – Trauma

Once you have found a therapist you can trust – I suggest one that is trained in trauma, PTSD and abuse – you also have to make sure that you get along together and can trust one another. You do have to be aware that they also have a code of conduct which means that if they suspect there is a risk of harm (including to yourself), they have a duty of care to report the matter. They will explain this when you begin your treatment.

One method that a psychologist might suggest to open up about some of the things that happened without going into detail is to 'hypothetically' discuss what might have happened. Also using the regression V-KD techniques without you needing to explain the trauma out loud. This method can help you gain trust with your therapist, whilst getting the support you need.

Be selective about your therapist. Look for one that understands trauma, can quickly understand the problem and for most of the time allow you to walk out of the therapy session feeling relieved or knowing how to improve in some way. If you don't think things are progressing fast enough or you are left emotionally raw – find another therapist.

Controlling your environment

Another aspect of recovering from abuse is the ability to control your own environment. Dependent on the level of control you have experienced in your relationship, you may have to re-learn how you prefer things.

For example, how might you like your drinks? Your environment? How tidy is your home? Where do you prefer to keep things? All these things, dependent on the level of abuse experienced, can take time and give you a sense of empowerment back.

Soothing yourself in moments of distress – Breathing and hand reflexology

Another option that could work for you is a mini hand reflexology treatment.

When you consider the automatic reactions you have to stress – wringing your hands – you automatically reach for the palm of your hands to sooth yourself. This series of movements will help to calm you down and is helpful when you are going into a stressful situation (e.g. before interviews).

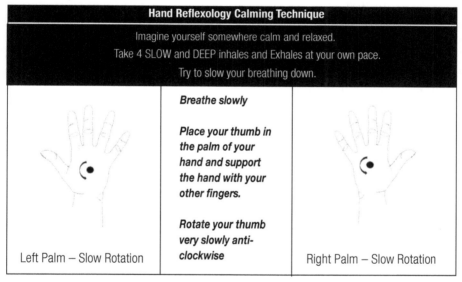

Hand Reflexology Calming Technique		
Imagine yourself somewhere calm and relaxed. Take 4 SLOW and DEEP inhales and Exhales at your own pace. Try to slow your breathing down.		
Left Palm – Slow Rotation	**Breathe slowly** **Place your thumb in the palm of your hand and support the hand with your other fingers.** **Rotate your thumb very slowly anti-clockwise**	Right Palm – Slow Rotation

Soothing yourself in moments of distress – Visualisation for acute emotional stress

The following visualisation is similar to that used by psychologists. I would suggest that you ask your therapist to help you. If, however, you are in immediate emotional distress, this visualisation may help, along with other resources mentioned.

Note of caution: This visualisation will only work if you are able to think about a trusted friend or family member – someone stable, logical, warm and loving. If this is not possible, please do not go any further and seek professional therapist help instead.

I would recommend that you record your own voice first and play it back

236 Section 3 – Now You Have Left – The Recovery Begins

(or get someone soothing to read it to you) so that you can concentrate on the visualisation.

Before you start I want you to imagine a place where you feel safe and relaxed, maybe outside near a natural stream in a green space, perhaps by a warm glowing fire. This is your safe space in your mind.

What to do	Record yourself saying this
Find yourself a quiet place to sit with no distractions.	Sit back, make yourself comfortable and relax. I am going to take the immediate emotional distress away.
Take a deep breath through your nose into your stomach, expanding your lungs and breathing out of your mouth. As you breath in and out try to regulate the speed of your breathing – aiming to breath until the breath is the same amount of time on both the inhale and the exhale.	Take some deep breaths.Count slowly 1, 2, 3 in through your nose. Count slowly 1, 2, 3 out though your mouth. Fill your stomach and lungs up with air and relax into your natural breathing rhythm.
Sit breathing until breathing is calm.	Continue to breathe in slowly and out slowly. In and out. In and out. In and out.
Close your eyes. Keep breathing rhythmically.	Now I want you to close your eyes and think about a place that makes you happy and smile. Perhaps in a green field with flowing water with streaming sunlight and fluffy white clouds crossing a brilliant blue sky.You are now in your happy space, feeling calm relaxed and safe. Breathe in and out. In and out. In and out.

What to do	Record yourself saying this
Go to your imagination.	Into your happy safe place walks in someone you love and who can protect you. You smile at each other in acknowledgement.
	Your protective loved one sees that you have come to your happy space because of something that has caused you distress. They want you to tell them what has happened so that they can help you. This might be your adult self if you see yourself as a child, or someone you know always protected and loved you.
	Describe the scene to your protective loved one – where are you?
	Who is there at this time?
	What is happening?
	What emotions are you feeling?
	Where in your body are you feeling those emotions?
	What were you thinking?
	What did you say?
	What did the other person say and do?
	How did that make you feel?
	How did the incident end?
	Now your protective loved one is coming back into the scene with you to protect you.
	What do you say or do differently now that they are there?
	What does your protective loved one do or say?
	How does that make you feel now?
	What do you want to say to the other person now?
	You walk away from the scene knowing that the situation ended with you being protected. You are going to go back to your safe space now with your protective loved one.
	Once you are back in your safe space, you know that the memory has changed to a positive one, and it is time for you to go home.

238   Section 3 – Now You Have Left – The Recovery Begins

What to do	Record yourself saying this
Open your eyes.	As you walk back, you start to feel yourself back in the room. You can feel your toes. You wiggle your hands, stretch a little and now you are back in the room. Open your eyes.
Take a moment to be fully present.	Sit for a moment.

Questions to ask yourself

How are you feeling about this incident now?

Thinking about your body, are you still feeling any tension and if so where?

If you are still feeling acute emotional distress, I suggest that you speak to someone straight away to comfort you – friends, family, therapist.

NLP V-KD, rewind hypnotherapy techniques, holographic kinetics and quanta freedom healing

If you are open to other alternative treatment methods, the quickest and least emotionally painful ways I found for long-term emotional relief was through NLP V-KD, rewind hypnotherapy techniques, quanta freedom healing or holographic kinetics. These alternative approaches may not be suitable for everyone, but worked quickly and brought fast, long-term emotional relief for me. These treatments look at how emotions are stored in the body and how these can be quickly re-programmed.

No boundaries to loving myself – Question to yourself

This is another visualisation, which I found useful to reconnect to my own needs. Take a piece of paper and ask yourself the following question:

'If there was no restrictions on my time, money or where I can go, I would like to totally honour and love myself today by ...'

Therapy/Treatment Types **239**

And see what you write.

This often would give me some insights about what I really wanted to do. Whilst it may not all be possible right away, it often gave me ideas such as pampering myself, going for a walk or nourishing myself in some way, and importantly made me smile.

Keeping a check on your painful emotional triggers/shadow emotional side

During the recovery process you might experience a lot of strong negative emotions and also have painful emotional triggers. These are your conscious mind's way of saying 'Listen to me,' and 'I need to be validated.'

When these moments happen, it is an opportunity to acknowledge the deep feelings, soothe them and finally let go of them through suitable psychological techniques. You do not have to continue to suffer flashbacks or extreme fears – there are excellent methods to 'erase' the painful connections, so that any similar experiences do not jettison you unconsciously into fight or flight mode.

An example of this might be if someone was screamed at/physically punished for accidentally dropping and breaking a dinner plate in an abusive relationship. Even after leaving the abusive relationship, there may be an unconscious association in the memory of extreme fear when a plate is accidentally dropped or broken. It is a 'trigger' and survival mechanism for the body and memory. The mind has 'programmed' itself to alert the body to danger and decided that dropping a plate will equate to extreme emotional and even physical punishment, so the body and mind automatically can 'freeze' or 'run'. This emotional 'trigger' in the present can continue for some time after an abusive relationship until it is addressed professionally.

These 'triggers' and the frightening feelings associated with them may resurface in safe environments – for example if a victim accidentally breaks a plate in their own home, it can send a victim into a terrifying 'fight or flight mode'. When these triggers occur, it is important to recognise what is happening, make a note and with good psychotherapist support (such as rewind techniques, trauma recovery techniques, NLP V-KD), you are able to re-train your brain to replace the fear response with no reaction.

To do this you may have to delve further into your unconscious mind.

What made sense to me (and perhaps to you) is the Carl Jung personality theory, which had three main aspects, the ego, personal unconscious and collective unconscious. The conscious mind is only a small proportion of the levels of consciousness, with the **overwhelming majority** in the unconscious mind. If the reactions are coming from the unconscious mind, you cannot **think your way out** of some of these triggers:

Ego	Conscious mind	Thoughts, memories and emotions people are **aware of.**
Personal unconscious	Unconscious mind	Quite close to the surface of the conscious mind. **People are not aware of.** Temporarily forgotten information and repressed memories. Less concerned with repressed childhood memories. About present and future.
Collective unconscious	Unconscious mind	This aspect had latent memories from ancestral and evolutionary past. **People are not aware of.** The human mind has innate characteristics 'imprinted' on it as a result of evolution.

Source: https://www.simplypsychology.org/carl-jung.html

If the majority of our memories come from our unconscious mind, it makes sense that the *unconscious thoughts, feelings and emotions are what need to be consciously observed and our response to them changed.*

With various psychotherapy or the other treatments mentioned above, you can de-sensitise these strong emotions. Some of the reasons you might be reacting can be *unconscious* and may well be related to something that has happened in your past as well as reactions to the abuse.

Keeping a check on those emotions and de-sensitising them will help over time.

Therapy/Treatment Types 241

This is a list of some of the negative emotions a victim may be experiencing.

Victims may feel		Keeping a check on your emotions – How strongly do your feel these emotions, where 0 = Not at all; 10 = Feeling it very strongly							
		Monday	Tuesday	Wednesday	Thursday	Friday	Saturday	Sunday	What was happening/why?
Terror and fear	Afraid								
	Horrified								
	Panicky								
	Terrified								
	Worried								
	Intimidated								
	Paralysed								
	Unsafe								
	Nervous								
	Other ...								
Confusion	Shocked								
	Trapped								
	Disturbed								
	Unsettled								
	Other ...								
Hurt	Abused								
	Degraded								
	In pain								
	Devastated								
	Tortured								
	Ridiculed								
	Punished								
	Other ...								
Loss of others	Alienated								
	Ostracised								
	Abandoned								
	Loneliness								
	Isolated								
	Other ...								
Hope	Hopelessness								
	Despair								
	Defeated								
	Destroyed								
	Dejected								
	Depressed								
	Other ...								

Always seek professional psychotherapy.

242   Section 3 – Now You Have Left – The Recovery Begins

Victims may feel		Keeping a check on your emotions – How strongly do your feel these emotions, where 0 = Not at all; 10 = Feeling it very strongly							
		Monday	Tuesday	Wednesday	Thursday	Friday	Saturday	Sunday	What was happening/why?
Loss of trust in self	Incapable								
	Hopeless								
	Powerlessness								
	Helpless								
	Valueless								
	Worthless								
	Weak								
	Insecure								
	Self-Pity								
	Self-Loathing								
	Incompetent								
	Vulnerable								
	Others …								
Shame	Humiliated								
	Embarrassed								
	Degraded								
	Ashamed								
	Other …								
Contempt	Disgust								
	Hatred								
	Resentment								
	Rage/Fury								
	Bitterness								
	Other …								
Sadness	Grief								
	Sorrow								
	Envious								
	Guilty								
	Other …								
Love of love	Jealousy								
	Humiliated								
	Discarded								
	Rejected								
	Other …								
Hypersensitive	Hysterical								
	Paranoia								
	Tearful								
	Vigilant								
	Petrified								
	Other …								

Always seek professional psychotherapy.

Which emotions have the highest ratings? These are the emotions that you need to work on.

I suggest you do a positive visualisation to help ease any raw emotions or talk to your therapist to work through how else you can help yourself.

My top four ways of dealing with painful emotions were:

1. **Traditional methods: NLP/psychotherapy:** Well-trained trauma psychologists who use cognitive behavioural therapy, NLP V-KD and EMDR – eye movement desensitisation and reprocessing – are extremely effective at results.

   What is amazing about some of the techniques used is that they allow you to go back to the painful experiences and 're-frame' them in your mind. It de-sensitises the memory, so that you are no longer experiencing painful emotional triggers.

2. **Practical/alternative methods: The UK Narcissistic Abuse Intensive Recovery Programme Course:** Using practical advice and visualisations to help speed up recovery after abuse.

3. **Alternative methods: rewind technique visualisations:** These are techniques to 'reframe' what has happened in the past – with no need to share what you experienced with the practitioner. Fast and effective.

4. **Alternative methods: Holographic kinetics/NARP:** Holographic kinetics is an Aboriginal-based treatment which I found worked swiftly to find emotions held in the body, eliminate the original cause of any emotional pain and release the emotional pain. It was a same-day treatment to get immediate relief from emotions.

   In the UK you can access a narcissistic abuse and trauma release programme from Melanie Tonia Evans. She has developed a healing process based on similar healing methods, which she calls a 'Thriver' movement. She has also developed an online support forum. The benefit of this is that you can do the emotional work the moment you need it. There is no need to wait for an appointment. Whilst Melanie is based in Australia, her training can be downloaded and used as and when you need it the UK. Again, this approach works swiftly and almost instantly and gives long lasting relief.

244 Section 3 – Now You Have Left – The Recovery Begins

Emotional reduction visualisation with your guardian angel

For this exercise you will need some quiet time alone. Somewhere you can peacefully write down your needs today.

Take a deep breath into your stomach through your nose, expanding your lungs and breathing out of your mouth. As you breath in and out try to regulate the speed of your breathing - aiming to breath until the breath is the same amount of time on both the inhale and the exhale.

What to do	Record yourself saying this
Find yourself a quiet place to sit with no distractions.	Sit back, make yourself comfortable and relax. We are going to ask your guardian angel to take the immediate emotional distress away.
Take a deep breath through your nose into your stomach, expanding your lungs and breathing out of your mouth. As you breath in and out try to regulate the speed of your breathing – aiming to breath until the breath is the same amount of time on both the inhale and the exhale.	Take some deep breaths as we tap into your unconscious mind. Count slowly 1, 2, 3 in through your nose. Count slowly 1, 2, 3 out though your mouth. Feel the air filling your stomach and lungs and relax into your natural breathing rhythm. Breathe in, breathe out. Breathe in, breathe out.
Sit breathing until breathing is calm.	Breathe in, breathe out. Breathe in, breathe out.
Give yourself permission to go deeper into your subconscious.	Now we are going to go a little deeper into your subconscious to meet your guardian angel.
Close your eyes Keep breathing rhythmically.	Now I want you to close your eyes and think about a special place that makes you happy and smile. Perhaps in a green field with flowing water. Maybe there is sunlight and fluffy white clouds crossing a brilliant blue sky. It's your special place. The place you feel relaxed and safe. You are there now.

Therapy/Treatment Types 245

What to do	Record yourself saying this
Your guardian angel joins you.	Your guardian angel now comes into your special place to talk to you.
Your guardian angel asks you.	'What is the emotion that you are feeling the strongest today that you would like me to take away?'
	'It is [emotion].'
Your guardian angel asks you.	And where do you feel that?
You.	You consider what the guardian angel is saying.
Your guardian angel asks you.	What does it look like?
	Breathing in. Breathing out.
	Breathing in. Breathing out.
Your guardian angel asks you.	Are you willing to let that emotion be gone?
You reply.	Yes.
You observe	The guardian angel walks over to you and takes the emotion out of your body.
Your guardian angel says.	'I am taking this emotion out of your body, out of your ego, out of your personal and collective conscious. 'I am going to take it away and transmute those emotions back to love.'
You.	You watch as the guardian angel takes the emotions away and fills you up with lighter feelings of love and light. There your guardian angel goes taking it away and away and replacing it with love and light. As you allow those emotions to flow away and be replaced you say to your guardian angel.
You say.	'Thank you for your divine help and for protecting and guiding me to my highest good and for transmuting these negative emotions.'
Your guardian angel.	Your guardian angel smiles and sends loving looks to you. Fills you again with love and light and then starts to walk away.

What to do	Record yourself saying this
You.	You are now still in your happy place, but you know that it is time now to come back into the room you are in.
	You start to walk back.
	As you walk back, you realise that you feel lighter and the emotions you were feeling a moment ago have been reduced.
Reconnect to the room.	We are gently going to come back into the room you are in.
	Starting to feel your toes.
	Your body.
	Connected back into the room.
	A deep breathe in and out. And become aware of the room.
	Open your eyes again, feel the ground beneath you and realise you are back in the room and you are here connected. Wait for a moment to be fully present in the room, but know now you are back and those painful emotions have been reduced.

Phase 4 – I'm Ready to Speak Up and Defend Myself

After you have spent time on Phase 3, getting some of the intense emotions down to more manageable levels, you can then start to speak up for yourself and also be heard and listened to.

This requires you to be able to speak up and defend yourself:

(1)   Constructively
(2)   Clearly
(3)   Calmly

The three Cs. If your communication is not done calmly, clearly and constructively it may be difficult for people to hear what you are trying to say and also help you.

Chapter 38 – Speaking up – Finding your voice

The ability to speak up for yourself and find your own voice becomes important if you need to defend yourself, particularly against an articulate narcissist. This may seem difficult at first but will become easier with time.

One of the ways to do this if you think you may get emotional is writing down what you are trying to say before talking about it. Remembering the three Cs, communication will help you do this. This is how it is done when writing something:

1. **Write down what needs to be said, including emotions:** Do nothing with this, do not send it, just use it as a first draft.
2. **Remove all emotions/blame and replace with just facts:** Take the same information and edit out all the feelings and accusations, so you are just left with statements of fact.
3. **State clearly the resolution you want and need constructively.**

Let's look at a practical example:

Harassment Example

Before editing
I was sick to the core when he followed me to work. I was so anxious and scared and didn't know what to do. He just sat in the car staring at me. I was terrified. This is not the first time either – he did it the other day. Please help me, I don't know what to do.

After editing
On the [date], xyz followed me when I was driving to work in his vehicle. I only noticed when I parked my car at the work car park and got out of the vehicle. Xyz was sitting in his car and staring at me in a menacing way. This caused me extreme alarm and distress because he had also followed me on the [date] and parked outside my work and watched me. I am recently out of a relationship with him. He has threatened to watch me, so I was concerned for my safety. I had stated on [date] that I wanted no further contact.

Chapter 39 – Practicalities of Defending Yourself

A narcissist is more than likely to be looking to seek revenge in some way after you leave an abusive relationship. For this reason, go back to Chapter 30 and make sure you have completed these:

1. **A SWOT abuse analysis:** to work out your current situation and working on your strengths, weaknesses, opportunities and threats.
2. **Friendship matrix:** Using the chart from Phase 1, keep to hand who you can trust.
3. **Work out possible influencing/defending options:** Work out what you could do to influence and defend yourself locally, socially, nationally or internationally if required.
4. **Work out financial implications:** Work out how you can support yourself/get help.
5. **Work out how you will defend yourself from narcissistic attack:** How will you defend against:
   a. Blackmail
   b. Stalking/harassment
   c. Smear campaigns
   d. False allegations
   e. Property damage
   f. Threats
   g. Violence/threats of violence
6. **Prepare a timeline of events:** Start to write down the timeline of events. When the relationship started, when the abuse started, what is was, what happened. Have evidence ready.
7. **Get ready for legal defence (or attack):** Get prepared to defend yourself strongly and include everything that has happened.

250   Section 3 – Now You Have Left – The Recovery Begins

For ease, these are your templates (from Chapter 30):

SWOT abuse analysis: Example

Strengths: What I have/support	Weaknesses: What they have over me, they could use against me
Finances: • [What financial support do you have?] **Illness/injuries/medical/counselling:** • [Have injuries been recorded?] **Home:** • [Do you need a possession order?] **Children:** • [Where are your children safe?] **Pets/Animals:** • [Are pets safe?] **The law – Legal:** • [Do you know your rights?] **Friends/family:** • [Who can help you?] **Work:** • [Is work aware of the abuse?] **Neighbours:** • [Can any neighbours verify the abuse?] **Wider social/political:** • [Can your community help?]	**Threats made:** [What are they?] **What am I scared of:** [Explain] **Finances:** • [What financial support do they have?] **Illness/injuries/medical/counselling:** • [Is there evidence?] **Home:** • [Do they own the house?/will they try to take your home?] **Children:** • [Will they try to take the children?] **Pets/animals:** • [Will they try to take or harm pets?] **The law – Legal:** • [Have they got evidence you have broken the law?] **Friends/family:** • [Will friends and family stand up for the abuser?] **Neighbours:** [Will neighbours support the abuser?]

Opportunities: What can be done to protect yourself?	Threats: What they might try to do:
Take all of the possible threats and weaknesses and write down what you can do :	**What is your biggest fear?** Whatever your biggest fear(s) are, a narcissist may have no hesitation in going for this. **Threats:** • [What are they?] **False allegations:** • [What are they?] **Humiliation:** • [What are they doing?] **Taking things/damage to property:** • [What damage/stolen goods?] **Harming/stalking/Harassment:** • [What happened and when?] **Refusal to agree:** • [What cannot be agreed upon?] **Financial compensation:** • [What money is being demanded?] **Reputational damage:** • [What happened and when?]

Who can you trust?: Example

From Phase 1, write down who you have to support you. This will help you in the darker moments to realise you are not alone.

Believes You – Supports you 100% • [Name] • [Name] • [Organisation] • [Therapist] • [Support groups] **Keep in your life**	Not really sure who to believe – Asks questions • [Name] • [Name] **Keep away**
May believe you – Doesn't want to get involved/'no fire without matches' belief • [Name] • [Name] **Remove them/minimise them from your life**	Believes the narcissist – repeats lies and false information about you • [Name] • [Name] **No contact/make them accountable**

EXAMPLE cease and desist letter to someone gossiping – Repeating lies and false information

Dear XYZ,

I was very shocked to hear what has been said about me. I realise that you are not aware of the full facts, or my side of what has happened.

I refute entirely these lies and false allegations of [state what it is].

The truth is that I [e.g. have left an abusive relationship] and will not now be subjected to an untrue smear campaign or victim blamed.

I would ask that you don't repeat these lies and false allegations as I consider it defamation of my good character. I believe you have innocently and mistakenly repeated this. However, I am asking you to please now cease and desist repeating these lies.

Thank you.

254 Section 3 – Now You Have Left – The Recovery Begins

How you defend yourself: Types of narcissistic attack

This is a list of options open to you when defending yourself from narcissistic attack. If applicable use the information from Chapter 30.

Type of narcissistic attack	Options to defend yourself
Stalking/harassment	• [I will ... to defend myself]
Smear campaigns	• [I will ... to defend myself]
False allegations	• [I will ... to defend myself]
Property damage	• [I will ... to defend myself]
Threats	• [I will ... to defend myself][What happened, on what date, what was the threat?]
Violence/threat of violence	• [I will ... to defend myself]

Legal aspects – Legal 'covering'

If you need to go down the legal route, the best way to prevent narcissistic attacks is legal 'covering'. This means that you need to find a good solicitor/lawyer who can articulate the whole problem, threats and put in writing anticipated actions and reserve all rights. This is the same as the information provided in Chapter 30.

For example, ask your solicitor to write a letter which covers all the abusive elements – which gives courts a fuller picture of what is going on. It may be necessary to take out civil proceedings against your abuser as another option.

So, for example, include subsections for:

Possible subsections	Things to cover
Physical abuse	• [I have suffered xyz type of physical abuse, over abc period and have jkl evidence of this.]
Psychological abuse	• [I have suffered xyz type of psychological abuse, over abc period and have jkl evidence of this.]
General abusive behaviour	• [I have had the following threats [name them] which has caused me distress and meant that I have had to ...]
Agreed under duress	• [Because I am afraid of xyz ... I have agreed to the following under duress ...]
False allegations:	• [Xyz has made false allegations regarding the following I refute these entirely and ask that evidence is provided to prove this allegation.]
Threats and blackmail – Disclosing information	• [I am being threatened with ...] • [I am afraid that ...]
Defamation of character	• [I have become aware that xyz said abc on [date] which is untrue.] • Request cease and desist untruthful and disparaging remarks that would amount to defamation.
Harassment and stalking	• [I have been stalked and harassed over [time].]
Money	• [We have a financial agreement of ... I am concerned that ... agreement will not be honoured.] • [I am concerned that there is a life policy taken out recently for £xxxx.]

256 Section 3 – Now You Have Left – The Recovery Begins

Prepare a timeline of events

A timeline of events in date order: If you are able to list the key points in date order, this will help a solicitor/lawyer, yourself and others with your case.

Your timeline of events:

Date	What happened	Consequence(s)	Evidence
On or around the [date]	• Met Xyz.	• Thought he was very charming and nice person, so started a relationship.	• Emails proclaiming his love.
Between [dates]			
On or around [date]			
[date]			
[date]			
[date]			
[date]			
[date]			
[date]			
[date]			
[date]			
[date]			
[date]			
[date]			
[date]			
[date]			
[date]			
[date]			
[date]			
[date]			
[date]			

When preparing a timeline of events, if you can not remember a specific date use the terms 'on or around'.

If something occured between dates, state between [date a] and [date b].

Chapter 40 - Narcissists' Weaknesses

Whilst a narcissist is very charming and can easily manipulate those around them, there are a few weaknesses which can help you when defending yourself. These are the weaknesses:

1. **Getting caught out with their pathological lies over time:** Whilst a narcissist is very convincing, because they cannot help pathological lying, after some time the lies they tell become more obvious. What they say is likely to change. This, however, takes time. Whilst they don't generally care if they get caught out, they do care if people start ignoring them.
2. **Public humiliation or shame:** A bad outcome for a narcissist is being publicly humiliated or shamed by their own actions, derived from facts. However, this can gain them the attention that they desire. This is why evidence is so crucial when defending yourself against a narcissist and being prepared to speak out publicly about what has happened.
3. **Needs an audience:** A narcissist needs an audience. So, the most powerful thing you can do is take that away from them. Silence and move on.
4. **Evidence of their actions:** A narcissist is likely to go to great lengths to create alibis and false witnesses; it is therefore crucial to have your own robust evidence.
5. **Trying to hide what they do:** A narcissist is going to try to hide the abuse, pressure, or manipulation from other people. They need secrecy to survive. The best methods to defend yourself from this might include:
    a. **Transparency:** Confirm what they have said to you back in writing and copy other people in (e.g. by email).
    b. **Speak out:** Speak to other people and say that is not what happened, and the truth is ...
6. **Accountability:** A narcissist is likely to not want to conform to rules and be accountable. If things are said verbally, they are more likely to deny it. Therefore, to defend against lack of accountability:
    a. **Put what was said in writing/record it:** A narcissist will not want to put in writing what they have said or agreed to as it is harder for them to deny.
    a. **Have an independent mediator:** Someone independent, such as a mediator or lawyer, is unlikely to be swayed by lack of accountability.

The protection/defending checklist

What might happen	How will I protect/defend myself?	Am I ready?	If not, what do I need to do?
Physical	• Self-defence • Rape alarm • Safety plan		
Emotional/mental	• Abuse charities • Counselling/psychologist • Friends/family		
Home	• CCTV • Security assessment/fix • Plan if they turn up • Plan if they move close • Who overlooks you? • Moving home plans • Post redirection • Change locks • Change entry • Is the house listed by police for previous domestic violence?		
Work	• Change route to work • Look for new job		
Friends/family	• Speak the truth about what happened • Keep friendships		
Children	• Speak to school • Are they safe with me		
Local Area	• Talk to neighbours/ others about what has happened		
Pets	• In safe boarding		
Belongings	• Precious items in storage		
Finances:	• Emergency funds • Bank accounts		

260   Section 3 – Now You Have Left – The Recovery Begins

What might happen	How will I protect/defend myself?	Am I ready?	If not, what do I need to do?
Communication:	• Get a new phone • Change numbers • Record phone calls		
Evidence:	• In a safe place • More than one copy • With my solicitor/lawyer		
New security measures:	• Do not let anyone in the house • Go out with other people or not alone • Changed your route to work • Burning receipts • Not putting anything in bins		
Defending false allegations:	• Cease and desist letters sent • Getting false allegations vigorously denied		
Defending social isolation from smear campaigns:	• Speak out about your side of the story		

Phase 5 – My Needs Are The Most Important, They Are ...

Chapter 41 – What are your needs and wants?

Defining your needs and wants is important as you move forward. You may use phrases like 'I don't know,' 'I'm not sure,' 'You choose for me,' and 'Whatever you want.' This can be reflective of the abuse that you have been through and it takes some time to actually know what it is that you need and want.

Needs are things that are important to you. They can be a need for your survival – such as food or a need to make yourself happy. Wants are desires. This is an important distinction because what you want may not be what you need.

262 Section 3 – Now You Have Left – The Recovery Begins

How to work out what you want and need after an abusive relationship actually starts the other way round to other people. You begin with defining what you don't like and don't need. This is because you may have become so accustomed to bending to someone else's demands, you may have suppressed your own. This is the process:

Defining wants and needs

Think of a towel screwed up on the floor in a colour you really dislike. It smells old and musty.

Now imagine you are in a luxury retreat for the night and to your amazement there are towels presented in exactly the colour you like, and the smell is just so relaxing.

What colour is the towel?

How is the towel folded?

Where is the towel placed for your enjoyment?

What does the towel smell like?

What type of fragrance is it?

What is the thickness of the towel?

Does the towel have any significant features (fluffy, design, personalised.)

How are you feeling knowing someone has done this for you?

Why? _____

From this exercise, you now know something simple like your preferences on towels.

Is this a want or a need for you or both? _____

Why? _____

When you take this process further, you slowly discover that you do actually have strong likes, dislikes, wants and needs, which have been suppressed or compromised.

Here are some of the areas that can help you define this for yourself. If you cannot imagine what it is that you like, then imagine the opposite and go from there:

Examples	Questions to ask yourself	What are your wants and needs?
Your perfect cup of tea	What size mug or cup? What make of tea or tea bags? How long does the tea brew? Do you take milk? What type of milk? When does the milk go in? How much milk goes in? Do you take sugar or sweeteners? How much? What colour is the tea? How hot is it? Where are you sitting to drink the tea? What time of day is this? Anything else? Spoon? Biscuits?	How do you feel? Why?
A cup of coffee	Think about type, colour, strength, aroma, the mug or cup, how the coffee is prepared, percolated and presented.	How do you feel? Why?
A glass of wine/ champagne	What type, flavour, colour, aroma, taste, type of glass, type of bottle, corked or screw top, size of glass, portion size?	How do you feel? Why?
Your favourite comfort meal	What type of meal, what does it taste like, what flavours does it have in it, how is it presented, what type of cutlery/crockery?	How do you feel? Why?
Your favourite going out meal	Where is the place you most want to go? What type of food? What is the atmosphere like? Where are you sitting? What type of furnishing is there? What makes it special for you? What is the smell? How is the food cooked? What is the ambient music? How does it taste?	How do you feel? Why?

264 Section 3 – Now You Have Left – The Recovery Begins

Examples	Questions to ask yourself	What are your wants and needs?
A programme/ film to make you laugh/feel good	What is it? What makes you laugh/feel good? Who is in the TV show? Where does the show take place? When did you last watch it?	How do you feel? Why?
A favourite day out	Where are you going? What is the scenery? What smells are there? What is so special for you? How long are you there? What do you do? What makes you smile?	How do you feel? Why?
A treat for yourself	What is the treat? What does it look like, smell like, taste like? Why do you love it?	How do you feel? Why?

The next way to integrate this into your life is to work out deservedness:

The Priority of Deservedness

Your deservedness to have the things that make you happy is important for you to consider. You may know what you want and need, but there may be resistance on actually doing it to make yourself feel special. You may still be putting up resistance because you have been used to meeting someone else's needs first. This will slowly change over time.

For each of the answers above, think about how often have treated yourself in the way that you want and need to be treated.

If you haven't treated yourself in the best way possible recently, what is the resistance?

_____

Why is that?

_____

Some of these answers may well give you schemas to consider such as 'I don't deserve it' or 'It's not a priority'.

The lesson here really is that you are a priority and the only person who can make you that priority is yourself.

'My needs are my priority.'

Chapter 42 – What Does a 'Normal, Healthy' Relationship Feel Like?

In Phase 2, Part 2 you started to consider your values and beliefs.

The next step is using that information to define your values and beliefs. Using this information gives you a way to define what you want in a normal, healthy relationship and be able to 'feel' the difference. I use feelings rather than anything else because you might logically know what a healthy relationship is, but you may not be able to describe how it 'feels'. It is also important to define what it is or not.

My values/beliefs	Do you know what that feels like?	Is there anyone in your life that has treated you this way so that you can relate to this feeling?
Trust • My partner earns my trust as I earn their trust. • Other:	Yes/No/Sometimes/ I don't know	**Trust** • [xyz] shows me trust in this way.
Integrity • My partner does what they say they will and means what they say lovingly. • Other:	Yes/No/Sometimes/ I don't know	**Integrity** • [xyz] shows me integrity in this way.
Financial • I trust my partner financially. • Other:	Yes/No/Sometimes/ I don't know	**Financial** • [xyz] shows me financial support in this way.
Respect • My partner respects my views, even if they don't agree. • Other:	Yes/No/Sometimes/ I don't know	**Respect** • [xyz] shows me respect in this way.

What Does a 'Normal, Healthy' Relationship Feel Like? **267**

My values/beliefs	Do you know what that feels like?	Is there anyone in your life that has treated you this way so that you can relate to this feeling?
Being Valued • I am valued for who I am. • Other:	Yes/No/Sometimes/ I don't know	**Being Valued** • [xyz] shows me that I am valued for who I am.
Faithfulness • My partner is totally faithful to me, as I am to them. This means there is never any need for jealousy. • Other:	Yes/No/Sometimes/ I don't know	**Faithfulness** • [xyz] makes me feel this secure in a relationship.
Kindness • My partner does their best by me, as I do the best for them. • Other:	Yes/No/Sometimes/ I don't know	**Kindness** • [xyz] is kind to me in this way.
Listens to me • My partner listens to what I have to say, hears what I have to say and understands my point of view. • Other:	Yes/No/Sometimes/ I don't know	**Listen to me** • [xyz] listens and hears me. • Other:
Honest • My partner doesn't tell me lies. • Other:	Yes/No/Sometimes/ I don't know	**Honest** • [xyz] has always been honest with me. • Other:
Living • My partner makes an honest living and works ethically. • Other:	Yes/No/Sometimes/ I don't know	**Living** • [xyz] always made an honest living • Other:

268 Section 3 — Now You Have Left — The Recovery Begins

My values/beliefs	Do you know what that feels like?	Is there anyone in your life that has treated you this way so that you can relate to this feeling?
Security • My partner makes me feel secure in the relationship • Other:	Yes/No/Sometimes/ I don't know	**Security** • [xyz] made me feel this way. • Other:
Physical • My partner lovingly cares for my physical needs. • Other:	Yes/No/Sometimes/ I don't know	**Physical** • [xyz] made me feel this way. • Other:
Mental • My partner takes care of their own mental wellbeing as I take care of mine. • Other:	Yes/No/Sometimes/ I don't know	**Mental** • [xyz] makes me feel this way. • Other:
Animals • My partner is kind to animals. • Other:	Yes/No/Sometimes/ I don't know	**Animals** • [xyz] was always kind to animals. • Other:
Health • My partner looks after their own health and we share the same health goals. • Other:	Yes/No/Sometimes/ I don't know	**Health** • [xyz] has shown me positive healthy goals. •Other:
Children • My partner loves children and is a loving parent. • Other.	Yes/No/Sometimes/ I don't know	**Children** • [xyz] has shown me loving parenting. • Other.

What Does a 'Normal, Healthy' Relationship Feel Like? **269**

My values/beliefs	Do you know what that feels like?	Is there anyone in your life that has treated you this way so that you can relate to this feeling?
Laughter • My partner and I have a lot of laughter in our relationship. • Other:	Yes/No/Sometimes/ I don't know	**Laughter** • [xyz] makes me laugh. • Other:
Hobbies • My partner encourages me to enjoy my own hobbies as they enjoys theirs.	Yes/No/Sometimes/ I don't know	**Hobbies** • [xyz] supported my hobbies
Other values and beliefs	**Do you know what that feels like?**	**Is there anyone in your life that has treated you in this way so that you can relate to this feeling?**

Putting this together

Now that you have a list of your own values and beliefs, you are able to look for relationships that match that – and discard the rest. You are worth all the values and beliefs you have just described and cannot afford to settle for anything less.

Where you find that you have no reference point in your life to how it feels to be loved, to trust someone or to have respect for your views (anything you answered no to above), then you have to rely on the mental explanation until you can understand what it feels like.

This approach does not mean that any relationship will be perfect. The difference with a healthy relationship is that your partner values you, respects you and takes into consideration your needs. They also take accountability for their own actions and genuinely and lovingly work together with you to build a strong foundation on both your needs.

One counsellor said to me that each relationship is like a pack of cards. You may want four aces, four kings or four queens, but the reality of relationships is that you can get any combination. What this translates to is that no one is perfect. Not even yourself. A loving partner, however, will love you for both your good points and your bad points, but the good points must outweigh the bad ones otherwise you are compromising yourself for someone else.

Using this approach is where you can slowly and cautiously meet someone new and not be afraid to end a relationship if your needs are not met.

Phase 6 - I've Changed and Recovered Enough

Chapter 43 - Have you Recovered Enough?

Phase 6 is when you have spent considerable time working on yourself and your value/belief systems and you are comfortable being in your own company. You might like to have someone else in your life, but it is not the be all and end all.

During this phase you will have gone through a transformation. These are the things that you are likely to have worked on, with your therapist.

272 Section 3 – Now You Have Left – The Recovery Begins

Fill in the following to see how you have changed.

	Before in abusive relationship your beliefs were:	Now your beliefs are:
Communication – Speaking Up EXAMPLE	I would not speak up because I was afraid of abusive consequences.	I speak up assertively about my needs and utilise the help of my support network to deal with any issues relating to abuse.
Communication – Speaking up		
Communication – Speaking out		
Trust in others		
Boundaries – Establishing		
Boundaries – Enforcing		
Validating yourself		
Believing in yourself		
Listening to your own needs		
Assertiveness		
Standing up for yourself		
Observing ACTION over WORDS		
Not guilt-tripped?		
Rescuing yourself before rescuing others		
Managing your emotions		
Dealt with emotional triggers		
Have a social network in place		
Have a support network in place		

	Before in abusive relationship your beliefs were:	Now your beliefs are:
Have substance abuse under control		
New friendships		
Identifying narcissistic behaviour early on?		
Know when you are lied to?		
Fully protected yourself		
Fully defended yourself		
Love yourself as you are		I am whole and perfect as I am. I love myself unconditionally.

When you reach a point where you smile when saying the following, you are in a very good emotional and psychological space:

'I am whole and perfect as I am. I love myself unconditionally.'

Congratulations.

Phase 7 – I Accept What Happened

Chapter 44 – Acceptance and Forgiveness

This is the final stages of recovery from an abusive relationship. It is where you can accept what happened to you (but not forget) and forgive yourself for being an unwitting victim because you did the best you could at the time.

I would say acceptance is necessary of what happened (you cannot change the past).

Some people have recovered beyond forgiving just themselves to forgiving their abuser. We don't all get there, but I hope that some of you will.

You might hear some say that it was a blessing in disguise and opportunity to make sure past hurts don't keep affecting the future. If that is so, it was an extremely painful blessing!

In my view, acceptance and forgiveness of yourself is the only thing that is important at the end of your recovery journey. It does not negate what happened, it does not forget what you went through, it makes the narcissist accountable but more importantly gives you your own power back.

One powerful thing that you can say to a narcissist should you ever meet another one is **'Your needs are not my priority – my needs are my priority.'** That statement is likely to make a narcissist want to avoid you.

And the most powerful thing you can do is not thinking about your abuser at all, with the freedom to get on with your new happier more fulfilled life.

In the end, I went from being a victim of narcissistic abuse to a survivor and victor of recovery.

I truly hope this book helps you on that journey too.

Phase 8 – I'm Ready To Move On With My Life

Now you are ready to move on with your life. Congratulations!. There may still be moments when you need to go back and deal with emotional triggers, but they get less and less frequent and less and less painful to deal with.

Let's just check you are not going to get caught up again with another narcissist.

Area of recovery	Statement to yourself	How confident are you moving forward with this statement?
Accountability	• I know how to take accountability for myself. • I know I cannot be accountable for other people's words, deeds or actions.	
Sad stories	• I ask pertinent questions if I hear sad stories to ascertain facts and if it is truthful or not.	
Validation	• I validate what I am thinking and feeling as a priority.	
Intensity	• I am not swayed by someone wanting to commit quickly in a relationship – I take my time.	
Values and beliefs	• I know my values and beliefs. • I use my values and beliefs to guide me in my life.	
Speaking up and speaking out	• I speak up confidently and assertively for myself.	
Defending myself verbally	• I know what actions to take or words to say to prevent verbal abuse.	

Area of recovery	Statement to yourself	How confident are you moving forward with this statement?
Words and actions	• I observe actions over words to make a decision about trusting another person.	
Manipulation	• I know when I am being manipulated. • I know what to say and do to prevent being manipulated.	
Negative emotions/ anger	• I have constructive ways to deal with my negative emotions/anger.	
Boundaries	• I know my boundaries.I maintain and defend my boundaries with others.	
Emotional triggers	• I know how to deal with any emotional triggers I experience.	
False accusations	• I do not tolerate false accusations and have a plan in place to deal with this.	
Abuse	• I do not tolerate abuse in my life. • I will defend myself with appropriate support.	
Acceptance	• I accept that I could not change a narcissist. • I accept that I did my best.	
Future dreams	• I believe the future will be more positive and I will create that.	
Trusting yourself	• I trust myself completely to know what to do or know where to go to get the help I need.	
Speaking about your needs	• I speak honestly and openly about my needs.	
Fearless dating	• I am not afraid to leave a relationship as soon as I know it is abusive in any way.	

Area of recovery	Statement to yourself	How confident are you moving forward with this statement?
My body language	• I know enough about my body language to understand my feelings.	
True friends	• I know who my true friends are.	
Normalising the normal	• I can differentiate easily between normal behaviour and abusive behaviour. • I normalise the normal now.	
Loving myself	• I love myself totally and unconditionally. • I am perfect as I am.	

I hope now that you have reached the end of this book you have more confidence and encouragement to leave an abusive relationship and seek the professional help you need to recover.

This is your own journey of recovery from abuse, from victim to survivor to being able to say, 'I recovered'.

I understand why I was chosen by a narcissist.
I understand what I have to do to protect myself.
I am now a survivor and victor and
the power narcissists once had over me is forever gone.

References and Other Resources

Behary, Wendy T. 2008. *Disarming the narcissist. Surviving & Thriving with the Self-Absorbed.* Oakland CA. New Harbinger Publications Inc.

Cooper, Diana. 1998. *Transform your life : a step-by-step programme for change,* London, UK. Piatkus.

Douglas, Kay. 1994. *Invisible Wounds : a self-help guide for New Zealand Woman in Destructive Relationships.* Penguin Books. North Shore, Penguin Group,

Evans, Melanie Tonia, *You can Thrive after Narcissistic Abuse, The #1 System for Recovering from Toxic Relationships.* Watkins.

Elgin, Suzette Haden 1995. *You can't say that to me! : stopping the pain of verbal abuse : an 8-step program.* New York. John Wiley & Sons, Inc.

MacKenzie, Jackson, *Psychopath Free Recovering from Emotionally Abusive Relationships with Narcissists, Sociopaths and Other Toxic People,* Berkley Books, New York

Levine, Peter A. *Healing Trauma* © *2008* Peter Levine, published by Sounds True Inc.

Images from *No-longer-here, Pixabay*

McLeod, S. A. (2018, May 21) *Carl Jung.* Simply Psychology. https://www.simplypsychology.org/carl-jung.html

Buck, A. M., The Intensive Recovery Programme – narcissitic abuse/domestic abuse, www.i-recovered.co.uk

Domestic Abuse Commissioner – for all UK charities – www.domesticabusecommissioner.uk

Young, Jeffrey E., Janet S. Klosko, and Marjorie E. Weishaar. 2006. *Schema Therapy: A Practitioner's Guide.* New York: Guliford Press

Lightning Source UK Ltd.
Milton Keynes UK
UKHW020809031022
409835UK00012B/1483